D0910610

"An excellent, insightful, and original approach to the faith formation processes. The artful and lively dialogue between faith and life, movies and Commandments, is sure to captivate. This creative resource will enrich catechetical ministry by offering practical ideas enabling us to teach, preach, and share God's word."

Edith Prendergast, RSC
Director, Religious Education,
Archdiocese of Los Angeles

"Pacatte and Malone give us insight into the deeper meaning of movies. Their book is a window into reflection and dialogue with God through film."

Luis Mandoki
Director of Innocent Voices, Message in a Bottle,
and When a Man Loves a Woman

"A help for growing in *spiritual* literacy by developing *media* literacy through the contemplation of popular movies. A most welcome resource for all—bravo to the authors!"

John J. Pungente, SJ
Co-author of Finding God in the Dark:
Taking the Spiritual Exercises of St. Ignatius to the Movies

"This book gave me a greater appreciation of the role of the Commandments in the Christian tradition, and a way to think about them as less punitive and more life-affirming. It will be a great resource for small group discussions as well as for individuals seeking a deeper appreciation of the resources embedded in their own faith tradition."

Lynn Schofield Clark, Ph.D.
Assistant Research Professor, Director of Teens & the New Media at Home,
School of Journalism and Mass Communication, University of Colorado

"What a handy tool for all people interested in teaching and learning about the Commandments, as well as those interested in film. I can't wait to run out and rent the movies they discuss within these pages!"

Laurie A. Trotta
Media Analyst and Author

"With this volume, Peter Malone and Rose Pacatte have responded to the pleas of postmodern and emerging church liturgists everywhere for additional *Lights, Camera...Faith!* volumes. Now, preachers, educators, and workshop leaders have even more options for stimulating vibrant theological reflection on film."

Teresa Blythe
Co-author of Meeting God in Virtual Reality: Using Spiritual Practices with Media,
Coordinator of Hesychia School for Spiritual Directors at the Redemptorist Renewal Center, Tucson

"Lights, Camera...Faith! The Ten Commandments reminds us to be engaged rather than passive participants of popular media. Exploring the meaning and messages of popular film demonstrates the richness and vibrancy of our religious Scriptures. Peter Malone and Rose Pacatte give people of faith—and people who *question* faith—an opportunity for meaningful dialogue about the challenges of being human."

Meryl Marshall-Daniels
Former President of the Academy of Television Arts & Sciences

"The movies and the guidance provided here present an opportunity to discuss significant life issues with the young adults in my parish group. Thanks...I could not lead these nights without *Lights, Camera...Faith!*"

Susan M. Wallace, FSP
Catechist

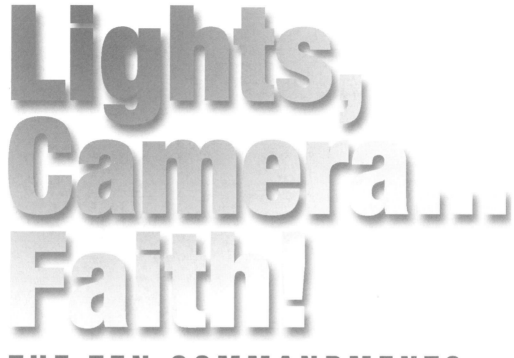

Lights, Camera... Faith!

THE TEN COMMANDMENTS

A MOVIE LOVER'S GUIDE TO SCRIPTURE

Rose Pacatte, FSP, and Peter Malone, MSC

Pauline
BOOKS & MEDIA
Boston

Nihil Obstat:
Reverend Francis R. Colborn, S.T.D.
Censor Deputatus

Imprimatur:
✠ His Eminence Cardinal Roger Mahony
Archbishop of Los Angeles
May 18, 2005

The *Nihil Obstat* and *Imprimatur* are official declarations that the work contains nothing contrary to Faith and Morals. It is not implied thereby that those granting the Nihil Obstat and Imprimatur agree with the contents, statements, or opinions expressed.

Library of Congress Cataloging-in-Publication Data
    Pacatte, Rose.
    Lights, camera— faith! : the Ten commandments / by Rose Pacatte and Peter Malone.
        p. cm.
    Edition of 2002 written by Peter Malone and Rose Pacatte.
    Includes bibliographical references and index.
        ISBN 0-8198-4520-5 (pbk.)
        1. Ten commandments. 2. Motion pictures—Religious aspects—Christianity. I. Title: Ten commandments. II. Malone, Peter. III. Malone, Peter. Lights, camera— faith! IV. Title.
        BV4655.M375 2006
        261.5'7—dc22
                          2005016538

Cover design by Rosana Usselmann

Cover photo: Magictorch/Getty Images

Movie photos courtesy of Photofest www.photofestnyc.com

Published by Pauline Books & Media, 50 Saint Paul's Avenue, Boston, MA 02130-3491. www.pauline.org

Printed in the U.S.A.

Pauline Books & Media is the publishing house of the Daughters of St. Paul, an international congregation of women religious serving the Church with the communications media.

1 2 3 4 5 6 7 8 9   12 11 10 09 08 07 06

Contents

Foreword

As president of Walden Media, and as a parent, I know first-hand the power of stories, which is why I cofounded Walden Media. Walden Media's mission statement lays the matter directly on the table: we believe quality entertainment is inherently educational, and we are dedicated to making family movies that inspire, engage, enlighten, and entertain. We think film is a great way to teach and that seeing good movies might help make us better people. Which brings me to this book.

A recent church ad campaign reminds the wary (and the weary) among us that "God is still speaking." There's probably no better corroboration of this statement than *Lights, Camera...Faith! The Ten Commandments* by Rose Pacatte and Peter Malone. The idea behind this volume in the *Lights, Camera...Faith!* series is so simple, it's revolutionary. It demonstrates what the Ten Commandments mean today by applying them to a well-chosen body of contemporary films.

This sounds easy enough.

But if you stop to consider accomplishing this task on your own, the magnitude of sheer effort and insight required (and here I'll speak for myself) might find you coming up short. Sure, there are plenty of cinematic examples to go around for the Sixth (do not commit adultery) and the Seventh (you shall not steal) Commandments, which is probably as telling about Hollywood as it is about the human condition.

But then try to name three films that examine the Third Commandment (keep holy the Lord's day), and I doubt you would come up with the titles Pacatte and Malone have included in these pages. More important I doubt you would explain the films' connection to the Third Commandment with as much wisdom as is offered here.

And that's the power of *Lights, Camera...Faith!* Applying films to the Ten Commandments makes some good movies even better by giving them more significance, more relevance, and by making them "holy," if you will. The discussion of each film becomes an instrument of grace, a means to a very important end: trying to grasp, through full-screen examples, what God asks of us day by day, on good days and bad, one step at a time. And the application does what art does best: it makes the all-too-familiar Ten Commandments new. In this context, we read them as if for the first time. And the result is thrilling and instructive.

A favorite film offered for scrutiny in this collection is Robert Redford's 1980 faithful screen adaptation of Judith Guest's novel, *Ordinary People,* here presented in the context of the Fourth Commandment (honor your father and mother). The dialogue between commandment and film is every bit as powerful as the film itself, particularly because there is so little about the mother at the center of the story's action, Beth Jarrett (portrayed with cutting brittleness by Mary Tyler Moore), that's worthy of honor. This particularly compelling exploration of the Fourth Commandment leads the authors to discuss understanding, tolerance, forgiveness, and reconciliation. Pacatte and Malone end this section with the observation that, "Some leaders in faith communities think that parenting is the greatest pastoral need in Western countries today," and ask the haunting question, "Why might this be so?" They ask the reader to consider Scripture—as they do throughout the book—in this case, different translations of Matthew 5:48, and what the word "perfect" does and does not mean in the context of the Fourth Commandment; as rendered in *Ordinary People,* being a "perfect" son is literally a matter of life and death. Each film discussion then closes with a short prayer.

You'll want to read this book in no particular order, or from beginning to end, or according to your favorite films, or as concerns the commandment that seems to offer no end of personal trial. *Lights, Camera...Faith! The Ten Commandments* is suffused with provocative discussion questions, applicable references to the *Catechism of the Catholic Church,* and a recommended reading list for further exploration and study.

Lights, Camera... Faith! reminds us, above all, that *The Ten Commandments* isn't simply a Hollywood blockbuster starring Charlton Heston and Yvonne DeCarlo. The Ten Commandments are a set of truths with which each generation must somehow find ways to engage—and apply. This book helps us do both.

MICHAEL FLAHERTY

The Ten Commandments

1. You shall not have other gods besides me. / Be authentically religious. / Destroy your idols.

2. Do not take God's name in vain. / Be authentic. / Do not presume or play God.

3. Keep holy the Lord's Day. / Develop a sense of the sacred in work and leisure.

4. Honor your father and mother. / Do not disrespect parents or children.

5. You shall not kill. / Respect life. / Do not encourage violence.

6. Do not commit adultery. / Be loving and faithful. / Do not violate others.

7. You shall not steal. / Be honest. / Respect others' goods.

8. You shall not bear false witness against your neighbor. / Be truthful. / Do not lie.

9. You shall not covet your neighbor's wife. / Be faithful. / Do not lust after another.

10. Do not covet your neighbor's goods. / Be content with what you have.

The word "Decalogue" means literally "ten words."
God revealed these "ten words"
to his people on the holy mountain.
They were written "with the finger of God,"
unlike the other commandments written by Moses.
They are pre-eminently the words of God.
They are handed on to us
in the books of Exodus and Deuteronomy.
Beginning with the Old Testament,
the sacred books refer to the "ten words,"
but it is in the New Covenant in Jesus Christ
that their full meaning will be revealed.

Catechism of the Catholic Church, no. 2056

Introduction

Using Movies to Explore the Ten Commandments

When we completed the three-volume series, *Lights, Camera...Faith! A Movie Lectionary* for Cycles A, B, and C of the liturgical year (and following in great part the revised Lectionary), Sister Rose Pacatte, FSP, and I were asked what the next topic might be for a book that promotes dialogue between life and faith, movies and the Scriptures. Because homilists and religious educators from a variety of Christian faith traditions form the greatest part of the audience for *Lights, Camera...Faith! A Movie Lectionary,* we thought that the four themes of the *Catechism of the Catholic Church* (English edition, 1994) would frame a whole new conversational approach to the dialogue between theology, spirituality, and cinema. The themes of the *Catechism* are Creed, Sacraments, the Commandments/Beatitudes, and Prayer. The Ten Commandments seemed the obvious theme with which to begin because of the role of morality in faith development.

By popular demand, a volume on the Beatitudes and the Seven Deadly Sins is to follow; others on the Sacraments, Creed, and Prayer are planned.

The Ten Commandments and Movies

In the 1970s, when critics of religious education were complaining that students were not being taught strong and sound doctrine, one of the examples they gave to support their point of view was the students' ignorance of the Ten Commandments. Walter Black, MSC, a moral theologian and colleague who taught ethical and moral issues in adult faith-formation programs, made the point that some of the critics simply wanted to be sure that young people could recite the Ten Commandments. Black suggested that the group he was teaching take about forty minutes to memorize the Commandments. They did. Then his telling question to them was, "Now, what...?"

This new volume of the series *Lights, Camera...Faith!* offers reflections on popular movies in pursuit of a deeper understanding of what "comes next" after we memorize the Commandments. Naming them is not nearly enough. We need to know what they mean and explore how to live them in our daily lives as individuals, communities, and societies. In doing this, we will understand more fully the role and formation of conscience, the nuances of their injunctions, the consequences of not following the Ten Commandments, and the blessings that come to us when we do.

Format

For the most part we have kept the format of the original *Lights, Camera...Faith!* series because it has proved useful to preachers, catechists, film and faith study groups, and individuals. However, the focus of the current series has now changed from the liturgical readings to the specific theme of the commandments. Therefore, we have introduced the Ten Commandments as a whole, with two films to evoke reflection and conversation on this fruitful topic. Following this, we begin the consideration of each commandment with a brief introduction that highlights contemporary aspects and relevant themes.

At its heart, this volume remains, like the volumes of *Lights, Camera...Faith! A Movie Lectionary*, a means to create a dialogue between the Scriptures and the movies. (See page 287 for a detailed outline for a group event or gatherings.) Therefore, we have chosen Scripture readings that relate to different aspects of each commandment. For each commandment, we begin with a reading from the Old Testament followed by one from a book of the New Testament and conclude with a key reading from the Gospels. One advantage in choosing readings that relate specifically to the commandments or their themes is that they can serve as a basis for catechesis and religious education, retreats, homilies, prayer experiences, ecumenical or interfaith gatherings or spirituality, and film events.

Listed for each film are:
- the credits;
- a synopsis for ready reference and refreshing memories;
- a clear statement that integrates the film and the Scriptures;
- a list of three key scenes and themes;
- material for conversation and reflection;
- a prayer.

The appendices offer many helpful tables, including a list of key sequence clips for each movie, which can be used when it is not possible to view an entire film. We have also correlated the movie titles from *Lights, Camera...Faith! A Movie Lectionary*, Cycles A–C, which can be used in exploring the meaning of each commandment. We have expanded the bibliography for relevant books as well.

Audiences and Ratings

We have chosen to consider three movies per commandment. Although we recommend this book for young adults age eighteen and up, the first movie option can be viewed by most audiences from high school and up. We urge the presenter to screen the film in its entirety and to invite parents to be part of the experience if the film is used with students. The second movie suggested presents and treats moral issues and dilemmas in a more mature way than the first film, and therefore requires a more developed moral sense in order to interpret the film in meaningful ways. The third film is the most difficult in terms of the issues treated and the ways people sin against or live the Commandments. These films are darker in nature, and the presenter will want to use them for select groups and circumstances, as they require more life and faith experience, as well as maturity in viewing and conversation.

All of these films have "ratings," that is, a content ranking that offers information for guidance. The MPAA (Motion Picture Association of America, www.mpaa.org) has given many of the suggested films an "R" rating. The rating system in other countries, such as the United Kingdom or Australia, have a higher or lower ranking; please consult the chart on page 282 for these ratings, as well as those provided by the United States Conference of Catholic Bishops Office for Film and Broadcast (www.usccb.org). "R" ratings do not necessarily mean "bad"; they signify that the films deal with subjects for mature audiences.

Presenting the Human Condition

Dealing with the commandments in conjunction with stories told through film means that many issues will be confronted: the complexities of moral dilemmas, various levels of conscience development, the universality of the human condition, and a variety of sins. Though some of these transgressions have parallels in the Bible itself, they are nonetheless difficult or disturbing to probe.

Yet understanding the nature of a particular transgression and sin, and finding ways for forgiveness and reconciliation, is the very mission and work of the Church. A number of these movies could be considered controversial, as are so many of the moral dilemmas that people face in everyday life.

The principle we have employed in choosing these films and examining them through the lens of the Ten Commandments is to make the distinction between "what" is presented on screen and "how" it is presented. This means that there is no limit to the topics that can be examined. All human experience, no matter how twisted or evil, is a legitimate subject for a movie.

As we read through the Old and New Testaments, we realize that the Bible tells stories about both virtuous and sinful behavior mixed with a wide range of human inconsistencies about good people who choose what is sinful over what is right and good. This is life and it can also make excellent drama. The Second Vatican Council said that moral evil should be presented in such a way as to lead to a deeper understanding of the human person and the value of truth and goodness (*Inter Mirifica,* no. 7). And this can, indeed, occur in film. The limits for the presentation of sinfulness arise when we ask "how" the material is presented.

Each family and culture has developed sensitivities and particular norms (often unarticulated) concerning what is acceptable or not regarding how visual media presents and deals with the dark and disturbing. As individuals, we all have a conscience. Pastoral theology and practice encourage teachers, homilists, and ministers to respect these sensibilities and norms. In dealing with movies that are open to such wide interpretations about controversial and sometimes disturbing issues, we, the audience, need to have both a delicate or well-tuned sensitivity to morality as well as a robust attitude about life and faith that does not wilt under pressure. Often a viewer can determine the difference between a film that treats difficult topics in a mature way and one that tends to exploit the audience with artistry, technical achievements, and the intensity of the presentation. However, every individual sees and interprets these elements differently, so at times it is challenging to arrive at a consensus. Seeking information and guidance from film reviews or checking film ratings (see page 297 for websites and ratings information) is always an excellent way to prepare to view a film.

In addition, not *every* person is obliged to see *every* movie. We all have particular emotional responses, interests, tastes, styles, and values, based on our family and faith formation, life experience, and education, which form our viewing lens. Because of our particular lens, we may choose not to watch a film no matter how useful for a faith and culture dialogue it may be. This applies, of course, to presentations of violence, sexuality, and the use of alcohol and drugs, as well as the language a screenplay employs. To discern and judge "how" a movie tells its story, we are called upon to use our mature powers of discernment, to consider the context in which objectionable behavior appears, and to gauge the artistry and intensity of the portrayal.

The Decalogue

Are the Ten Commandments, or the Decalogue, relevant today? In an era in which institutional religion is losing its credibility and influence, especially because of inconsistent behavior on the part of a religion's representatives, people the world over still look to churches and Scriptures for moral guidance. This is also true in parts of the world where the predominant religion's faith systems do not include the Decalogue. Indeed, people of all religions and no religion search for objective moral norms to guide them. In an age when many fear that morality is losing ground, the Ten Commandments offer clear general laws providing a basic structure to guide the human family. Men and women of all religious persuasions as well as people who seek authentic secular solutions can subscribe to the Ten Commandments.

By studying the Commandments and the Scriptures and gaining an understanding of the joy and pain of human experience as told through film, we can discern their deeper meaning and better understand their nuances. In this way, after memorizing the Ten Commandments, we can respond to Father Black's question: "Now, what?" In other words, how do we live the Commandments today? The Decalogue is a moral structure that remains modern and relevant.

The Decalogue as Covenant

At Mount Sinai, God did not simply give his people some moral injunctions, a set of rules. Mount Sinai is the sacred place where God made a covenant with the Israelites and all their spiritual descendants. "Covenant" is a sacred word that characterizes the mutual responsibilities of the partners who enter into it. In the Hebrew, the word is "Brit" (pronounced "breet"), and it appears over fifty times in the first five books of the Bible alone. It is a word of promise, of pledge, of deep commitment on the part of God, whose faithful love demands faithful action in return from the Israelite community. The Sinai Covenant has always been seen as the initiative of God, who loved all peoples but chose Israel as his special partner: "...if you hearken to my voice and keep my covenant, you shall be my special possession, dearer to me than all other people, though all the earth is mine" (Ex 19:5).

The Ten Commandments are, therefore, the blueprint for the way of life for people who have said "yes" to God's promise of fidelity, justice, and loving kindness. Those who live by these laws are indeed God's covenant people. Long after God established the covenant with the Israelites, the prophet Micah spoke words of covenant spirituality when he said:

> You have been told, O man, what is good,
> and what the LORD requires of you:
> Only to do the right and to love goodness,
> and to walk humbly with your God (Mic 6:8).

Rabbi Michael Resnick of Adat Shalom in Los Angeles once said:

> Because of the covenant, Jews are supposed to live by the highest standards. We are commanded to be a model community—a "light to the nations." While this sometimes comes at a cost—remember the words of Tevye in *Fiddler on the Roof:* "We are your chosen people. But, once in a while, can't you choose someone else?"—it is a price worth paying.

At the Last Supper, Jesus renewed the Old Covenant. The New Covenant he offers us also has its requirements, which, of course, do not cancel the old law. Rather, Jesus fulfilled the Old Covenant with a new focus to the law, a new motivation for keeping the Commandments:

> I give you a new commandment:/ Love one another./ Such as my love has been for you,/ so must your love be for each other./ This is how all will know you for my disciples:/ your love for one another (Jn 13:34–35).

To think of the Ten Commandments in terms of a covenant of love can help us to consider God in new ways, giving new life to our spirituality.

Ethics, Morality, and Conscience

When speaking of right and wrong, some people use the language of ethics, others the language of morality. In general, ethics refers to the philosophical, sometimes abstract, consideration of principles of right behavior and their application. We speak of expectations of ethical conduct by governments, police forces, advertisers, and the media.

Morality refers more to the exercise of conscience as a norm for right behavior and is the part of theology that deals with human behavior. Christianity respects ethics, but finds the core of right action in God's revelation, especially since all Christians believe that Jesus' teaching confirms the Ten Commandments. Jesus' teaching, grounded in the two great commandments of love of God and love of neighbor, gives us deeper motivation for obeying the Ten Commandments. Jesus' teaching brings morality closer to spirituality because it contains the two essential bonds that help us to develop and maintain our relationship with him. Through faith-filled Christian discipleship, we will find the means to ask for God's grace in every situation so that we may see and understand the loving, right choice and, when we sin, to beg for God's grace so that we may have the humility and strength to repent and be forgiven.

Conscience, that still small voice that speaks in the place where we are alone with God, tells us what is right and wrong and helps us to apply this knowledge to our thoughts and actions. As human beings, we are always informing and reforming our consciences so that we can conform more closely to God's presence and teaching in light of ever-new situations. Conscience teaches us that we are to act morally, that is, with love toward God, self, and others, and that it is sinful to choose to act against moral norms by choosing self and sin over love. Societies and communities betray both ethics and morality when they establish sinful structures that systematically offend human dignity.

The Nature of Evil

Evil is a popular word used to describe that which is bad in itself or people who do things that are inherently wrong. Mature, responsible, and thoughtful people will want to use this word wisely. Philosophers traditionally understand evil as the absence of good or, as one popular novelist* defined it, the absence of empathy. Another description defines evil as the opposite of benevolence or refusing to wish that oth-

---

* John Connolly, *The White Road* (New York: Simon & Schuster, 2003).

ers do well. Evil is mired in malevolence: the desire that disaster, cruelty, and failure befall others. Evil can also permeate societies and the structures by which those societies live. Evil is spoken of in abstract terms, but it manifests itself through real people's choices and the systems they create.

Dialogue between Scripture and Cinema

Cinematic evil manifests itself in the malicious attitudes of a character's (the protagonist or antagonist) mind and heart and his or her subsequent behavior. This is why it is useful to establish a dialogue between the Scriptures and popular movies that dramatize real moral dilemmas. The Ten Commandments are written on our hearts, and, if we are theologically and spiritually attuned and open, they can help form our viewing lens.

From our own experience, we know that, by its nature, morality is dynamic and dramatic, for we are always confronted with the choice between good and evil. The films in this volume mirror the drama, pain, and joys of all human living through the presentation of temptation, choices, motivations, consequences, and often the ambiguity of what constitutes the good and just response to a situation.

Why ought we obey the Ten Commandments? The first motivation is love; God revealed the Commandments in love, and love for God is the only reason for observing them that transcends our human limitations. In this book, we will treat the dilemma and moral tension of choosing between what is good or bad.

Cinema as a Moral Laboratory

The contribution of this book to religious and moral education is through its theological reflection and discernment as presented in the moral laboratory of popular, contemporary cinema. Through the exercise of our moral imagination, we can explore what moral theologians call "case studies" and learn to appreciate the complex nuances of moral behavior. By considering real or hypothetical cinematic stories, we can see people and issues from different perspectives of responsibility, sinfulness, and guilt, as well as how the characters have formed their consciences to begin with. It is hoped that we will learn empathy and, at the same time, "fine tune" our consciences through the process of listening, dialogue, and action. We can compare and contrast our own moral norms and values with those of the Church, the Scriptures, and our culture so that we can choose rightly and walk justly in the light of the Lord.

The formation of conscience is a challenge for people of faith. Some people only want to be told what to do or to have their views confirmed. They have found a place of moral safety and feel it comforting to obey blindly. This can lead to a loss of empathy for others. Other people seem to base their moral decisions on what feels good and right to them regardless of any moral and ethical arguments that might counter their views. This leads to moral relativity, which Pope Benedict XVI, while still Cardinal Joseph Ratzinger, described on April 18, 2005, as "letting oneself be tossed and swept away by every wind of teaching." Contemporary culture expresses this as: if it feels good or right, no matter what anyone says, just do it. Filmmakers who give voice to conscience in their movies often use this kind of moral relativity to create the dramatic counterpoint to a protagonist's struggle.

Movies are the dramatic moral case studies of today. The aim of this book is to explore the issues, motivations, choices, and consequences involved in the stories we have chosen, not to rearticulate laws that people already know. Movies tell stories and enable us to identify with the characters and their struggles. As the films tell their stories, they offer us images, metaphors, symbols, and analogies that open up our intellects to more concrete meanings than mere abstract reasoning could offer (cf. *Vigilanti cura,* [*On Motion Pictures*], no. 23).

Although these film stories do not cover every aspect of each commandment, they give us quite a bit to reflect on, both emotionally and rationally. Sometimes the stories have happy endings with repentance, reconciliation, and restitution. At other times, the more complex moral stories do not give us easy solutions. They take us "into the depths" (*de profundis*) with the sinner and immerse us in the protagonist's struggles and his or her choice to do evil rather than good. Nevertheless, these stories continually remind us of how much human beings are in need of redemption. Psalm 130 reminds us that God is attentive to the pleading of those who cry out to him from the depths of their need for redemption.

We now offer two movies that are indeed case studies for the Ten Commandments as a whole. The first film is Cecil B. DeMille's blockbuster movie, *The Ten Commandments.* This film remains relevant because it is a classic saga that includes a cinematic interpretation of the Sinai event when God gave the Decalogue to Moses. The second film is based on a John Grisham novel, *The Client.* This film shows how contemporary movies can subtly dramatize the issues and values inherent in the commandments as well as their purpose in our lives.

Charlton Heston in *The Ten Commandments*.

THE TEN COMMANDMENTS

Exodus 20:1–17; Deuteronomy 5:1–6:13

Romans 12:8–10

Mark 10:17–22

The Ten Commandments

U.S.A., 1956, 240 minutes

Actors: Charlton Heston, Yul Brynner, Anne Baxter, Yvonne De Carlo, Edward G. Robinson, Debra Paget, John Derek, Nina Foch, Judith Anderson, Cedric Hardwicke, John Carradine, Douglass Dumbrille, Martha Scott, Vincent Price

Writers: Aneas MacKenzie, Jesse L. Lasky Jr., Jack Gariss, Fredric M. Frank

Director: Cecil B. DeMille

The Ten Commandments

The Covenant and the Law

The Hebrews have been slaves of the Egyptians for 400 years. About the year 1525 B.C.,[*] when the high priest claims that a deliverer of the Hebrew people has been born, Pharaoh Rameses I declares that all newborn Hebrew males are to be killed. In order to save her infant son, Yochabel places the boy in a basket and sets him adrift on the Nile River. The childless princess Bithia (Nina Foch) finds him and raises him as her son. She names him Moses. Her brother, the Pharaoh Sethi (Cedric Hardwicke), has a son named Rameses II. The boys grow up together as princes of Egypt. They compete for the love of Nefretiri (Anne Baxter), who wants to marry Moses.

When Rameses II (Yul Brynner) fails to build the city Sethi wants, Moses takes over. Shocked at the condition of the Hebrew slaves, he opens the granaries to feed them. He rescues a woman when she falls under a huge stone. When he discovers that he is a Hebrew, Moses goes to find his family. He becomes a slave among slaves and kills Baka (Vincent Price), the master builder of the city. He meets Joshua

SYNOPSIS

---

[*] This is the date used in the film. Contemporary biblical scholarship sets the date at approximately 1300 B.C.

1

(John Derek) and admits he is a Hebrew. When Sethi discovers the truth about Moses, he gives Nefretiri to Rameses and lets Rameses banish Moses to the desert.

Moses wanders in the wilderness until he comes to the well at Median. Jethro and his daughters take him in. He becomes a shepherd, marries Sephora (Yvonne de Carlo), and has a son, Gershom. Moses sees a fire burning on Mount Sinai and knows it is God. He approaches the burning bush and demands to know why God is not helping his people. He also asks God's name and receives the reply, "I am that am." God gives Moses a mission to rescue the Hebrews. Joshua arrives to call Moses back to Egypt to save their people.

Moses goes to Pharaoh Rameses and tells him he brings the Word of God. To prove it, his staff turns into a serpent. Aaron (John Carradine) tells Moses the people want to leave Egypt. Moses returns again and again to Pharaoh to ask that he release the Hebrew people, and seven times God sends a plague to convince him: water turns into blood, a hail storm strikes down everything, locusts destroy the crops, and, finally, the firstborn son of every Egyptian family is to die.

Nefretiri goes to Moses to bargain for her son's life, but it is too late. The Hebrews put lambs' blood on their doorposts so the angel of death will pass them over. There is great lamentation in the land as the sons of the Egyptians die. The Hebrews pack their things and eat a supper of lamb and bitter herbs before they flee. Rameses has finally decreed they can go.

Joshua organizes the people into tribes. His girlfriend, Lilia (Debra Paget), is now with the treacherous Dothan (Edward G. Robinson), an Egyptian. Joshua forces Lilia and Dothan to go with the Hebrews. They begin their trek, but when Pharaoh realizes his slaves are leaving, he regrets his decision, and he and his army give chase. At the Red Sea,

Moses lifts up his staff to part the waters. The Hebrews follow a pillar of flame through the sea. When Pharaoh and his men follow, they drown.

The Hebrew people walk through the wilderness to Mount Sinai. When Moses climbs up the mountain to speak with God, Dothan leads the people to commit idolatry. Aaron helps them make a golden calf. Dothan wants to offer Lilia as a sacrifice. Meanwhile, God announces the Ten Commandments to Moses and engraves them on stone tablets. If the people obey these laws, God will bless them. This is God's covenant. When Moses comes down the mountain with the tablets, Joshua is waiting. They hear the revelry in the camp and realize that many of the people have lost faith in Moses' return and in God. When they enter the camp, Moses breaks the tablets in anger, and Joshua rescues Lilia.

Moses and the people wander in the desert for forty years. When those who had been unfaithful had all died, they finally reach the Promised Land. Moses sees it from a mountain and tells Joshua and Sephora that he cannot cross over the Jordan River because he did not obey when God tested him at the rock of Horeb. Joshua is to lead the people. Moses gives him the five scrolls of the Law that are to be put in the sacred chest, the Ark of the Covenant, that the people carry with them. Moses tells Joshua, "Go, proclaim liberty to the land and the inhabitants." Moses stands in the light of God.

COMMENTARY

The Ten Commandments turned out to be the climax of Cecil B. De Mille's directing career. His 1923 silent version of the Exodus epic, also called *The Ten Commandments,* was very popular. In the 1930s he directed spectacular productions containing a combination of action, sex, and religion, among them *The Sign of the Cross, Cleopatra,* and *The Crusades.* He turned his creative attention to Americana in the late 1930s and early 1940s with *The Plainsman, Union Pacific,* and *Reap the Wild Wind.* In 1949, he returned to the Bible with *Samson and Delilah.* Next, he portrayed the circus in *The Greatest Show on Earth,* which surprisingly won the Oscar for Best Film of 1952.

For *The Ten Commandments,* De Mille drew on an enormous amount of talent in stars, photographers, and set designers. The film is quite a mammoth event. De Mille even appears at the beginning of the film (as he did with *Samson and Delilah*) and solemnly announces that the film's authenticity is based on the Sacred Scriptures, the writings of the statesman and philosopher Philo (20 B.C.–A.D. 50), and the historian Josephus (ca. A.D. 37–100). Charlton Heston, who was still in the early years of his acting career when he portrayed many famous characters, including Judah Ben-Hur in *Ben-Hur* (1959), Rodrigo Dìaz de Vivar in *El Cid* (1961), and Michelangelo in *The Agony and the Ecstasy* (1965), is convincing and effective as Moses.

Some people find difficulty in watching *The Ten Commandments* because it sometimes takes the literary forms of the Exodus and its saga style too literally, and at other times adds fictional elements. This is the stuff of movie spectacles, but it is still an interpretation of events and not necessarily recorded "history." Today, some of the movie's sequences, such as Moses' encounter with God in the burning bush, the parting of the Red Sea, and the actual giving of the Ten Commandments, seem more like technical displays of special effects than a deep and religious dramatization of the events. On the one hand, this is a pity, as these events are central to the theology of the Book of Exodus: the revelation of the name of Yahweh to Moses, the beginning of the Exodus to the Promised Land, and the pledging of the covenant by the Decalogue. On the other hand, *The Ten Commandments* remains one of the most popular biblical epics. Younger audiences might enjoy more the 1998 animated *Prince of Egypt,* although the giving of the Commandments plays a lesser role and impact in the story.

> *Focus:* The Ten Commandments *is a spectacular re-creation of the Exodus that enables us to enter the world of Moses and to experience the Decalogue event. Jesus is the New Covenant who gave us his law of love. As with the rich young man, Jesus invites us all to live the Commandments and to give everything to God in love.*

DIALOGUE WITH THE SCRIPTURES

Exodus, chapter 20, is one of the key chapters of the Jewish Scriptures. It presents us with the formulation of the Decalogue and gives us the guarantee of its authenticity: the fact that God so loved the Israelite people that he pledged to be faithful to them. He brought them out of their slavery in Egypt to guide them to their Promised Land. The Decalogue was to be the way of life for the people of Israel. The Ten Commandments still have a pride of place among the Christian churches because "[t]hey are pre-eminently the words of God... [and] must first be understood in the context of the Exodus, God's great liberating event at the center of the Old Covenant" (*CCC,* nos. 2056, 2057).

In the seventh-century B.C., the inspired Hebrew writers looked again at the Decalogue tradition. In Deuteronomy 5 and 6, while incorporating material from the tradition that would become the Exodus formulations, the principal theme is that of the covenant. The beginning of Deuteronomy 5 amplifies descriptions of the role of Yahweh in making the covenant pledges. The latter part of the chapter amplifies the role of Moses as mediator of the covenant. The emphasis is on handing on this covenant tradition to succeeding generations. The culmination of this exhortation is to be found in the classic call, "Hear, O Israel! The LORD is our God, the LORD alone! Therefore, you shall love the LORD, your God, with all your heart, and with all your soul, and with all your strength...." It is the "Shema Israel" of Deuteronomy 6:4—to love God wholeheartedly. The verses continue: this law is to be repeated, fixed before the people's eyes, written on the doorposts of their homes.

This is where *The Ten Commandments*, with all its spectacle, stars, and special effects, can be helpful. It is difficult to imagine the world of Moses and the Exodus. By dramatizing the Exodus, De Mille creates an ancient world and immerses his audiences in it. To that extent, it becomes real. In this film, the oppression of the Hebrews and the order for all male infants to be killed, Moses and his life at Pharaoh's court, the violence of the times, the experience of God in the desert, and the plagues are all there for us to relive and imagine. The characters from the biblical texts of Exodus and Numbers appear, sometimes breaking the Commandments, especially when the people worship the golden calf.

Jesus is the New Covenant and his law of love is the new law. Paul, in his Letter to the Romans, takes up the themes of Deuteronomy, especially the law of love as the fulfillment of every other law.

Living the Ten Commandments every day is generally not as spectacular as a De Mille movie. As Christians, we strive to live the Commandments and the law of love in our daily lives, responding to the challenges of the world around us. The Gospel story of the rich young man brings this home to us. When he approached Jesus to ask how he should live his life, Jesus reminded him of the Commandments. The rich young man was a good man and assured Jesus that he had observed them all his life. Jesus went a step further and invited the youth to follow him and rediscover the Law in the person of the Master, who is its perfect fulfillment. A person of great wealth, the young man decided to remain with the basic laws of God to guide him to eternal life. He understood the Decalogue but was not able to interpret it in the light of Jesus' invitation to sell his possessions, give to the poor, and follow him.

- Moses fleeing to Midian, meeting Jethro, settling with him and his family, caring for the flocks; Moses' courting of Sephora; his solitude in the wilderness and experiencing the presence of God, hearing his name and sensing his mission to lead the people of Israel.

- The flight from Egypt; the Passover preparations, the meal, and the children of Israel ready to leave; the angel passing over the houses of Israel but destroying the firstborn of Egypt; Moses leading the people on the Exodus, parting the waters of the Red Sea, and the people passing safely through; the pursuit by the Egyptians and their drowning.

- Mount Sinai and the thunder and lightning of the theophany; Moses and his going into the clouds to receive the Law; his coming to the people, pledging God's covenant, and the people of Israel pledging themselves to fidelity as God's chosen people.

KEY SCENES AND THEMES

1. From the beginning of *The Ten Commandments* when Cecil B. De Mille appears to present the film, we get a sense of its relevance in relation to the Scriptures and to the modern world despite the fact that the film is fifty years old. No work of art is created in a cultural vacuum, and neither was *The Ten Commandments*. It was released barely ten years after World War II, when the Jewish people in Europe were enslaved and their population almost annihilated by the Nazi regime because of racial hatred. Therefore, we have this reality playing in our consciousness as we watch the film. How and when do the characters in the film, for example, Moses, Yochabel, Jethro, and Joshua, speak to issues of social justice (e.g., when Moses says

FOR REFLECTION AND CONVERSATION

that all people are to worship God in freedom, regardless of their race or creed)? Why don't Rameses and Nefretiri understand Moses' actions both before and after his time in the wilderness? How are the commandments, the covenant, personal and social at the same time?

2. When Jesus spoke to the rich young man about the Law of Moses and his law of love (cf. Mt 19:16–21), Jesus invited him to embrace the example of his own life of love for self and others. Later, religious orders read this passage as encouraging a life that embraces poverty, chastity, and obedience. These virtues or words of guidance for a happy, holy life counter the vices that encourage the abuse of money, sex, and power by individuals and societies. Which characters in the film express the desire for wealth at the expense of others, indulging in unchecked lust and unbridled power over others? Why do these characters make certain choices, and what are the consequences for them and the nation and community of the Hebrews? Talk about how Jesus came to fulfill the Law of Moses through his law of love. How did Jesus integrate these laws in his teaching? What do they mean for you?

3. A "theophany" is an epiphany or a manifestation of God. Moses' encounter with God in the burning bush on Mount Sinai remains one of the most intensely religious and spiritual moments recorded in the Scriptures. What do you think Moses' image of God was before this encounter? What do you think Moses' image of God was afterward? How does Moses "theologize" about God in the film? Have you ever had a "theophany" or a moment of insight into

God's presence in your life? How would you articulate your image of God? Who is the God of the covenant, the God of Moses, for you? What difference does this image of God make in your life and how you live the Ten Commandments and Jesus' law of love?

Prayer

Lord, you gave the law to your Chosen People as a way of life and of fidelity to you, and now you have given us Jesus, your Son, and his law of love. Help us always to be faithful to your law. Amen.

For Catechists

Catechism of the Catholic Church

The Decalogue in Scripture and the Church's tradition, nos. 1961–1974, 2052–2074

Susan Sarandon and Brad Renfro in *The Client*.

THE TEN COMMANDMENTS

Proverbs 12:12–28

1 John 5:1–5

John 14:21–24

The Client

U.S.A., 1994, 119 minutes

Actors: Susan Sarandon, Tommy Lee Jones, Mary-Louise Parker, William H. Macy, Anthony LaPaglia, J. T. Walsh, Anthony Edwards, Brad Renfro, Will Patton, Bradley Whitford

Writers: Akiva Goldsman, Robert Getchell

Director: Joel Schumacher

 *The Client*

Moral Compass

SYNOPSIS

A young, poor, single mother, Diane Sway (Mary-Louise Parker), tells her boys not to play in the woods while she's at work. Eleven-year-old Mark (Brad Renfro) promises not to, but he and eight-year-old Ricky go anyway and sit down on the river bank to smoke. A man drives up and tries to kill himself by hooking up a hose to the car's exhaust pipe. Mark realizes what is happening and tries to stop him. The second time Mark pulls the hose out, the man grabs him, hooks up the hose again, and forces Mark into the car with him. He says he is Jerome Clifford, a lawyer for the mob in New Orleans. He tells Mark where the body of a murdered senator is buried. Clifford, high on pills and alcohol, is afraid of the mob. Mark escapes from the car, and he and Ricky run through the woods to hide. Clifford gives chase but quickly loses them. He shouts that their escape does not matter: the mob will find and kill Mark because of the secret he has told him. Then Clifford shoots himself.

Mark calls 911. His mother comes home to find Ricky in a catatonic state. A policeman asks Mark if the man spoke to him before committing suicide. Mark denies that Clifford told him anything, but the policeman is suspicious. An ambu-

11

lance takes Ricky to the hospital. Mark decides he needs a lawyer and finds Reggie Love (Susan Sarandon), a divorced, recovering alcoholic who has only been a lawyer for two years. She always wears a small compass around her neck.

The egotistical, Scripture-quoting U.S. attorney from Louisiana, Roy Foltrigg (Tommy Lee Jones), becomes involved. Foltrigg wants the senator's body so he can win a case against the mob and advance politically. He and his assistants try to convince Mark that he doesn't need a lawyer, but Mark is wearing a hidden recording device that Reggie has given him to tape their lies. Reggie Love arrives and confronts them with the incriminating tape, saving Mark from a forced confession. The mob in New Orleans pursues Mark and threatens his family, so he decides not to talk to the police and continues to hide the whole truth even from Reggie.

Foltrigg and the FBI have Mark put in custody so they can question him in court. At the hearing, Mark takes the Fifth Amendment to protect his family. Mark escapes from custody, calls Reggie to pick him up, and they discuss the witness protection program. But before Mark can be sure Foltrigg will offer his family this protection, Reggie and Mark must go to New Orleans to make sure that the body of the murdered senator is really there. Foltrigg and the mob follow, but Mark and Reggie outwit everyone. Reggie gets Foltrigg to agree to Mark's terms for witness protection in return for the location of the senator's body. As they say goodbye, Reggie gives Mark her compass.

COMMENTARY

The Client is the third of lawyer-author John Grisham's novels to be made into a motion picture. The first two, *The Firm* and *The Pelican Brief,* were both released in 1993. Grisham's novels ring true because he writes from his own experiences as an attorney working in the American South, and he weaves in the interesting and relevant ethical issues that lawyers face. His fifteen novels to date have been published in twenty-seven languages, and over 60 million copies are in print internationally.

Director Joel Schumacher has an impressive filmography that includes another Grisham book-into-film, *A Time to Kill* (1996); *Flatliners* (1990); the social-psychological drama *Falling Down* (1993); and, more recently, *Phone Booth* (2002) and *Veronica Guerin* (2003). Much of Schumacher's recent work is a social commentary about people who seek justice and truth. He also directed *Batman Forever* (1995) and *Batman & Robin* (1997), but is blamed for the demise of the franchise, perhaps because he changed Tim Burton's dark vision to a brightly colored, flamboyant treatment. He won the Golden Bear at the Berlin Film Festival in 1999 for *The Thin Red Line,* and his film version of Andrew Lloyd Weber's musical, *Phantom of the Opera,* came out in 2004.

The screenplay for *The Client* is by Robert Getchell (*Alice Doesn't Live Here Anymore*) and Akiva Goldsman (*A Beautiful Mind, A Time to Kill,* and several of Schumacher's other films).

Susan Sarandon, who went on to win an Oscar in 1996 for her role as Sr. Helen Prejean in *Dead Man Walking,* was nominated for an Academy Award for her role as the divorced, recovering alcoholic attorney Reggie Love in *The Client.* Sarandon's intelligent femininity stands in stark contrast to the male lawyers and criminals who test the limits of the law in this film.

Joel Schumacher worked before (*Batman Forever*) with Academy Award winner Tommy Lee Jones, who plays "Reverend" Roy Foltrigg, the ambitious, vain, Bible-quoting district attorney in *The Client.* Brad Renfro was twelve years old when Schumacher cast him as Mark. William H. Macy, Anthony LaPaglia (*Without a Trace*), Mary-Louise Parker, Bradley Whitford, Anthony Edwards, and Will Patton complete the multi-award-winning ensemble cast.

Focus: Attorney Roy Foltrigg needs the words of Proverbs as much as anyone. Mark Sway ponders the meaning of "The truth shall set you free" graffiti on the wall. The Client *uses "truth" to explore and unify all the commandments as the guide or map to right human living, as symbolized by Reggie Love's compass.*

The Book of Proverbs is part of the wisdom genre of Sacred Scripture that uses a poetic literary form. "Lying lips are an abomination to the LORD, but those who are truthful are his delight" (Prov 12:22) shows the act-consequence relationship of this Wisdom teaching. Foltrigg wrongly attributes the quote to the Psalms, but the judge in the story quickly puts him right. In Hebrew this kind of poetic saying is called a *mashal.* Foltrigg, the representative of the state's laws, uses Scripture to manipulate his subjects; the judge, also a representative of the state, has integrated the law of God and civil law in a just way. Nevertheless, the meaning of this proverb is not lost on the audience as the tension in the film plays out. The entire reading fits Mark's situation, and we can imagine him, Foltrigg, Reggie, and the criminals in the story all struggling for power through the use of the language of Proverbs: the consequences of lies over truth and truth over lies.

Mark, a mere child, ponders the words on the wall: "The truth shall set you free." The reading from the First Letter of John: "[w]e can be sure that we love God's children when we love God and do what he has commanded" (5:2) fits the relationship between Mark and Reggie. She loves and cares for Mark and teaches him in an almost Socratic fashion, engaging him in argument and dialogue about how the truth can be a compass for life. When he first asks about the compass she wears, she explains its role in her life. Later, she gives it to him, saying it is so "you won't lose your way." Thus Reggie shows how she loves this child who is caught between wanting to be truthful and protecting his family.

The Gospel reading is from John's Last Supper discourse that ends with Jesus telling Judas, "[h]e who obeys the commandments he has from me is the man who loves me; and he who loves me will be loved by my Father" (Jn 14:21). In *The Client*, God's love appears in Reggie's love for Mark and in the religious visuals that form the rich background of the film: pictures of the Sacred Heart of Jesus, the crosses on the wall, stained glass windows, and even the fact that much of the action takes place in a Catholic, that is, faith-based hospital.

Trying to do the right thing, to be among the just, is a difficult struggle for the child and adults in *The Client*. The traitors in the film are those who break the laws of God and society as well as those who manipulate the law for their own gain at the expense of the innocent. Reggie Love's intelligent and right use of the law to protect the innocent achieves salvation, the reward of the just.

KEY SCENES AND THEMES

- Dianne Sway telling Mark and Ricky not to go to the river; their promise and later disobedience; the lawyer Clifford driving up and trying to kill himself; Mark trying to stop him; Clifford dragging Mark into the car, confessing his secret, and shooting himself; Ricky collapsing.

- At the hospital; the police trying to get Mark to talk; the reporter sneaking in; Foltrigg arriving with his entourage and the media; Mark hiring Reggie Love because he is afraid to talk about what Clifford told him; Reggie's story and the compass; Foltrigg lying to Mark, and Reggie unmasking him; Foltrigg revealing Reggie's story to Dianne; the mob threatening Mark.

- The courtroom and the judge's rules and wisdom; Mark refusing to speak, and the police taking him into custody; Mark ordering pizza with a stolen cred-it card; escaping with Reggie; deciding to go into protective custody; finding the body of the senator and making a deal with Foltrigg; the terms of the deal and Reggie giving the compass to Mark.

FOR REFLECTION AND CONVERSATION

1. *The Client* is a film about all the commandments, including Jesus' law of love. Identify the words, scenes, symbols, and visuals in the film that refer to each of the commandments, e.g., truth, lies, the meaning of "swearing," oaths, killing, suicide, theft, marriage, parent-child relationships, the false gods of celebrity and fame, hope, despair, promises, the worship of God (or not), bearing false witness, mate-rial poverty, love for self and neighbor, etc. Which of the characters exemplifies divine love in the movie? Talk about how these symbols, characters, and themes interact to create the meaning of the film. What did it mean to you?

2. The reading from Proverbs contrasts righteous-ness/uprightness and wickedness/evil. What virtue and vice, wisdom and foolishness are contrasted in *The Client?* How are the moral or cardinal virtues, such as prudence, justice, fortitude, temperance, truthfulness, and patience, present in the film? Write a proverb of your own inspired by the film.

3. *The Ten Commandments* is *explicitly* about the Commandments as the Sinai Covenant between God and the Hebrew people: he will be their God, bring them into a land of milk and honey, and save them from their enemies. They will be God's Chosen People and obey God's law. *The Client,* however, is about the Commandments *implicitly.* What kind of

covenant does *The Client* imply? What did Reggie's compass symbolize? What did it mean when she gave it to Mark? Have you ever entered into a covenant with God or another person? Talk about that relationship and what it means for you, your family, and for society.

Prayer

Lord, be with us as we seek to live everything that you have revealed to us in the Commandments and your law of love. Amen.

For Catechists

Catechism of the Catholic Church
Moral or cardinal virtues, nos. 1803–1809
Moral conscience, nos. 1776–1794

The First Commandment

Introduction

You shall not have other gods besides me./Be authentically religious./Destroy your idols.

"You shall not have other gods besides me" (Deut 5:7).

"You shall not follow other gods...for the LORD, your God, who is in your midst, is a jealous God" (Deut 6:14–15).

"Idol" is a word that people toss around easily these days. Originally, the word meant a false god, the same meaning it has in the expression of the First Commandment in Exodus and Deuteronomy. However, "idol" is now used for anyone who is put on a pedestal, be it a sports figure or an entertainment celebrity. In fact, to become an "idol" has now become a desired goal made popular by the television shows *American Idol* in the United States and *Pop Idol* in the United Kingdom.

Why is it that so many people seem to have lost a sense of the sacred in their lives to such an extent that they are eager to fill the void with idols? We develop a "cult" following for celebrities, we participate in newly established "rituals" of television watching, voting for them, then buying their music; we "worship" these idols and eagerly read any gossip associated with them—which some of us go so far as to take as "gospel" truth. It is not as if the human race were not religious, but the question is, who are the gods we adore?

In order to get an idea of the priorities in peoples' lives, it would be very interesting to list in one column those people they admire and put on pedestals (celebrities) and in another column those people who are essential to their daily lives (family and friends, co-workers). The list could also include a column for such goals as money, fame, and success, because these are associated with the cult of celebrity. Then the list-maker would cross-reference the columns. One has only to look at the outrageously high figures paid to football, baseball, and basketball players, famous recording artists, and movie stars to realize that we, as their audience, all share in this idolatry.

In contrast to this, the First Commandment is primarily about the requirement (yes, requirement) to love God above all things and to serve and adore God alone.

All of us need to look at our individual lives and ask ourselves about our own idols. These idols might be our family or groups to which we belong—including our churches. Anything and anyone we put on a pedestal and venerate can become an idol when we let this object or person usurp the place of God in our lives.

This can be particularly true of causes. The twentieth century saw the rise of the "worship" of idealism with the creation of the socialist state and its failure decades later. We have seen statues toppled from their "pedestals": Lenin, fascist leaders, and, most recently, Saddam Hussein.

One of the dangers of placing faith on a pedestal through a fundamentalist approach to religion by good people who want to secure an unbreakable faith is that "faith," or the "act of believing," rather than the person of God, becomes the object of worship. Religious people who eagerly point out the misdirected idolatry of others often fail to appreciate that this can happen to them.

In recent decades, some people have taken refuge in the new idols of New Age movements and activities. They place crystals, meditation practices, and self-help programs on pedestals. It is true that while some of these activities may be beneficial for the person, they can also be a substitute for authentic religion and worship.

The Book of Deuteronomy contains many condemnations of superstitious rituals such as those that seduced the people of Israel. In our own day, numerous superstitious practices are available via newspapers, magazines, the telephone, and the Internet. Normally common-sensed, even skeptical people turn to astrology, palm reading, and tarot cards for guidance (see *The Gift,* page 36).

Other sins against the First Commandment are indifference to our faith, abandonment of our faith, presumption or despair, or hatred of God in our neighbor through envy, sloth, ingratitude, and scandal, etc.

The First Commandment is the fundamental divine decree from which all the others proceed. It challenges us to acknowledge who our God is, the nature of our commitment to God, and how to identify and topple our idols.

The three films we have chosen for the First Commandment are *Princess Caraboo,* which deals with the cult of celebrity; *Simone,* which is about false gods; and *The Gift,* which deals with the world of superstition.

Genesis 3:1–13
Romans 13:8–10
Matthew 20:20–21

Princess Caraboo
U.S.A./U.K., 1994, 90 minutes
Actors: Phoebe Cates, Stephen Rea, Wendy Hughes,
Jim Broadbent, John Lithgow, Kevin Kline, John Sessions,
John Lynch, Steven Mackintosh, Anna Chancellor
Writers: Michael Austin, John Wells
Director: Michael Austin

Princess Caraboo

Fantasy, Ambition, Celebrity

SYNOPSIS

In 1817, just outside the port city of Bristol, England, a young and very beautiful woman (Phoebe Cates) is walking the roads. She gets a ride in a hay wagon. At a nearby village, the authorities almost arrest her for vagrancy, which is a crime in England. She speaks no English, but only an exotic sounding language that enchants the wealthy Worrals, who take her in. She says "Caraboo" and Mrs. Worrall (Wendy Hughes) believes this is her name. A reporter, Mr. Gutch (Stephen Rea), becomes interested in her story and starts to investigate it based on a prayer book she has with her. Frixos (Kevin Kline), the Greek butler, is suspicious and unfriendly to her, but the maids like her.

Soon the Worralls convince themselves that she is an East Indian princess who has escaped from a slave trader's ship. They engage a linguist from Oxford to discover her origins and to see if the tattoos she has on her body mean that she is an authentic princess. He agrees that she is.

Mrs. Worrall introduces the princess to society to increase her own social standing. Mr. Worrall (Jim Broadbent) and his friends create a business scheme that promises profit from trade with the princess's father. They invite their colleagues to invest. Mr. Gutch travels to London and discovers that the princess is really Mary Baker, a poor homeless girl who is just trying to survive.

When her true identity is revealed, Mr. Worrall and his friends imprison Mary Baker with the intent of having her hanged for fraud. That night she tells Mr. Gutch how she imagined the life of the princess everyone thought her to be. Mrs. Worrall, who is really kind, and Frixos, who admires Mary Baker, help her to escape. Mr. Gutch joins her on a ship to America.

COMMENTARY

Princess Caraboo is based on a true story from early nineteenth-century England. It's somewhat difficult to pin down the film's genre, and reviewers in both the United States and the United Kingdom have called it a fable, a fantasy, a mystery, or a social commentary. But it is actually a romantic comedy firmly rooted in the above because the main characters must give up something for one another. Other reviewers think it similar to *Sommersby* (1993), because the film deals with identity; still others think it is more like *A Little Princess* (1995), because it is about self-esteem and belief in oneself.

Princess Caraboo is a small-budget film that looks and feels like a storybook. It is only the second film Michael Austin has directed. The majority of his film credits are as co-writer, a role he also had in this project with John Wells. Wells published a book called *Princess Caraboo: Her True Story* in 1994.

For such a small film, *Princess Caraboo* has a stellar cast. Phoebe Cates, who plays the princess, made her motion picture debut in Amy Heckerling's *Fast Times at Ridgemont High* in 1982. She also stared in *Gremlins* (1984) and *Gremlins 2* (1990). She plays the mysterious princess very well, and much of the film's comedy emerges from the way she aggravates Frixos, played by real-life husband and Academy

Award-winner Kevin Kline (*Life As a House, The Emperor's Club, A Fish Called Wanda*). Stephen Rea of *The Crying Game* is excellent as Mr. Gutch, the ardent journalist/hesitant suitor and love interest. Jim Broadbent (*Moulin Rouge*), Wendy Hughes (*Paradise Road*), and John Lithgow (*Shrek, The Pelican Brief*) round out the cast.

DIALOGUE WITH THE SCRIPTURES

Focus: Mary Baker dreamed up the exotic Princess Caraboo in her fantasy life. The Worrall family and local society put her on a pedestal for their own purposes. The mother of James and John was ambitious for her sons, but Jesus tells her that those who wish to be truly great must serve the rest.

The mother of James and John dreamed of power and prestige for her sons, imagining that they would be princes at the right and the left of the Lord Jesus. Jesus tells her that she and her sons do not know the implications of what she is asking. Whatever our vocation in life, it is God who calls us, and humility is a requirement for greatness.

Mary Baker, who weaved her stories about Princess Caraboo for children, succumbs to the temptation of the mother of James and John. She wants to rise from her poor state and become a princess. She wants to live out the exotic stories she imagined, to be a person feted by society, even by the Prince Regent. For a while, her dream becomes a lavish reality. But, rather than living the life she deserves as a member of the human family, she creates a fantasy world and worships an idol of her true self. It is a world that has to come tumbling down before she can be truly free to follow her destiny. Fortunately for Mary, her charming pretense never takes in John Gutch, who loves her for herself. He saves her and, in so doing, saves himself. Mrs. Worrall does believe Mary's story, but her main motives are kindness and generosity rather than greed. She, too, helps save Mary from the consequences of escaping into her pretend world.

Princess Caraboo offers a whole gallery of people, mostly men, who make up stories about the princess and believe them. They make an idol out of Princess Caraboo for their own greed and to further their ambitions, and they are responsible for the success of the princess's disguise. The movie presents, in a gently satiric way, how foolish and cruel people can be when they indulge in such idolatry. Mr. Worrall and the magistrate create a speculating trade scheme at their bank based on information they have fabricated about the princess. Professor Wilkinson becomes obsessed with the princess, first academically and then personally. The Worralls and their neighbors exploit her at court. Their disillusionment is all the greater because of the large amount of money they have invested in a scam as well as their reputations, which they have staked on Princess Caraboo's authenticity.

The frightening aspect of the unmasking of Princess Caraboo is that Mr. Worrall and the magistrate blame her for their own stupidity and are determined to hang her as quickly as possible to save their own names and necks. Going back to the Genesis story of the Fall, we see how quickly the man blames the woman for his eating of the forbidden fruit.

The Genesis story of the Fall recounts how God created the woman as man's companion. Adam was delighted at first, but soon he becomes vindictive toward her and makes her a scapegoat for his own wrongdoing. Men have frequently idolized women and, disappointed, found them wanting. Legends, myths, and stories told from time immemorial through the spoken and printed word, cinema, and television, show that a common reaction of the thwarted man is to destroy the woman. The violence and execution planned by the men at the movie's end is more powerful than this kind of light entertainment usually portrays, but it reminds us what can happen to women who are set up as "goddesses" for the purposes of others.

Mrs. Worrall treats Mary Baker kindly and tells her the truth about the men's evil intentions. She saves Mary Baker from death and gives her the opportunity to begin a new, free life because, through her, Mrs. Warrall has been saved from the deceit of her husband. John Gutch, whose only desire was to free Mary from the consequences of her own folly, is finally free enough to acknowledge his love and begin a new life with her. Paul's Letter to the Romans seems an appropriate epitaph: "Love does no evil to the neighbor; hence, love is the fulfillment of the law."

- The beautiful young girl walking along the English countryside; the men in the wagon giving her a ride; the authorities at the village questioning her and taking her to court; the journalist watching from the balcony; the prayer book.

- The court scene; going to the Worrall's and their welcome; the reaction of the staff; the Worrall's creation of the princess's story; the professor's visit and conclusion; Mr. Worrall and associates creating a business scheme; Mr. Gutch's investigation and trip to London; the Magdalene institution.

- The party and meeting the prince; Mr. Gutch's attempt to save her; the princess posing for her portrait and being confronted with the truth; Mrs. Worrall's reaction; Mr. Worrall and his associates' reaction; the staff's reaction; Mary's imprisonment in the barn and telling her story to Mr. Gutch; Mrs. Worrall's kindness and decision; Mary's departure and Mr. Gutch's decision.

1. The Beatitudes are the heart of the teachings of Jesus, and "Blessed are the poor in spirit" seems especially applicable to all the characters in this film.

KEY SCENES AND THEMES

FOR REFLECTION AND CONVERSATION

Further, the Beatitudes fulfill the promises of the covenant by extending their effects beyond geography to the kingdom of heaven. When Princess Caraboo is exposed as an imposter, all people turn on her except those who have been kind to her and love her for herself. How are the princess and those who seek to exploit her for profit "poor in spirit"? Is the princess really to blame for what happened? Who is responsible for turning Mary Baker into a princess? Who lives the Beatitudes in *Princess Caraboo?* How?

2. Men and women view *Princess Caraboo* differently. Young women identify with Mary Baker's imaginative struggle to survive; young men identify with Gutch's ambivalence about making a commitment to Mary, and they see his decision to risk everything for love as a model. Talk about the obstacles that both Mary and Gutch faced in their search for meaning and a happy life. Given the social structures of that time and place, what choices would you have made if you were in their place? Does anyone in the film make a wrong choice, an evil choice? Why do the characters do what they do? What motivates them?

3. The First Commandment is about offering God authentic worship. What is the place of worship in the lives of those who are trying to survive in the world that the film creates? Of those who are trying to make it big in that world? What kind of relationship with God can you imagine the characters in the film to have if any? What was the image of God or the false gods that guided them? Do you think they tempted God? How? Are people who make a god out of possessions and live life by the "bottom line" practical atheists? Why or why not?

Prayer

Lord, we make our own idols every day, set them up for our worship, and then find that they have feet of clay. Help us to see you more clearly as our one and only God. Amen.

For Catechists

Catechism of the Catholic Church
Our vocation to beatitude, no. 1716
"You shall not make for yourself a graven image..."
  nos. 2129–2132
Atheism, no. 2123

Al Pacino in *Simone*.

THE FIRST COMMANDMENT

Exodus 32:11–14; Psalm 113
Acts 14:8–18
Luke 12:16–21

Simone

U.S.A., 2002, 117 minutes

Actors: Al Pacino, Winona Ryder, Jay Mohr, Catherine Keener,
Evan Rachel Wood, Rachel Roberts, Darnell Williams

Writer: Andrew Niccol

Director: Andrew Niccol

 Simone

An American Idol

SYNOPSIS

Film director Viktor Taransky (Al Pacino) is frustrated when Nicola (Winona Ryder), the spoiled lead actress of his film, throws a tantrum and quits. He wants to save the picture, but the studio boss, his former wife, Elaine (Catherine Keener), refuses and even declines to renew his contract.

An old acquaintance, Hank (Elias Koteas), visits Viktor and tells him he has invented something that will help Viktor make movies with artistic integrity. But Viktor brushes him off. When Hank dies a few days later, a lawyer brings Viktor a package with computer disks of a CGI (computer generated image), a v-actress (virtual actress) known as SimulationOne, or SimOne. Nine months later, Viktor has replaced Nicola with Simone and releases the film. It is an instant success.

Celebrity reporters demand to see Simone, but Viktor always has an excuse for her non-appearance. Two reporters are especially suspicious. Viktor begins to make another film starring Simone. During an interview, the reporters realize Viktor is faking the background in the image and accuse him of embezzlement and kidnapping. To appease them, Viktor stages Simone staying at a hotel and even fakes her performance at a concert. There is a tie for Best Actress at the Oscars—Simone has won for both her films. Viktor's enthusiasm starts to fade when his daughter realizes Simone didn't thank him for being her director—he has forgotten to program that into her acceptance video.

Viktor concludes that he has to stage Simone's death. He destroys her image with a virus and sinks the disks in the ocean. At the funeral, he is arrested for murder when the police open her casket and find it empty. The police find no trace of Simone, and just as Viktor decides to plead guilty to her murder, his daughter manages to restore Simone to the computer.

Viktor, Elaine, and their daughter reunite and decide to continue making films with a whole cast of simulated characters. In her virtual world, Simone has a child and then decides to go into politics.

COMMENTARY

New Zealand-born Andrew Niccol had a very successful year in 1998. He directed a stylish futuristic thriller, *Gattaca,* which explored a totalitarian state and its need for a rebel, and he also wrote the screenplay for Peter Weir's *The Truman Show.* In the futuristic planned community of Seaside, Jim Carrey's Truman Burbank is an unwitting celebrity in his own reality show. The television producer, Christof (Ed Harris), "plays God" with Truman's life, controlling his every mood and reaction to every situation.

It is not a huge step from *The Truman Show* to Niccol's screenplay for *Simone,* which he also directed. He stays with the world of movies and television to comment on the public's need for celebrity, its craving for entertainment glitz, and the industry's willingness to respond in kind.

Academy Award-winner Al Pacino (*Scent of a Woman*), who often plays men in powerful positions (*The Godfather I, II, III, Serpico*), portrays the down-on-his-luck film producer Viktor Taransky with just enough angst to give *Simone* its comedy status. Simone (SimOne) is played by real-life actress Rachel Roberts.

Simone, the television celebrity, is a construct, as is the movie we watch. We assume all kinds of things in moviemaking. We know that computer graphics reproduced huge armies for *Braveheart* and a coliseum full of Roman spectators for *Gladiator* (these are called CGIs—computer generated graphics). But what if the star exists only in a computer-controlled machine and only appears to be lifelike through the process of computer graphics and computer-controlled action? It is fun to watch the stupidities of pragmatic producers like Viktor's wife, Elaine, and the reporters, who are desperate to meet and to associate with Simone.

Although the movie was not a commercial success, Niccol has given us an entertaining fantasy and satire about the tensions between our craving for reality and our idolization of technology and celebrity.

Focus: Simone is a technologically manufactured idol, similar to the golden calf described in the Exodus reading. The reporters are like those who extol Barnabas and Paul as false gods. The reading from Luke challenges Viktor to look at the emptiness in his life.

DIALOGUE WITH THE SCRIPTURES

Simone is an extraordinary idol of the twenty-first century, the completely manufactured movie star. She is the product of technological ingenuity. She is merely a digital image enhanced into the likeness of a real person. She is glorified by the media, her fans, and the critics. She is a beautiful conglomeration of aspects of real movie stars, but she is a phantom, an idol. Psalm 113 speaks of the emptiness of idols.

The movie parallels the Scripture passages about having false gods before our actual God.

One of the earliest stories of idolatry is that of the making of the golden calf by the Israelites in the desert. This event appears only twelve chapters after the declaration of the Decalogue in Exodus 20. The people feel abandoned by Moses and, consequently, by their God. To have some sense of identity, they panic and create a god to worship.

Movie director Viktor Taransky feels abandoned. He needs a hit, with the cooperation of a star, to get back on top, restore his reputation, save his sense of identity, and make some money.

Just as the calf was made out of the gold from the people's jewelry, so Simone is a modern construct, a golden-blonde image of many ingredients. No longer is molten metal used to make an effigy of an animal, but microchips, software, a computer keyboard, and digital technology produce this effigy. In the desert, the people worshipped the calf, offered sacrifice, ate, drank, and amused themselves. Once the public sees Simone onscreen, people worship her image, sacrifice their self-esteem to be seen with her, and amuse themselves by identifying with her status and movies.

Jesus tells the parable of the man who had everything but wanted to have more. Once Viktor creates Simone and sets her loose on the public, he manipulates her "appearances" at parties, at concerts, and in hotel rooms. He even manufactures her acceptance speech at the Oscars. Just as the Wizard of Oz is the mere human behind the "Great Oz," Victor is the human behind Simone the idol. Viktor is hooked. He has to have more and more. His equivalent of the barns mentioned in the Gospel of Luke is nowhere big enough to contain his gains from Simone's success.

But, like the wealthy man in the Gospel reading, he really does not have control over what he has put in motion; Simone could cease to exist, and he would be accused of her murder. Viktor's success with Simone's movies help him achieve cult status. People also worship and idolize him as a Hollywood mega-success. *Simone* is reminiscent of the story in Acts about Paul and Barnabas being so successful in their preaching and healing that the people of Lystra thought they must be gods. They were feted with garlanded oxen that were to be sacrificed in their honor. It took all of Paul and Barnabas' efforts to dissuade the people from worshipping them. "We are only human beings like you," they cried. Celebrities have to remind themselves of this truth.

The principal characters in the film can be explored in the light of these Scripture passages: Viktor's wife, Elaine, and her desperation to be associated with the idol; the fanatic detective and his associate who were prepared to sell themselves for Simone; the actor who thinks he is performing with a real person; the screaming fans.

In the Book of Exodus, Moses comes down from the mountain and topples and destroys the golden calf. Simone must be destroyed or she will destroy Viktor and his family. Although he succeeds in Simone's destruction, Viktor's daughter "resurrects" or restores her, and we are left wondering if Viktor and his family have learned anything at all.

KEY SCENES AND THEMES

- Nicola throwing a tantrum and demanding to be treated as royalty; her quitting and Viktor helping her load the car; Viktor trying to salvage the picture with the studio producers; Elaine chiding him and then telling him she will not renew his contract; Hank's appearance and words of appreciation for Viktor's talent; Viktor refusing to listen.

- The lawyer delivering the package from Hank; Viktor's realization of what Hank has created; the empty studio on the lot and Viktor's working arrangements; his creation of Simone and his relationship with "her."

- The media circus and the two suspicious reporters; Viktor's many ways of deceiving the reporters, fans, and his own family; the death and burial of Simone; the funeral and Viktor's arrest; Lainey restoring Simone and rescuing Viktor; Lainey's words on honesty; Viktor and Simone's future.

FOR REFLECTION AND CONVERSATION

1. Hollywood has made many movies that contrast money, sex, and power idols with the positive values revealed by the Commandments—worship of God over things being the first. The First Commandment can also include choosing what is human and of God over greed, lust, anger, and blind ambition. Some of these films are *Wall Street, Glengarry Glen Ross, Gandhi, Schindler's List, Regarding Henry, The Doctor, Home for the Holidays,* and *Nine Months.* List other films that deal with the issue of choosing God (or transcendent values) and one's fellow human beings over things or status. In what way are the dilemmas of the main character(s) like those of Viktor Transky? What other commandments does *Simone* deal with? What did Viktor mean when he said, "Our ability to manufacture fraud now exceeds our ability to detect it"?

2. "The proper artistic response of digital technology," wrote author Ralph Lombraglia, "is to embrace it as a new window on everything that's eternally human, and to use it with wisdom, passion, fearlessness and joy." Do you agree with this statement? Why or why not? What are some of the very human concerns people of faith and good will have about films with computer-generated images? How important is the ontological question about what is real and what isn't in information and entertainment media productions?

3. We live in a technological era that needs a spirituality that can transform us from living a life of individualism to one of community and from a system of relentless capitalism to a global economic system with a conscience. Moral integration—to recognize ourselves as sinners, to repent and live according to the Ten Commandments and Jesus' law of love—is the first step toward living the spiritual life. Where then does this leave Viktor Taransky? Where is he spiritually by the end of the film? How does Viktor wrestle with his conscience? Who is the voice of conscience in the film? Is there one? Do you think that Viktor made Simone or that Simone made Viktor—or both? Why?

Prayer

We are tempted every day, Lord, to put our heroes on pedestals, to amass possessions, to worship the idols we set up in place of you. Help us to look beyond these idols and see you, our loving and fulfilling God, and our brothers and sisters in need. Amen.

For Catechists

Catechism of the Catholic Church
"Him only shall you serve," nos. 2095–2103
Graven images, nos. 2129–2132

THE FIRST COMMANDMENT

Deuteronomy 18:9–22

Acts 17:23–31

Mark 9:14–29

The Gift

U.S.A., 2001, 112 minutes

Actors: Cate Blanchett, Giovanni Ribisi, Hilary Swank, Keanu Reeves, Greg Kinnear, Katie Holmes, Michael Jeter, Gary Cole

Writers: Billy Bob Thornton, Tom Epperson

Director: Sam Raimi

 *The Gift*

To an Unknown God

SYNOPSIS

Annie Wilson (Cate Blanchett) lives in Brixton, Georgia, with her three sons, Mike, Miller, and Ben. She is a psychic and supports her family by reading tarot cards for people. She does a reading for Valerie Barksdale (Hilary Swank), whose husband, Donnie (Keanu Reeves), is physically abusive and unfaithful. Annie urges Valerie to leave Donnie before he puts her in the hospital. Annie is very kind to the people who come to her. She has visions and dreams that disturb and frighten her.

Wayne Collins (Greg Kinnear) is the principal of Mike's school. He calls Annie in for a conference because Mike is acting out his anger over his father's death. Mike wants to visit his father's grave. Wayne and Annie feel an attraction for one another. When she takes her car to the garage for repairs, the mechanic, Buddy (Giovanni Ribisi), is grateful for her psychic help.

One night, Donnie Barksdale threatens Annie because she has told his wife to leave him. He tells her that she is doing Satan's work. Annie's dead grandmother (Rosemary Harris) appears to her in a psychic vision and tells her to listen to her instincts. When Annie goes to the country club with her friend, she sees Wayne's fiancé, Jessica (Katie Holmes), having sex with another man. When Donnie Barksdale frightens Miller the next day, Buddy comes along and rescues him.

Jessica's father comes to Annie for a reading because Jessica is missing. Annie sees Donnie's pond, and they find the body there. Donnie stands trial for the murder, and the jury convicts him. When Annie gives her testimony, the attorney reviles her. Buddy goes to her for help, but she is too upset. That night, Buddy tries to kill his father, and the police take him away to the state mental hospital. In a psychic vision, Annie sees that someone else has killed Jessica, but does not know who. Wayne asks her to go back to the pond with him to see if it will help her to identify Jessica's murderer. She sees that Wayne is the murderer, and he tries to kill her. Buddy saves her and explains that he has escaped from the hospital. They drive Wayne to the sheriff's office, and Annie goes in alone. Later, the sheriff tells Annie that Wayne has confessed. Annie swears that Buddy helped her, but the sheriff tells her that's impossible. Buddy committed suicide earlier that same night.

Annie and her sons go to visit her husband's grave.

The Gift was co-written by Billy Bob Thornton and his friend, Tom Epperson. The film seems very believable, probably because Thornton's own mother claims to be a psychic who is said to have foretold several events on the path of his career.

COMMENTARY

Director Sam Raimi, known for his horror and nightmarish films, began to explore the darkness of humanity when confronted with the reality of the struggle between greed, murder, and truth in his excellent and Coen Brothers-like 1999 film, *A Simple Plan*. In 2004, he explored humanity and character in the entertaining and high-concept film *Spider Man II*. *Spider Man III* continues the series. *The Gift,* while still a thriller, takes a different turn because it gets inside the head and soul of a woman with the dubious gift of being able to see the darkness in others. Australian actress Cate Blanchett once again shows her ability to assume any role and play it to perfection. Here she believably plays a woman of the American South with little means who is a deeply caring mother and neighbor.

DIALOGUE WITH THE SCRIPTURES

Focus: The Gift raises issues of superstition. Deuteronomy condemns all superstition and urges people to faith in God. This is the message Paul has for the Athenians, and Jesus urges it on his disciples who unsuccessfully try to heal a boy.

The First Commandment condemns idols, that is, anything finite set up as an alternate to God. One of the sins this commandment addresses is superstition. It is always surprising and strange to find people who call faith in God irrational while they indulge in superstition, whether reading tea leaves or horoscopes, attending a séance, or asking about the future from a fortune-teller. Deuteronomy reveals that superstition was sometimes rampant in Israel, and chapter 18 condemns all kinds of divination and fortune-telling, use of charms, and calling up the dead. It also highlights the role of the true prophet who listens to God's word and communicates it. Anyone who speaks in his or her own name is a fraud.

There is a saying that when someone does not stand for something, they will fall for anything. At times of loss of faith, this is evident, and the latter part of the twentieth century seems to have been such a time. When there was speculation in the mid-1960s that there should be a moratorium on the use of the word "God," and when the slogan "God is dead" became popular, filmmakers produced a series of rather serious movies about the devil, including *Rosemary's Baby, The Exorcist, The Omen,* and many, many more.

The Gift is an entertaining piece of thriller hokum, a murder mystery solved by clairvoyance that certainly raises issues about superstition in a contemporary context. Annie Wilson has some kind of gift, some capacity for intuition and "second sight." Annie's neighbors rely on her to look at the tarot cards or other signs to discover what will happen to them. They entrust their future to a superstition.

The movie, however, takes us beyond this fortune-telling "gift" to question the reality of gifts that are part of some people's psychological makeup: an ability to read people, signs, and their own hunches. Annie gives healthy, common-sense advice to battered wives and others who come to her door. When she assists the police in their investigation, her gift for being able to sense evil more deeply helps her unmask the killer. The denouement of the film is when the ghost of her friend Buddy saves her life.

Acts 18, which describes Paul's visit to Athens, is a normative chapter on how believers can relate to people who are sincere in their beliefs but do not share our faith. He commends the Athenians for their devotion to the gods, and he quotes their literature. When he notices how they have hedged their theological bets by erecting a statue to the unknown god, he preaches the Gospel to them. As we consider current practices of beliefs or superstitions, we have to ask whether it is a matter of idols or a matter of people seeking something beyond themselves, seeking the God they do not know. And when they choose superstition, is it because they don't know any better?

Jesus' disciples discovered the sin of idolizing superstition when they tried to heal a man's son who was subject to violent seizures. They could not do it because they idolized their healing powers. They did not acknowledge how Jesus prayed for healing for others; instead, they relied on a kind of magic to heal the boy. Jesus is very stern in his rebuke. He says this kind of healing can come only by prayer and faith. If we have faith in God, everything is possible.

- Annie reading the tarot cards for a client; Annie at home with her children; Valerie's visit and plea to have Annie read; Annie's meeting with Wayne at the school; her relationship with Buddy at the garage; Donnie's threats; the town's disbelief in Annie.

- The party at the country club; Annie meeting Jessica and her relationship with Wayne; Jessica's infidelity; Annie and Wayne talking; Jessica's disappearance; Annie's fear; the intruder and Annie's nightmare.

- The search for Jessica and the sheriff's visit; Annie's dream and vision; dredging Donnie's pond; Donnie's arrest and the trial; Buddy and Annie; the unexplained apparitions; reading for Wayne; the discovery of Jessica's body and the true murderer.

FOR REFLECTION AND CONVERSATION

1. Reading tarot cards is a form of fortune-telling called *cartomancy,* that is, using special cards to predict or tell the future. Tarot was probably introduced into Europe during the time of the Crusades in the twelfth century, though most certainly these cards were in use there by the fifteenth century. The *Catechism of the Catholic Church* says that all forms of divination, including clairvoyance, that is, trying to find out the past, present, and the future through unusual insight or the aid of supernatural powers, are to be rejected, because all these means (including the reading of horoscopes) "conceal a desire for power over time, history, and, in the last analysis, other human beings, as well as a wish to conciliate hidden powers, They contradict the honor, respect, and loving fear that we owe to God alone" (*CCC*, no. 2116). Annie uses tarot cards, which the Second Commandment forbids, believing this to be a way

for her to express her second sight, "the gift." As a believer, what could Annie have done to help others without resorting to the tarot?

2. Almost every film in this volume deals with more than one of the Ten Commandments. What other commandments come into play in *The Gift?* What other sins? Spousal abuse, adultery, murder, envy, lying, anger, and gossip all play a role in *The Gift*. On the other hand, what moral virtues does Annie live? How does this antagonism between sin and virtue create drama? What does Annie learn by the end of the film? What do the citizens of the town learn? Does anyone grow and change by the end of the story?

3. If Annie were your neighbor, how would you relate to her and her family? How are believers to conduct themselves in a world where people engage in activities contrary to God's law, but at the same time do things that are in accord with the Ten Commandments and Beatitudes? Besides original sin, what accounts for this paradox? To what can it be attributed? What do you really think Jesus would do?

Prayer

Lord, we are so often bewildered by our world and the things people do. Help us to trust you always and increase our faith. Amen.

For Catechists

Catechism of the Catholic Church
Superstition, idolatry, divination, and magic, nos. 2110–2128
Serving God alone, nos. 2096–2097

The Second Commandment

Introduction

Do not take God's name in vain./Be authentic./Do not presume or play God.

"You shall not take the name of the LORD, your God, in vain" (Ex 20:7).

"You have heard the commandment imposed on your forefathers, 'Do not take a false oath'... What I tell you is: do not swear at all..." (Mt 5:33–34).

In Ronald F. Maxwell's 2003 Civil War film, *Gods and Generals,* Confederate Lieutenant General Thomas "Stonewall" Jackson studies the Old Testament Book of Joshua with a magnifying glass. His over-literal reading of the text on Joshua's battles is, for him, both a religious act and a rationale for his service in the Confederate Army. He praises the text for its military savvy and for God's goodness in taking the side of the people of Israel against the Canaanites. He advises his soldiers and officers to read the books of Samuel and Kings as the religious grounding and rationale for his counsel to kill the enemy.

Jackson never reads the New Testament passage in which Jesus communicates the ideal of turning the other cheek. However, the name of the Lord is holy, and to use God's name to bolster troops for war is presumption. At best it is rash and misdirected; at worst it can have terrible, unalterable consequences. Jackson presumes God's help for the Confederate cause just as the Union does for its own.

Jesus extends our understanding of presumption with his powerful words, especially in Matthew's Gospel; in chapter 23, his words, directed at the religious leadership of the day, the scribes and Pharisees, are particularly scathing. Jesus accuses them of breaking the Second Commandment because they play God by laying down their strict and burdensome interpretation of Jewish law for ordinary people while hypocritically acting in the opposite way.

There is much presumption—"playing God"—in today's world. We get an idea of what presumption is whenever an authority commands us to do something without listening, but simply exercising power over us without even a justifiable rebuke. Parents do it. Civil authorities do it. Church authorities do it. And all of them often take the name of the Lord in vain by using it as the justification or punctuation mark for their words and actions, their presumption.

Two other areas of presumption have stirred people all over the world. The first is the arrogance of science when individuals, groups of doctors, or biological engineers go beyond ethical limits in trying to control human life. Ever since Mary Shelley's 1818 classic novel *Frankenstein,* about a man who attempts to play God, novels, movies, television series, radio programs, and documentaries have featured Frankenstein-like stories as warnings about the dangers of finite human beings presuming to have infinite wisdom and power.

Another area of presumption is that of political dominance. This is particularly true in wartime and is reflected in the presumptive prayer that declares God to be on "our side." Christian armies presume it. Muslim combatants presume it. Military followers of other religions, small or great, assume this stance and turn their prayer into blasphemy as they invade, massacre, and kill with the resulting "acceptable" losses, collateral damage, and injury or death by friendly fire. Although soldiers rightly ask for God's protection as they go into war, it is presumption to assume that God takes sides.

The Second Commandment also forbids the cursing of God, uttering angry oaths, and taking God's name in vain because these are an abuse of God's name. Another word for this is blasphemy. Blasphemy is not a list of expletives or profanities that slip too easily off the tongue, but rather the contempt of God that gives rise to taking God's name in vain. Limiting the commandment to the prohibition of curses and foul language when we have a bad day or lock our keys in the car is tempting, but our repentance would have a more lasting effect if we pondered what our thoughtless cursing says about our spiritual health.

There is so much more reflected in the Second Commandment than a casual, flippant, or irritable curse: blasphemy, false oaths, and perjury.

The three films we have chosen to explore the Second Commandment are *Bruce Almighty,* which is all about "playing God" and watching our language; *Glory,* which highlights the sin of presumption in war; and *Absolute Power,* a harrowing tale about how power corrupts.

THE SECOND COMMANDMENT

Job 1:1–2:10

2 Corinthians 12:7–10

Luke 18:9–14

Bruce Almighty

U.S.A., 2003, 104 minutes

Actors: Jim Carrey, Morgan Freeman, Jennifer Aniston, Philip Baker Hall, Sally Kirkland, Steve Carell

Writer: Steve Koren, Mark O'Keefe, Steve Oedekerk

Director: Tom Shadyac

Bruce Almighty

A Difficult Game: Playing God

Bruce Nolan (Jim Carrey) is a forty-year-old local television reporter in Buffalo, New York, who is angry with God. He gets no respect and must take all the crummy reporting jobs. Bruce aspires to become an evening news anchor, but loses out to his humorless rival.

Bruce lives with his long-term girlfriend, Grace (Jennifer Aniston), who wants to get married, but Bruce is too self-centered to see the need or her desire. Nothing goes right for him; he gets caught in traffic jams, he gets to work late, thugs beat him up when he helps a poor man, and his dog urinates all over the house. Bruce is self-absorbed and jealous.

Bruce loses his job when he deliberately messes up a "Maid of the Mist" story about a historic tourist boat ride at Niagara Falls. It is a very low moment for him. When he gets home, his pager goes off. Bruce eventually calls the number and a man invites him to come for a job interview. The caller knows everything there is to know about Bruce because it is God speaking. When they meet, God (Morgan Freeman) gives Bruce his own powers for a week to see if Bruce can do a better job at being God. Bruce, however,

SYNOPSIS

45

cannot tell anyone he is now "God," and he cannot interfere with anyone's free will. As God walks away, he tells
Bruce that because of free will, he cannot force anyone to
love him.

Bruce uses his powers as if they were magic, and then he
starts to hear people praying. After a few days God visits him
again and asks him what he has done to help people, knowing that he has mostly helped himself. Bruce (mis)uses his
powers to get the news anchor job. When Grace catches
Susan (Catherine Bell), the other news anchor, kissing
Bruce at a party, she leaves him. Bruce is devastated. As he
finally surrenders his life to God, he is hit by a truck and
thinks he has died. Bruce and God have a long conversation, and Bruce wakes up in the hospital. Grace is there.
Bruce apologizes to anchorman Evan (Steve Carell), whom
he tormented, and goes back to his old job with dedication
and humor.

COMMENTARY

Film director Tom Shadyac is a practicing Catholic,
which might come as something of a surprise for those who
know that one of his earliest movies was *Ace Ventura: Pet
Detective* (1994). Shadyac is probably best known for his
broad, popular comedies with Jim Carrey, Eddie Murphy
(*The Nutty Professor*), and Robin Williams (*Patch Adams*). He
did try his hand at a serious movie with themes of near-
death experiences and communication from beyond in the
movie *Dragonfly* (2002), starring Kevin Costner and Linda
Hunt, who played a nun. The general consensus is that
Shadyac is far better with comedy.

Bruce Almighty is the third in a series of comedies with
Jim Carrey. After *Ace Ventura*, Shadyac and Carrey collaborated on an effective comic moral fable, *Liar Liar* (1997).

With the combination of a witty script and Carrey's control of both serious humor and manic clowning, with *Bruce
Almighty,* Shadyac and Carrey found themselves with a popular religious film and a box-office hit. It is not easy to make

a credible movie about God, God's providence, human free will, and prayer, but the team succeeded. Carrey's television reporter, Bruce Nolan, is a latter-day Job who learns some profound lessons.

Morgan Freeman is an actor with great nobility and gravity and a speaking voice full of dignity, and he brings those qualities to his convincing portrayal of God. *Bruce Almighty*'s God also has a fine sense of humor, and some of his witty one-liners invite us and Bruce to see the world rather differently: through God's eyes. Jennifer Aniston (*Friends*) plays her role as the faithful but wronged fiancé just right.

> *Focus: Bruce Nolan complains about how God treats him. Only by God's intervention does he learn to be enduring like Job, humble like Paul, and acknowledge the truth about himself like the tax collector in Jesus' parable.*

DIALOGUE WITH THE SCRIPTURES

"Curse God and die" (Job 2:10). These are the words of advice that Job's wife offered him when he was afflicted by all kinds of tragedies: the loss of children, the loss of property, his whole body covered in sores. It is the extreme cry of someone baffled by their suffering: God is to blame.

Yet, despite his questioning, in the end, Job did not curse God. We speak of the patience of Job or, better still, his endurance. He remained faithful in the face of horrendous personal disasters, in the face of his wife's criticism, and in the face of the callowness of his so-called comforters, whose theology told them that Job's great suffering meant he must be a great sinner. Job was not a sinner. He is the exemplar of encouragement to trust in God no matter what.

Compared with Job, Bruce Nolan's personal problems, even the loss of his job, are really very small. Yet they seem significant for Bruce, and he is only too happy to "curse" God. He feels that God has it in for him, and that this is unjust.

Ultimately Job (in chapters 29 and 38) had a profound experience of God's majesty and power. His final words in chapter 42 still stand as one of the best prayers for those who have experienced great suffering. Job says he had not understood God at all. Now that he does, he retracts his bitter questions and offers to repent in dust and ashes. This is the prayer of an innocent man. Bruce Nolan also has an experience of God. Bruce's first meeting with God is rather mundane—they mop floors together—but Bruce does have a cosmic moment with God on top of Mount Everest. Unlike Job, Bruce is a constant complainer with a short fuse. Even when he experiences God, he is so self-centered (which is a form of taking the Lord's name in vain) that he uses his godlike powers for his own petty purposes. Only when he starts really listening to people's prayers and tries to pray himself, especially for Grace, does he realize that he *can* be and *must* be less selfish. As Bruce resumes his life at the end of the movie, it is his small Job-like acceptance of God that gives him happiness.

Paul also had a constant reminder that God seemed to be being hard on him. But he knew that this "thorn" in his flesh would keep him grounded. In fact, he tells the Corinthians what God had revealed to him: "My grace is enough for you, for in weakness power reaches perfection" (2 Cor 12:9).

The Second Commandment is not simply about taking the Lord's name in vain as Bruce Nolan does. It takes us deeper into the narcissism in which Bruce indulges. Following this commandment does not mean simply cleaning up one's language, but something more profound; it is about becoming truly humble. Job's final prayer is humble and deeply sincere. Once a very proud and domineering religious leader, Paul was struck to the ground by God's presence and had to learn to be a humble apostle. Humility is a virtue that helps us to know ourselves and to be grateful for the good within us.

Jesus makes the same point in his parable of the Pharisee and the tax collector. The Pharisee, who should have known better, was self-absorbed while he ostensibly used humble words. He boasted of his righteousness. In fact, one translation of Luke's Gospel says that "he said this prayer to himself." The tax collector, meanwhile, acknowledged who he really was as a sinful person. Bruce Nolan, in his complaining days, had a lot of this Pharisee in him. However, in the end he becomes the equivalent of the tax collector and asks God to have mercy on him, a sinner. Jesus says that those who exalt themselves will be humbled. This is not a bad thing, for those who are humble will be exalted.

KEY SCENES AND THEMES

- Bruce's meetings with God: answering his pager message and going to the seventh floor of the Omni Presents building, finding God as the janitor and electrician; God appearing in the diner after he had parted the red tomato soup; God giving Bruce powers but instructing him to respect others' free will; walking on the water as God goes on vacation; God challenging Bruce on Mount Everest to think of others; God asking Bruce to pray and sending him back to earth after the accident.

- Bruce hearing the buzz of people's prayers in the restaurant; Bruce trying to find ways of cataloging them: files, posters, e-mail files; their volume and his trying to cope with answering them, his carelessly giving everyone what they want; his looking at Grace's prayers.

- The finale with Bruce back where he started, interviewing the cookie bakers, doing the humorous piece, pointing out Grace—but his life transformed and his being content to do well in the things that he does best.

1. Bruce is angry because he thinks God won't do anything to help him, from the little things to the big things, like his career. He yells at God in anger, like the psalmist, but then bargains with God like a child. Bruce suffers from an arrested faith development. What other elements in the story seem to indicate this? Do you ever find yourself, frustrated and tired, asking God, "Why do you hate me?" Does anyone really think this, or is it a cry for mercy and compassion? How does Bruce begin the journey toward moral integration by recognizing his sinfulness, asking forgiveness, and choosing to follow the way of God?

2. Spirituality in the Judeo-Christian tradition is about the nature of a person's relationship with God as known through divine revelation. This relationship begins for us with the rites of Christian initiation— which we assume Bruce has had some experience with, since he knows God well enough to blame him for his misfortunes. Inspired by how the saints interpreted the Gospels, some people try to live in relationship to Jesus according to the inspiration they receive from the saints: St. Francis, St. Benedict, St. Clare, St. Angela Merici, Blessed James Alberione, St. John Bosco, St. Ignatius of Loyola. Others follow the example and teachings of holy people like Dietrich Bonhoeffer (1906–1945), who lived and taught the spirituality of the Beatitudes, or Gandhi (1869–1948), who admired and sought to live Jesus' teachings on peace. But poor Bruce—his spiritual life is pretty dry. He believes in God enough to get mad at him, but he does not truly live in relationship to him. What is the nature of your spirituality? How

do you live in relationship with God? How do you nurture this relationship? What would you tell Bruce by word and example if you knew him?

3. The Second Commandment tells us very clearly that we are not to presume to play God. The spiritually and theologically naive Bruce, however, barely hesitates to take on the role of the All Powerful. The film's comedy stems from Bruce's playing at manipulating the universe just because he can (the moon, the lottery, parting his bowl of soup, etc.). What makes him take his role more seriously? What do all the "signs" in the film tell Bruce, and us the viewers? How does Bruce change from the beginning of the film to the end? What makes him change? Other than comedy, what genres might *Bruce Almighty* fit? Why?

Prayer

Lord, help us not to blame you when things seem to go wrong, but to trust you and to take responsibility for our actions. Amen.

For Catechists

Catechism of the Catholic Church
The name of the Lord is holy, nos. 2142–2149
"You shall love your neighbor as yourself," no. 2196
Marriage in God's plan, nos. 1602, 1604, 1605
Fear of impending evil, no. 1765
The nature of love, no. 1766

Morgan Freeman, Cary Elwes, and Denzel Washington in *Glory*.

THE SECOND COMMANDMENT

Exodus 17:8–16

Ephesians 6:10–17

Luke 14:30–33

Glory

U.S.A., 1989, 122 minutes

Actors: Matthew Broderick, Morgan Freeman, Andre Braugher,
Denzel Washington, Raymond St. Jacques, Jane Alexander,
Cary Elwes, Cliff De Young, Jihmi Kennedy

Writer: Kevin Jarre

Director: Edward Zwick

 Glory

God Is on Our Side!

SYNOPSIS

In September 1862, the Union Army defeats the Confederate Army at Antietam, Maryland, in one of the bloodiest battles of the American Civil War (1860–1864). A young Union officer from Boston, Robert Gould Shaw (Matthew Broderick), is wounded and left for dead. He recovers and finally returns home. There he learns that the Union is forming a regiment of black soldiers only: the 54th Regiment of Massachusetts Volunteer Infantry. Shaw accepts command of this regiment and persuades his good friend Major Forbes (Cary Elwes) to join him.

The regiment goes to Readville, Massachusetts, in February 1863, to begin training. One night, Private Trip (Denzel Washington) goes off to visit a local farmhouse. He is caught and treated as a deserter, and Shaw orders him flogged. Shaw is dismayed when he finds out that Trip was not a deserter, but only looking for a pair of shoes. Shaw outwits the quartermaster, who refuses to distribute the 700 pairs of shoes sent for the regiment, and obtains them for the men. The men really want to fight, but it is rumored that because they are African Americans, the Union Army will only use them for manual labor. Other brave soldiers of various backgrounds emerge among the volunteers: Jupiter Sharts (Jihmi Kennedy), Thomas Searles (Andre Braugher), and John Rawlins (Morgan Freeman).

When their paychecks come, the members of the regiment receive only ten dollars a month instead of the thirteen dollars that white soldiers receive. Private Trip encourages the men to tear up their checks, and Shaw does likewise. They finally receive their Union uniforms. Rawlins is made a sergeant major.

The Union deploys the regiment to Beaufort, South Carolina, in June 1863. The men want to fight, but the Union uses them for labor and orders them to raid a local town for no cause, much to Colonel Shaw's distress.

Finally, the regiment receives orders to go to Charleston, South Carolina. To take the city, the Union Army must first subdue the forts guarding the harbor. The men pray for God's help before the battle. Colonel Shaw volunteers the 54th to lead the charge against Fort Wagner, which lies at the mouth of the harbor across a narrow sand causeway. Shaw and almost half the regiment die and are buried in the sand.

COMMENTARY

Glory is a fine film that expertly recreates the American Civil War period by taking a little-known story of a black Massachusetts regiment along with the conflicts, prejudice, training, and ultimate bloodletting in a vividly staged battle sequence that brings home the violence of all war.

Glory is based on *One Gallant Rush* by Peter Burchard (1965), and *Lay This Laurel* by Lincoln Kirstein (1974), as well the letters of its principle protagonist, Colonel Robert Gould Shaw. The film portrays Boston society, the role of Frederick Douglass and the abolitionists, as well as the ethos in the North as it went to war against the South.

The American Civil War has been the setting for a great number of movies, including *Gone with the Wind* (1939), *The*

Good, The Bad, and the Ugly (1967), and *Cold Mountain* (2003). There have also been screen versions of classics that depict the war, like *The Red Badge of Courage* (1951), or have the Civil War as a background, like *Little Women* (1994). Ken Burns directed an Emmy and Humanitas prize-winning, ten-hour miniseries for television titled *The Civil War* in 1990. In 1993, Ronald F. Maxwell made the five-hour-long *Gettysburg*, which is told from the Union perspective, and followed it in 2003 with *Gods and Generals*, which is about the major battles leading up to Gettysburg from the perspective of the South. *The Last Full Measure* (2004), based on the book by Jeff Shaara, is in long-range development as the final film of Maxwell's trilogy.

The effective screenplay for *Glory* is by Kevin Jarre. James Horner composed the atmospheric music and choral work. The director is Edward Zwick, best known for his television series, *Thirtysomething*, and the film *About Last Night*. During the 1990s, Zwick took a greater interest in war themes, looking back at tensions and cover-ups during and after the Gulf War in *Courage Under Fire* (1996), and at terrorist attacks in New York City in *The Siege* in 1998. He then won acclaim for directing *The Last Samurai* (2003) in New Zealand with actor Tom Cruise. The quality writing, the strong plot, and the persuasive performances of Matthew Broderick, Morgan Freeman, and Denzel Washington, who won an Oscar for Best Supporting Actor for his role, all contribute to the film's success. Zwick has made an excellent war film that vividly revisits a popular theme while offering a cinematic interpretation of a unique aspect of the Civil War.

Focus: Glory *shows the presumption of the blind faith of believing that God is on our side in war. St. Paul uses the imagery of battle to describe our own struggle against the flesh. Jesus' parable is about the need to negotiate peace.*

DIALOGUE WITH THE SCRIPTURES

Where does God stand as armies line up against each other for battle? Whose side is God on? In wars between Christians and Muslims, Christians invoked God with confidence on the one side, while Muslims invoked Allah on the other. In any war, it is the same no matter the religion of the warring parties. The Second Commandment forbids us to take the name of the Lord in vain and is a key indicator of presumption on the part of any army that claims to have God on its side. Wars are complex issues, and it is often difficult to assess blame.

The invocation of God on both sides of the American Civil War is a powerful example of this presumption. The North was confident that God supported its westward expansion and the crusade against slavery. The South was confident in its righteous history, believing that God had blessed them in their prosperity. In fact, many of the Southern leaders were devout Christian men.

Glory is a particularly fine example of a Civil War movie. While it takes its stand with the armies of the North, it shows the fierce battles and slaughter that divided Americans from 1861 to 1865. It also depicts the efforts of the abolitionists, especially campaigner Frederick Douglass and those who supported his stand against slavery. What is distinctive about the film is its portrayal of the black regiment that fought for the North and the ultimate laying down of life, black alongside white. This equality of black and white soldiers on the battlefield highlights the hypocrisy of the Union Army. It had double standards and a latent racist attitude while at the same time holding the belief that it was taking God's side for the liberation of the slaves. This forms a significant part of the plot development.

Some of the Old Testament's bellicose language seems to support the belief that God could be identified as a divine ally in any conflagration. The Psalms and the Prophets often speak of the mighty victories of the Lord using the language of war. The famous passage in which Moses intercedes with God for Israel's victory, even to the point of having his arms held up, and God himself makes the sun stand still, seems to reinforce that belief. Yahweh's message to Moses after this battle is alarming because it seems to endorse a religious, that is, a divine, rationale for war.

This passage has often been misinterpreted over the centuries. Just as it was discredited as a scientific proof that the sun rotated around the earth rather than the other way around (the Galileo incident of 1633), so it can be discredited as a simplistic theological argument for divine support for "our" cause in war.

In addition, the misinterpretation and incorrect application of the *lex talionis* of "an eye for an eye" (see page 121) has to give way to Jesus' teaching of forgiveness and turning the other cheek in human relationships if we are to be true disciples. The just war theory articulated by the Church continues to teach that war is a last resort for a country trying to defend itself.

At the end of the Letter to the Ephesians, St. Paul offers the imagery of battle armor as a metaphor for the spiritual struggle between the flesh and the spirit. Paul, like Jesus, used language the people could understand: "Our battle is not against human forces" (Eph 6:12). We are to triumph over the power of evil, especially our own selfishness and sinfulness. If there must be war, then let the weapons be those of truth, integrity, and eagerness to show by example the truth and love of the good news of Jesus.

Jesus does not often speak of war. In his brief parable in Luke (14:30–33), his perspective is that to negotiate for peace is the right way to solve problems rather than to risk battle with its subsequent loss of life.

The spirit of the Civil War—a conflagration of brother against brother—did not conform to this teaching of

Jesus. *Glory* shows us battles to the death, including the deaths of the central characters. More recent experiences of war, especially in the Middle East, remind us that we must work and negotiate for peace by looking at the causes of aggression. We must seek just solutions rather than assume that might is right and victory belongs to the most well-armed and lethal of armies. This holds true not only in the battle, but also in the rebuilding of enduring peace. It is in openness to God that people will discern what is right and just.

KEY SCENES AND THEMES

- Boston, 1862; the Shaw family and their welcoming of Frederick Douglass and their listening to the arguments of the abolitionists; Douglass' influence on Robert Shaw and Shaw's preparation for military service.

- The members of the regiment: Searles and his educated and somewhat snobbish attitude when sharing with Trip and Rawlins; Rawlins, his humble beginnings and response to the regiment; Trip and his seemingly rebellious attitude; the use of the Negro regiment for the needless preemptive assault on the defenseless village.

- The assault on Fort Wagner; black and white men fighting together; Trip taking up the standard; their dying together with belief in the justice of the North's cause.

FOR REFLECTION AND CONVERSATION

1. "Theology of God and psychology of belief reinforce each other.... So when war clouds gather, religious belief electrifies the air," writes James Hillman in his 2004 treatise, *A Terrible Love of War* (p. 182). "When our belief is in the republic and the republic is declared endangered, we rally around the flag 'for

which it stands.' Whatever the object of belief—the flag, the nation, the president, or the god—a martial energy mobilizes." Hillman continues, "In the midst of...a recent war, a ranking American lieutenant general declared in uniform to a church congregation that the satanic foes in Islam 'will only be defeated if we come against them in the name of Jesus.' In that general's statement—'If there is no God, there is no hope'—we can see how the values of religion can fuel the will to fight" (p. 186). As any soldier would, the soldiers of the American Civil War, North and South, called upon the same God for help. But what is the image of God that fueled the Civil War for the North and the South? Were the soldiers guilty of hubris and presumption? Consider the unprovoked attack on the little Southern town in *Glory*. What is the inherent contradiction in Western theology that asserts truthfulness and unlimited charity, yet at the same time is used to justify war with all its side effects?

2. Pope John Paul II laid out the basic premise for universal peace when he said that it was "a serene and resolute commitment to shared human values; in the absence of such a commitment neither war nor terrorism will ever be overcome" (Pope's Address to U.S. President Bush, June 4, 2004). What were the "shared human values" that could have created peace in the United States in the years leading up to the Civil War (and today)? Was slavery the only issue that caused the Civil War? Compare the Christian elements of Ron Maxwell's 2003 film *Gods and Generals* with *Glory*. How would you describe the righteousness of any religious faith in these contexts?

3. When Constantine declared Christianity the state religion of the Roman Empire in the fourth century, heretics, especially those that disturbed the public order, were considered enemies of the state. Although early on the Catholic Church generally disapproved of the permission this gave the empire to persecute and punish people for their beliefs, St. Augustine gave his grudging approval. Thus was born a culture that blended church/religion and state and justified the use of faith for state action. It was this type of culture that fueled the Crusades (eleventh to thirteenth centuries), the medieval Inquisition, and the Spanish Inquisition (1231 to the nineteenth century) that are universally condemned today, and for which Pope John Paul II apologized in the years leading up to the Jubilee Year 2000. What is your opinion of the role of one's personal faith in the public life of a nation in relation to war? Recall the film *A Few Good Men* (1992). What were the four principles the accused marines lived by? ("Corp, Unit, God, Country—in that order.") Is this kind of code helpful toward eliminating war? How might this statement create a "them" and "us" perspective that sets up the possibility for war? In the Gospel reading, was Jesus justifying war by using it as an analogy? Why or why not?

Prayer

Lord of peace, where there is conflict, let us not presume that we are always right. Open our hearts and our minds to discern and choose what is good and right and to avoid what is wrong and evil. Amen.

For Catechists

Catechism of the Catholic Church

The name of the Lord is holy, nos. 2142–2155

Avoiding war, nos. 2307–2316

Causes of war and peace, no. 2317

Legitimate conditions for defense, no. 2309

The fruits of charity, no. 1829

Absolute Power

U.S.A., 1996, 120 minutes

Actors: Clint Eastwood, Ed Harris, Gene Hackman, Laura Linney, Judy Davis, Scott Glenn, E. G. Marshall, Denis Haysbert

Writer: William Goldman

Director: Clint Eastwood

Absolute Power

Absolute Presumption

SYNOPSIS

Luther Whitney (Clint Eastwood), a professional thief, has spent years in prison. His wife is dead, and he lives alone in his Washington, D.C., apartment. His estranged daughter, Kate (Laura Linney), is a prosecuting attorney.

One night he breaks into a mansion, mostly because he can. He goes to a bedroom, discovers a secret vault, and starts to steal jewelry and money. When he hears people coming, he closes himself in and watches what happens through a two-way mirror. A drunken couple enters the room to have sex. The man becomes violent and the woman stabs him with a letter opener in self-defense. Two men race into the room and shoot her. Whitney watches in horror but does nothing to help the woman. Another woman, Gloria Russell (Judy Davis), joins them. They collect all the evidence and leave, but Russell drops the bloody letter opener. Whitney comes out of hiding, grabs the letter opener, and escapes. Russell and the men realize they have lost the weapon; they discover Whitney and chase him, but he eludes them. The drunk man is U.S. President Allen Richmond (Gene Hackman), and the dead woman is Christy Sullivan, wife of Richmond's oldest political mentor,

Walter Sullivan (E. G. Marshall). The two men, Bill (Scott Glenn) and Tim (Denis Haysbert), are the president's Secret Service detail, and Russell is his chief of staff. She tells the men to find the potential witness and cover everything up.

Detective Seth Frank (Ed Harris) investigates what seems to be an ordinary murder. Whitney becomes a suspect because of his past, and Frank wants to interview him. Whitney begins to leave hints with the White House that he knows what happened. Frank visits Whitney's daughter, Kate, and gets her to set up a meeting with Whitney. At the meeting, both the Secret Service men and an assassin that Walter Sullivan hired try to kill Whitney, but he escapes in disguise. The Secret Service team goes after Kate and runs her car off a cliff because of what Whitney might have told her about the night of the murder. Later, Tim tries to kill Kate in the hospital, but Whitney gets him first.

Whitney is ashamed that he did nothing to help Christy. He tells Walter Sullivan that he has returned everything he had stolen and then gives him the weapon. Sullivan confronts the president in the White House. The president commits suicide it seems. Secret Service agent Bill, ridden with guilt, also commits suicide. Gloria Russell is arrested. Whitney and Kate reconcile.

COMMENTARY

Clint Eastwood directs this adaptation of David Baldacci's skillful novel (1996) and takes the central role of the thief, Luther Whitney. The film is an engaging conspiracy thriller with a top-notch cast. Who better to portray the amoral, power-hungry president than Gene Hackman, masking evil with earnest concern? Judy Davis has a plum role as his devoted, even infatuated, chief of staff who can be ruthless. Scott Glenn and Dennis Haysbert (who played the U.S. president in the television drama *24*) are the Secret Service guards. Ed Harris brings integrity to his role as the chief detective.

Laura Linney, who later appears with powerful effect in Eastwood's 2003 *Mystic River*, plays the daughter.

Perhaps some audiences will not find *Absolute Power* as intense as other political thrillers, but it is both stylish and absorbing. It offers its audiences the opportunity to assess the skills that Clint Eastwood has brought to a number of movies in his later career. After the seeming vigilantism of the Dirty Harry series and the dramatic explorations of good and evil in his Western series, beginning with the extremely violent *High Plains Drifter* (1973) and ending with his Oscar-winning *Unforgiven* (1992), Eastwood has made a number of movies that draw his audiences into examining social issues in the context of the thriller. He deals with the underside of Savannah society in *Midnight in the Garden of Good and Evil* (1997), media and capital punishment in *True Crime* (1999), and the aging detective in *Blood Work* (2002). *Mystic River* is emerging as his masterpiece in this genre. Eastwood went on to win a second Oscar as Best Director in 2004 for *Million Dollar Baby*.

DIALOGUE WITH THE SCRIPTURES

Focus: The elders who attacked Susanna in the Book of Daniel and the president in Absolute Power *abused their status and power. Paul urges us to have the same minds and hearts as Jesus, and the Gospel of Matthew urges us not to flaunt authority, as do the characters in the film.*

In the opening scenes of *Absolute Power*, the president of the United States must be protected in order to protect his status and office. No one is to know about the criminal behavior of the president, thus he does not have to accept responsibility. The specious motivation is that covering up the president's pernicious habits and crimes is for the good of the government and the people.

The movie title reminds us that we are watching people who believe that they have absolute power, that they have the right to "play God." Authority figures that rely on their status, their wealth, and their influence to manipulate truth and justice for their own benefit are guilty of blasphemy. John Calvin's theology of predestination, one tradition of the Protestant Reformation, was brought to America in the sixteenth century. It is rooted in the principle that as long as God is seen to be blessing you with material benefits, God is with you. Perhaps this explains America's history of political cover-ups, including Richard Nixon's failure to own up to his guilt and resign until the media broadcast the truth about Watergate to the American public. Arthur Miller saw this principle as partly explaining the 1950s "black list," and why he used the notorious Salem witch hunts and executions (c. 1692) to illustrate this kind of "scoundrel time" in his 1952 play, *The Crucible*.

Absolute Power reminds us that scoundrels can exist at any time.

The Book of Daniel, in which two men try to seduce Susanna and threaten to ruin her reputation if she refuses to submit, provides us with a leadership and sexual misconduct scandal. In both the Book of Daniel and the film, the woman does not deserve to be abused or killed. The two old men who have usurped their power for their own lusts lie when they are questioned about Susanna, but the wise Daniel finds the truth. With Daniel, the truth must win out, the victim must be vindicated, and the guilty must be condemned. When Luther Whitney becomes the fall guy for a crime he did not commit, a sincere detective takes on the role of Daniel as he follows the clues to unmask the criminals and the dire execution of justice, leading to another cover-up for the security of the state.

Gene Hackman's portrayal of President Richmond shows us the secret face of depravity and the extent to which presumption can corrupt. Two other characters offer haunting dramatizations of this same corruption, giving their hearts and souls to the government in order to fulfill their ambitions: Judy Davis as the co-conspirator of the cover-up and Dennis Haysbert as the ruthless Secret Service man. Both overreach themselves and destroy their careers.

Although Susanna calls on God as her witness and relies on the truthfulness of her life as her defense, her story highlights the negative aspect of the Second Commandment because it focuses on the consequences of the sin of pride. The other readings, however, lead us to this commandment's more positive perspectives. Paul's Letter to the Philippians urges us to have the same minds and hearts as Christ Jesus, and the Gospel from Matthew tells us not to flaunt authority. The virtue and strength of the Second Commandment is a humility that reflects a true understanding of one's gifts and weaknesses, that is, an acknowledgment of the good we do while confessing our sinfulness. To be humble means to be truly "of the earth," or grounded and self-aware, as the Latin origin of the word suggests. Humility means that arrogance has no part in our life, that in God we trust, and our actions follow this conviction in charity. To be humble means that we live out the qualities that Paul praises with his words, "do nothing out of selfishness or vainglory." Those in positions of leadership or power are meant to serve the rest, remembering that it is a godless thing to lord power over others and make one's authority felt. Jesus says to his disciples, "It cannot be like that with you" (Mt 20:26).

KEY SCENES AND THEMES

• Luther Whitney and the audience sharing the close view of the sexual encounter turning into an assault; the struggle and killing; the actions of the leader of the United States and his presumption that the law cannot touch him; Gloria Harris taking control of the cover-up and the Secret Service agents who follow her orders without question.

- Luther Whitney seeing President Richmond's address to the nation on television; his decision not to leave the country, but to do the right thing; his efforts to unmask the president and his part in revealing the truth.

- The White House social; Gloria Russell thinking she had been given the bracelet by the president as a reward for her loyalty and lies; her realization that both she and the president had been found out; the collapse of President Richmond's confidence and his attack on Gloria.

1. In the nineteenth century, British historian Lord Acton noted that power corrupts, but absolute power corrupts absolutely. The film shows the corrupt power that resides in the office of the fictitious president of the United States, Allen Richmond, a power that his close advisers enable and the Secret Service protect. Political power is meant to be at the service of the people. When someone at the top commits a callous and bloodthirsty crime, people may not think of justice or restitution. Rather, the immediate strategy may be a cover-up to protect the powerful. How does character education, which is living by the Ten Commandments and ethics, come into play in public life? In the opening part of the film, what ought each of the key characters have done morally, ethically, and legally in the face of such criminal actions? If any one of them had chosen to act ethically, how might the film have developed differently and still been an absorbing tale?

2. In *Absolute Power* there is an interesting and complex father-daughter issue running parallel to the

FOR REFLECTION AND CONVERSATION

detection and conspiracy plot. This thread gives the movie a deeper human dimension by looking at power relations in a family on a micro level, and on the macro level in the government. How would you describe the adult-to-adult relationship between Whitney and his daughter? How are Whitney, father and citizen, and the president, leader and citizen, alike or different? What does the film mean for you as a son, daughter, father or mother, and as a citizen?

3. Each character in the film has sworn or promised to be faithful to a commitment through marriage, political life, civil service, and ordinary employment. How important is it to keep one's word, especially if one has made vows or promises under oath? We hear God's name taken in vain every day at home, in the office, and through the media—at times in jest, at times in anger. Talk about how the misuse of God's name shows a lack of imagination and civility. What are some ways that we can be more mindful of our language as well as the promises we have made in God's name?

Prayer

Lord, bless those in authority so that they may serve their people in justice and in truth. Amen.

For Catechists

Catechism of the Catholic Church
Taking the name of the Lord in vain, nos. 2150–2155
The morality of the passions, nos. 1762–1770
Atheism, no. 2126
Promises, no. 2147
False oaths, nos. 2150, 2151
Perjury, no. 2152

The Third Commandment

Introduction

Keep holy the Lord's Day./Develop a sense of the sacred in work and leisure.

The Third Commandment grounds its injunctions for Sabbath rest on the creativity of God in Genesis, chapter 1. God worked for six days creating the world and rested on the seventh. God saw that creation was very good: the world itself, the natural environment, all that lives in the seas and on the land, and man and woman, who are made in God's very own likeness. With this achievement, God could relish the wonder and beauty of his work and rest.

Rest has also been an image, especially in the Psalms and in the prophets, of a goal for people faithful to God's covenant. Because Adam and Eve disobeyed God in Eden, they were sentenced to a life of labor "by the sweat of their brow." This is the human condition. Work occupies at least one third of our waking lives. Life has become a struggle to make ends meet, to survive, to find some hope of prosperity.

In the spirit of this commandment, movements are at work in the world to obtain just wages for workers, more humane and healthy working conditions, and contracts that respect justice for the human person and the family. Another effort aims at establishing reasonable working hours and childcare provisions so that parents may have more quality time with their families. All of these contribute to a holistic work ethic as well as foster a sense of the sacred.

The Scriptures offer images of good, solid work. The patriarchs tended their flocks, as did David. The industrious wife of Proverbs, chapter 31, is a model of a householder. Jesus came from a working family, laboring in a carpenter's shop. Paul often exhorts his followers to work for their living and gives the example of his own tent making. But while work is a creative activity, an essential aspect of human dignity, and necessary for human existence, work is not to be an end in itself. Otherwise, work becomes an idol, and we become workaholics with all the characteristics of other addictions. God graces us with the opportunity to find rest after our work.

This goal of rest provides us with the opportunity to find time to put our priorities in order and worship God, to acknowledge God's place in our lives, and to be a family together. The Sabbath rest implies the need to create adequate practical and emotional space to carry out spiritual activities such as a retreat, to engage in spiritual direction, or to keep a journal.

For many Catholics, the obligation of Sunday Mass is a reminder that worship is significant in their lives and that prayer is a priority. One of the consequences of the traditional understanding of the Sabbath rest and worship is respect for the sense of the sacred inherent in people's lives and work. It also promotes the understanding that there is a divine purpose and time for everything under the sun (cf. Eccles 3:1–8).

History teaches us that the seven-day work and rest cycle has a basis not only in Scripture, but in nature as well. Napoleon proved this in 1793, when his Republican Convention created a new calendar with a ten-day week. The new system only lasted thirteen years before Napoleon decided to separate his new empire from any association with the French Revolution and allowed the calendar to revert back to the seven-day cycle and the Gregorian calendar. It is said that people and animals could not withstand the burden of working nine days straight before they could legitimately rest. For a country whose citizens were predominantly Christian and Jewish, this was undoubtedly an additional burden.

The pace of contemporary life often seems like a continuum of workdays that weighs against the development of a sense of the sacred. We have more access than ever before to opportunities for leisure. We can travel, relax, or simply watch television or a DVD. However, people keep on working. Modern technology enables us to work constantly. Rest, worshipping, and developing a sense of the sacred are hurried over or forgotten.

We live in an environment created by media images and sounds, so many people have lost the facility for quiet, stillness, reflection, and meditation. Prayer movements within churches and the influence of meditative practices from the major world religions such as Buddhism have flourished, indicating that there is a deep human need for the quiet acknowledgment of God and the sacred in our world and in our lives.

The films we have chosen for the Third Commandment, *Tuesdays with Morrie, Witness,* and *Cold Mountain,* allow us to explore themes of contemplation, values, family, religion, God, work, leisure, and how to choose priorities that give life meaning.

THE THIRD COMMANDMENT

Exodus 31:12–17

Hebrews 12:22–25

Mark 2:23–3:6

Tuesdays with Morrie

U.S.A., 1999, 85 minutes

Actors: Jack Lemmon, Hank Azaria, Wendy Moniz, Caroline Aaron

Writer: Thomas Rickman

Director: Mick Jackson

Tuesdays with Morrie

Eternal Rest

SYNOPSIS

In the summer of 1994, Mitch Albom (Hank Azariah) is a successful sports journalist based in Detroit. By chance, he sees his old sociology professor from Brandeis University, Morrie Swartz (Jack Lemmon), being interviewed on *Nightline* by Ted Koppel. Morrie has ALS, or Lou Gehrig's disease.

Mitch lives his life by the clock. He takes on all kinds of jobs in addition to writing for the newspaper and has no time for his long-time girlfriend, Janine. At his graduation, Mitch had promised Morrie he would stay in touch, but he never did. Now he suddenly goes to see his old teacher in Boston so he can say good-bye.

One visit grows into many, always on Tuesdays. Morrie speaks of his love for teaching and dancing and expresses his belief that love goes on. Soon, Mitch decides to bring a tape recorder so he can save Morrie's aphorisms and wisdom. He calls Morrie "Coach," and they joke that what they talk about is like a curriculum. Morrie agrees to be recorded. He asks about Mitch's girlfriend and indicates that he would like to meet her. Mitch has problems with relationships, commitments, and prioritizing in his life. When

Janine (Wendy Monitz) breaks up with him, it throws him off balance. It's a wake-up call.

Over their Tuesdays together, Morrie tells Mitch about his immigrant father, his stepmother, and his own father's death.

On one of Mitch's visits, he learns how to lift and move Morrie. He brings Morrie his favorite foods even though it becomes increasingly difficult for Morrie to eat. On another visit, Morrie celebrates his funeral—before he dies. Mitch realizes that he cannot lose Janine, and he proposes to her. He brings her to visit Morrie. Janine is a backup singer who has just gone solo. Morrie sends Mitch away and then asks Janine to sing to him.

Finally, on the last visit, Mitch and Morrie say good-bye, and Morrie tells Mitch he loves him. After Morrie dies, Mitch attends the funeral.

COMMENTARY

Tuesdays with Morrie is a telefilm based on the book, *Tuesdays with Morrie: An Old Man, A Young Man, and Life's Greatest Lesson* by Mitch Albom, published in 1997.

Jack Lemmon plays Morrie, Mitch's mentor, and gives an extraordinarily persuasive performance as the creative sociology lecturer with an impoverished background and sad memories of his difficult relationship with his unaffectionate father. Some of these sequences appear as flashbacks, which remind the audience of the difficult past of immigrants in New York. Since Jack Lemmon died in 2001, this film is something of a last will and testament from the venerated actor. It makes the audience reflect on his extraordinary forty-five year career on television and the silver screen, during which he acted in such classics as *Mister Roberts* and *Some Like It Hot,* moving later to more serious films, such as *The China Syndrome* and *Missing.* His partnership with Walter Matthau in *The Odd Couple, The Front Page,* and others also comes to mind. The teleplay is by Thomas Rickman, who won both an Emmy Award and the Humanitas Award for the script.

The film is quite moving. The taped interviews between Mitch and Morrie contain a great deal of wisdom and common sense as well as a realistic approach to the experience of death. Hank Azariah is just right as Mitch. Azariah has appeared in many films including *The Birdcage, Godzilla,* and *Along Came Polly.* For many years, *The Simpsons* has featured him as one of the character voices. Englishman Mick Jackson, known best for his most successful movie, *The Bodyguard,* directs.

DIALOGUE WITH THE SCRIPTURES

Focus: The Sabbath is for the sake of men and women so they can worship, rest, and anticipate the heavenly feast that is to come. Morrie has learned these human and divine values and, as he prepares for death, he helps Mitch to discover them on his Tuesday visits.

Holiness is central to the Third Commandment. The other significant themes are rest and putting first those things that help people to grow in humanity and holiness. The sacredness of the Sabbath connects with creation and God's rest on the seventh day. Rest, instead of work, was to be the hallmark of the Sabbath. On the Sabbath, God's people would worship and rest. Exodus, chapter 31, offers a small charter for the observance of Sabbath rest.

Two consecutive stories in all three Synoptic Gospels dramatize these themes. The first is the Sabbath story of the disciples eating the ears of corn and the Pharisees spying on them and complaining to Jesus. Jesus offers them a lesson in law and casuistry, or explanation of the law. He says that the law is not rigid, and that there are times of need when the spirit of the law is kept while its letter is broken. For example, David and his men were in need of food and ate the sacred loaves. Jesus' conclusion is that the Sabbath law is at the service of people. Therefore, people are not to be unthinking slaves of it.

The next story shows Jesus illustrating this life-giving Sabbath observance as he heals the man with the withered hand.

What is the relevance of this commandment to contemporary experience? Men and women in the Western world suffer from stress and fatigue. Many are workaholics. Advances in technology, instead of offering opportunities for leisure, rest, reflection, and service for one's neighbor, are new means of working even harder and longer. The sense of the sacred, even on Sundays, is losing out to work and to business pressures.

The advantage of a movie like *Tuesdays with Morrie* is that the film directly tackles the themes of work, of letting go, and of the value of reflection and preparing for eternal rest.

Morrie has worked hard all his life as a sociology professor. His student, Mitch, is a slave to the contemporary work ethic and to protecting his job. Morrie is aware that he is dying and accepts that he must rest and prepare for death. This involves remembering his past, especially his childhood and his father. He knows he must come to terms with his early hardships and, in his memories and in his heart, reconcile with his father. It also means letting go of what he had achieved in his career so as to become fully human.

Morrie celebrates on his way to eternal rest. The Bible gives us many images of heaven, from the rich banquet to the colorful symbols of the Book of Revelation. It is the small passage in the Letter to the Hebrews that is pertinent here, because it describes a celebration, a heavenly festival of Sabbath worship and rest.

- Morrie's appearance on television, the program and its issues, his reaction to his terminal illness, his preparing to stop and take stock, to rest and appreciate the meaning of his life and of his death.

KEY SCENES AND THEMES

- Mitch and his hectic schedule; phoning his editors, staking out celebrities, interviewing them in the hope of exposing a scandal, meeting deadlines; joining the media hunt of personalities and finding himself flat on his face in a hotel vestibule.

- The Tuesday conversations between Morrie and Mitch, the talk about work and leisure, about letting go and what life really means; Mitch trying to let go, listening to Janine sing Gershwin to an appreciative Morrie, learning how to massage and touch Morrie with strength and tenderness; the funeral ritual with Morrie preparing him for death and eternal rest.

FOR REFLECTION AND CONVERSATION

1. When we see Morrie during the television interview and hear his thoughts on death, we are invited to think about what it means to be work-driven, the cost of not having a sense of the sacredness of life and rest. This is what catches Mitch's attention. He has to face these issues before it is too late. He falls flat on his face while chasing a celebrity and wonders what life is all about. How does Mitch come to an awareness about what is important in life, about not making work an idol? Have you ever experienced an epiphany like Mitch's? What are the priorities in your life? What is essential to your life of holiness?

2. In his conversations with Morrie, Mitch becomes aware of the importance of not making work an idol and of experiencing rest. He realizes that Morrie has moved from being an intelligent man to being a wise man. How is the living funeral a symbol of Morrie's teaching? What makes Morrie so spiritually free? How does his telling the stories of his mother's death, his father, and his stepmother help to prepare him for death and to understand what is important?

3. Recall some of Morrie's aphorisms from the film ("The way you get meaning into your life is to devote yourself to loving others"; "Love wins, love always wins"; "Once you learn how to die, you learn how to live"). Which one is your favorite? Why? How do these sayings change Mitch? Whose story is *Tuesdays with Morrie*? Which character grows and changes? How has *Tuesdays with Morrie* impressed you?

Prayer

Lord, you invited your disciples to come away and rest a while. Help us not to succumb to the temptation of being too busy to worship you and to learn to take time to contemplate your creation and to love others. Amen.

For Catechists

Catechism of the Catholic Church
A day of grace and rest from work, nos. 2184–2185
The family in God's plan, nos. 2201–2206
The family as community, nos. 2207, 2208

THE THIRD COMMANDMENT

Zephaniah 3:11–13
Revelation 21:1–8
Matthew 11:25–30

Witness
U.S.A., 1985, 112 minutes
Actors: Harrison Ford, Kelly McGillis, Lukas Haas,
Josef Sommer, Danny Glover, Viggo Mortensen
Writers: William Kelley, Earl W. Wallace
Director: Peter Weir

Witness

All Creation Is Made New

SYNOPSIS

Soon after her husband's funeral, Rachel Lapp and her son Samuel go to visit Rachel's sister in Baltimore. They are Amish.

Rachel (Kelly McGillis) and Samuel (Lukas Haas) are delayed while changing trains in Philadelphia. When Samuel goes to the men's room, he witnesses a murder and sees the man who did it. Detective John Book (Harrison Ford) and his partner, Detective Carter (Brent Jennings), interview Samuel and his mother, and then Book takes them to his sister's house for the night. The next day Samuel recognizes the perpetrator, Lieutenant McFee (Danny Glover), from a photo at the police station. Book tells Chief Schaeffer (Josef Sommer), and they decide to investigate quietly. That night, McFee tries to kill Book. Although injured, Book escapes and takes Rachel and Samuel home to their farm in Amish country. He tries to leave but collapses and wrecks his car.

Book recovers while Schaeffer and McFee search for him. He and Rachel feel a mutual attraction. When he fixes the car, they dance. Eli, her father-in-law (Jan Rubes), warns her that she risks being shunned by the community for her association with "the English." Book helps with milking the cows and carpentry, and he joins the community for a barn raising. Book dresses "plain" and goes into town with Eli to use the phone, and he learns that his partner has been killed. He calls Schaeffer and tells him he knows about him, the drugs, and the dirty cops. On the way home, the "English" stalk the Amish, and Book fights them off, breaking the nose of one of the ruffians. The sheriff reports this anomaly back to Schaeffer, suspecting Book is probably involved.

Schaeffer and McFee come to kill Book. Eli shouts a warning to him, and Book sends him to Daniel's (Alexander Godunov) farm, but he doesn't go. McFee and another cop are killed. As Schaeffer takes Rachel and Eli away, Eli signals to Samuel to ring the bell to call the community. When the people from the neighboring farms come, Schaeffer has to give himself up. Book bids farewell to Samuel, Rachel, and Eli.

COMMENTARY

Witness is Australian director Peter Weir's (*Gallipoli, The Year of Living Dangerously, Dead Poets Society, Fearless, Master and Commander: The Far Side of the World*) seventh feature film. As in most of his films, *Witness* bridges two worlds, contrasting light and dark, technology and countryside, right and wrong, good and evil. In *Witness,* he parallels the Amish world with the secular world where people speak "English." He effectively shows the disparity between people who live by peace and those who try to keep the peace through violence.

Witness was nominated for eight Academy Awards in 1986 and won two: Best Editing and Best Screenplay. William Kelley and television writers Earl W. Wallace (*How the West Was Won, War and Remembrance*) and Pamela Wallace (*Love with the Perfect Stranger, Single Santa Seeks Mrs. Clause*) scripted the film.

Witness is one of those nearly perfect literate films, with its conventional story structure, visual and moral contrasts, and cast. There are no secrets in the film; indeed, the film invites the audience to visit a secluded and tranquil place rarely experienced by outsiders. Child actor Lukas Haas was seven years old when he played Samuel, through whose eyes the audience considers the way of life described in the reading from Matthew.

Harrison Ford, whose movies have collectively grossed more box-office receipts than any actor in Hollywood history, is more than effective as John Book, who has to struggle between the film's two worlds. He was nominated for an Academy Award for *Witness,* and in 2000 he received a lifetime achievement award from the American Film Institute. Kelly McGillis, who went on to play the attorney in *The Accused,* was nominated for a Golden Globe for her role as Rachel.

Witness was ballet dancer Alexander Godunov's first film, and he is convincing as Rachel's suitor. Danny Glover, one of Hollywood's busiest actors (he has acted in seventy films to date and has won many awards), is one of the bad cops, playing counterpoint to his good-cop image in the *Lethal Weapon* franchise. *Witness* gives a very different impression of the Amish community from the television reality series, *Amish in the City* (2004).

DIALOGUE WITH THE SCRIPTURES

Focus: The Amish community exemplifies God's faithful remnant—those hard workers whom the prophet Zephaniah, the Book of Revelation, and Jesus himself describe as truly childlike. They are the new creation with a sense of the sacred and of Sabbath rest.

There are many levels of meaning in *Witness.* It works as a police and crime thriller, as a murder drama, and as a portrait of the Amish people who are dedicated to a life of work and integrity. This dialogue with the Scriptures acknowledges the thriller elements of the film and the picture of police corruption, of drug and money deals, and of violence. These are the ways of people who lack integrity as described by the prophet Zephaniah. Their fate is destruction on a great and terrible day, "A day of wrath...of anguish and distress...destruction and desolation...darkness and gloom" (1:15). The bad cops are the "proud braggarts" who "exult themselves" on God's holy mountain.

The Amish way of life, in direct opposition to this materialistic and corrupt way of life, exemplifies the Third Commandment. Not only do the Amish keep holy the day of the Lord, but they also have a sense of the sacred that underlies the positive dimensions of this commandment. Samuel witnesses the murder in the Philadelphia station, but, at the same time, he is a childlike witness to the values of the Amish. The Amish community itself is also a witness to the honorable way of life described by Zephaniah; they need have no sense of shame, for there will be no wrong, no lies, and no perjury in their mouths.

The movie offers many images of decent, hard work in the scenes in the home and the fields and, most significantly, in the sequence of the barn raising. It is a wonderful picture of a community working together constructively and building something that will last and serve everyone. There is a fine sense of joy as the men lift the beams and bolt them together. The spirit of labor draws in John Book, the outsider, welcoming him into the community and enabling him to share a drink with Daniel.

The whole community—men, women, and children—celebrate by breaking bread together, sharing refreshment, and taking some respite from the work. Samuel's central role in the film shows how the children are important to this life of work, celebration, and rest.

Jesus addresses his words of comfort and encouragement to children and the childlike. The wonder and reality of the God of blessings is revealed to those with childlike faith and trust. Samuel is a boy of truth and honesty; there is no deception in him. The childlike are those whom Jesus invites to come to him when the labor seems too much, too hard.

Jesus does not say he will take the burden of our labors away. Rather, he promises to share the load and invites us to share his burden as well. What follows is comfort and rest, a "Sabbath" for those who have borne the heat of the day and heavy burdens.

The Book of Revelation offers beautiful images, an ideal version of the New Jerusalem, a promise of Sabbath rest. This is a sacred vision with overtones of the love and union of bride and groom. For those who have remained faithful, it is a new earth and a new heaven. All creation is made new. Just as God rested on the Sabbath after the creation of the world in the Book of Genesis, so now, at the culmination of creation, God, the Alpha and the Omega, the beginning and the end, dwells with his people.

As Zephaniah promised rest, Revelation promises refreshing water to God's true children. The Amish have always tried to create an ideal community of fellowship and of prayer while resisting the temptations of the world.

Just as the passage from Revelation ends with a condemnation of sinners, so *Witness* ends with the destruction of the violent and corrupt police. It is the vision of sacred rest after labor, however, that remains in the memory.

- The funeral and the Amish community; Eli accompanying Rachel and Samuel to the train; the presence of Daniel; the delay at the Philadelphia train station; Samuel witnessing the murder in the men's room.

- John Book and Carter at the murder scene; Samuel as the witness; Rachel's discomfort and worry; staying with John's sister; Samuel looking at mug shots, recognizing McFee's photo and pointing at it; Book's report to the police chief; the agreement to keep it quiet; McFee attacking and wounding Book; Book's realization that corrupt cops are behind everything.

- Book taking Rachel and Samuel back home; his collapse; Rachel and the community caring for Book; Samuel's discovery of Book's gun and his grandfather's conversation with him; Book's trip into town to use the phone and his defense of the Amish; his relationship with Rachel; the arrival of the police chief and McFee; the fighting; the bell and the community.

1. "Just as God 'rested on the seventh day from all his work which he had done,' human life has a rhythm of work and rest. The institution of the Lord's Day helps everyone enjoy adequate rest and leisure to cultivate their familial, cultural, social, and religious lives" (*CCC,* no. 2184). The film shows the funeral in the Amish community, but does not reveal how they spend their Sabbath. It focuses on their work ethic and how their regard for the Lord influences everything they are and do. How does the Amish community reflect the above citation from the *Catechism of the Catholic Church?* What does the film say about what characterizes the Amish value system and their culture? Why do they not have machinery or telephones or cars? How does their external living reflect their relationship with the Lord and their lives in the community?

FOR REFLECTION AND CONVERSATION

2. The Amish have their origins in the Mennonite faith, Swiss Evangelical Protestants. They came to Pennsylvania in the early eighteenth century to escape persecution. The Amish derive their name from that of a Swiss bishop, Jakob Amman, who insisted on adhering strictly to the faith and punish-

ing the wayward by excommunication and shunning them. The rural, agricultural Amish are distinct because of their religious, peaceful, non-technological, community-centered lifestyle. Given this, what explains their attitude toward the violence Samuel experiences among the "English"? Talk about Samuel's discovery of the gun and his grandfather's conversation with him. Do you agree with the Amish perspective as explained by Eli? Why or why not? How does our national attitude and culture toward guns and violence as a way to solve problems conflict with that of the Amish? Is it really possible to hold the Amish perspective? How might it be good for public life to consider the way the Amish interpret the Scriptures?

3. Some of the most appreciable aspects of *Witness* are its use of symbols, music, and sound, and its integration of establishing shots to form the background of the action to come. What do you think Rachel's cap, the bell, the gun(s), the bullets, the angel, the doors, the car, the telephone, the birdhouse, and the other symbols mean? Why has the filmmaker taken such care to introduce John Book to the farm? How does this relate to the final resolution of the film's conflict? What does John Book learn from the Amish over the course of the film? What did the film mean to you in the context of the Third Commandment?

Prayer

Those who are faithful to you, Lord, will rest in security. Give comfort and courage to those who are overwhelmed by their labors. Amen.

For Catechists

Catechism of the Catholic Church
The Sabbath day, nos. 2168–2173
A day of grace from work, no. 2184
Peace, nos. 2302–2306
Avoiding war, nos. 2307, 2308
Intentional homicide, nos. 2268, 2269

Renée Zellweger and Nicole Kidman in *Cold Mountain*.

THE THIRD COMMANDMENT

Isaiah 2:1–5

Ephesians 2:13–18

Matthew 13:44–46

Cold Mountain

U.S.A., 2003, 152 minutes

Actors: Jude Law, Nicole Kidman, Renée Zellweger, Kathy Baker, James Gammon, Ray Winstone, Charley Hunnam, Eileen Atkins, Philip Seymour Hoffman, Natalie Portman, Giovanni Ribisi, Jena Malone

Writer: Anthony Minghella

Director: Anthony Minghella

Cold Mountain

A Time to Work and a Time to Rest

SYNOPSIS

In July 1864, Union troops dig tunnels under Confederate lines at Petersburg, Virginia, to lay explosives. A horrific battle follows, and several soldiers from Cold Mountain, North Carolina, are killed or wounded. One of them, Inman (Jude Law), is shot in the neck while trying to save his Indian friend. He recovers in a hospital but cannot leave. One day, he escapes through a window and becomes a deserter.

Not long before the war broke out, Ada Monroe (Nicole Kidman) and her father (Donald Sutherland), a retired preacher, had moved from Charleston, South Carolina, to Cold Mountain. Ada and Inman met and felt immediately and deeply attracted to one another. Inman is a carpenter and very shy. They barely speak to one another. When Inman decided to join the Confederate Army in 1861, Ada gave her word that she would wait for him. She gave him her picture and a book.

Teague (Ray Winstone), who desires to possess Ada, heads up the Home Guard. His special duty is to look for Confederate deserters and pacifists and kill them. He lets Ada know he wants her land and continually bothers her.

Ada's father dies, and she can barely fend for herself and tend their small farm. Ruby Thewes (Renée Zellweger), a lively, eccentric young woman, hears about Ada from a neighboring woman whose whole family has been killed by Teague. Ruby appears at the farm one day and says she is moving in to help Ada, but as an equal, not as a servant. Ruby is very earthy, and she brings new life to Ada and the farm. Ada lives in hope of Inman's return and often whispers, "Come back to me." She writes him letters all the time he is gone.

Inman, meanwhile, struggles toward home. He meets several people and families on the way: some are cowards, others traitors, and others survivors who are as war-weary as he is. When he reaches Cold Mountain, he runs into Ruby's musician father (Brendan Gleason), who is in hiding. Ada discovers Inman is home. They marry without witnesses and spend one night together. The next day, Teague kills him.

Years later, Ada and her daughter celebrate a meal with Ruby, her family, and the other survivors on Cold Mountain.

COMMENTARY

British playwright and filmmaker Anthony Minghella wrote and directed the award winning *Cold Mountain,* for which Renée Zellweger won an Academy Award for Best Supporting Actress. The film is based on Charles Frazier's 1997 best-selling novel and winner of the National Book Award. *Cold Mountain* is a visual tour de force that captures the fine details of the rural South on the verge of a war that pits brother against brother. Minghella constructs *Cold Mountain* in nonlinear ways that are reminiscent of his *The English Patient* (1996). Minghella also wrote and directed the 1991 award-winning romantic drama, *Truly Madly Deeply,* and *The Talented Mr. Ripley* in 1999.

The British stage-turned-screen actor Jude Law is credible in the role of Inman, who struggles with the ideology of war as he journeys home to find his true love. He was nominated for an Academy Award for this role. Nicole Kidman plays the polished young Southern belle who waits for him. Kidman was also nominated for an Academy Award for her portrayal of Ada.

The film was released at Christmas 2003, on time to be considered for the Academy Awards. Although an excellent piece of filmmaking, *Cold Mountain* lost out to the already crowded landscape of excellent films released in 2003.

Minghella did the principal photography for the film in Romania, for which some people criticized him. Others thought that the few African Americans portrayed and the lack of any treatment of the issue of slavery limited the film as a Civil War picture.

Focus: Cold Mountain *is a story of the hard work and struggle to survive of those left at home during the Civil War. Isaiah and Paul speak of peace, and Jesus reminds us that the kingdom is like a treasure hidden in a field.*

DIALOGUE WITH THE SCRIPTURES

Cold Mountain opens with the violence and horror of the Civil War and the confidence of both the North and South that God is on their side. Through Inman's outward journey, we see the struggle to return home to find peace. Through Ada's interior journey, we witness a woman who learns to genuinely care for and bring peace to others.

The classic text from Isaiah (repeated in Mic 4:13), in which swords are turned into ploughshares and spears into pruning hooks, expresses the symbolism of the transition from war to peace. In the sacred rest that comes after battles, there will be no more training for war. Of course, this is an ideal. Succeeding generations become aggressive, and war starts again. However, the ploughshares vision is one that has inspired many peace movements, and this citation is the title of a bronze statue in the United Nations Garden in New York City.

Cold Mountain effectively dramatizes the horror of war and Inman's odyssey of hope as he travels home to find Ada, love, and peace. In the meantime, it also dramatizes Ada's plight: the loss of her genteel way of life and her pride that prevents her from asking for help. Ruby's arrival and the need to work transform her. Ruby represents the "normal" way of human life, which includes hard work and the effort to survive. As the somewhat spoiled daughter of a minister, Ada must learn the "sacredness" of hard work by building fences, tending animals, and growing crops. Ada and Ruby live out what it means to turn "swords into ploughshares" and "spears into pruning hooks" (Is 2:4). They earn and share their rest and peace.

The women find their treasure hidden in the life-giving crops of their own fields. Working alongside Ruby, Ada learns to value friendship and, in so doing, finds her pearl of great price. Jesus says that this is what the reign of God is like. When people come together to work and live in peace, God is present. People are then able to repent of their sins, receive forgiveness, and hear and understand the good news, the Gospel of peace and love.

Ada's intense labor and her constant hope that Inman will return are consummated in her "marriage" to him. His tragic death might have meant the end for her, but she is no longer a fragile woman. Her years of work and communal living have given her strength. After Inman's death comes the birth of their daughter, her true pearl of great price.

Years later, Ada and her child along with Ruby and her husband, children, and father, who has survived the brutality of Teague and his followers, are ready for their rest, their Sabbath. The movie's final images glow with this atmosphere of peace. They symbolize what America hoped for after the Civil War and the hope that has followed every war ever fought.

The Letter to the Ephesians is so relevant because it gives a Christ-focused meaning to those who work for peace. Jesus, "breaking down the barrier of hostility that kept us apart," has reconciled us to God through his death and resurrection, which has given us the good news of peace after the battle. *Cold Mountain* shows us the rest and peace that will be ours at the end of our earthly exile.

- The laying of explosives; the battle and the carnage; Inman's book; Inman trying to save his friend and being wounded; Inman in the hospital; his escape and desertion; the pre-story of the Monroe's arrival at Cold Mountain; the town; Ada meeting Inman; his work as a carpenter; their attraction; the announcement of war while at church; Inman's decision to go to war and Ada's promise to wait for him; the book and the photo.

- Ada and her father; his death; the kindness of Mrs. Swanger; Teague's lust and cruelty, especially toward the Swangers; Ada's inability to cope and selling possessions to buy food; Ruby's arrival as an equal; their hard work and friendship; the arrival of Ruby's father.

- Inman's journey and the people he meets: the ex-minister, the deceitful woodsman and the loose women, the frightened widow and her child, and the lone woman in the woods; Inman's return; the wedding; the meal that Ada and her daughter prepare years after.

KEY SCENES AND THEMES

1. Talk about *Cold Mountain's* many themes (journey, war and peace, loyalty, friendship, poverty, the integrity of work, death, love of neighbor, perseverance, hope, etc.). Which themes touched you the

FOR REFLECTION AND CONVERSATION

most? Why? How are the themes of keeping holy the Lord's day—or religious faith—and work related in the film? Could *Cold Mountain* be called an anti-war film, a love story, or both? Why?

2. Jesus rose from the dead on the first day of the week. The Book of Exodus tells us that the Lord labored for the six days of creation, and on the seventh day he rested (Ex 20:11). The Christian Sabbath and day of rest "symbolizes the new creation ushered in by Christ's resurrection" (*CCC*, no. 2174). How were the years of the Civil War like a long, laborious Lenten season of suffering for the characters in the film? How was Ruby's coming like a resurrection for Ada? What was Mrs. Swanger's experience of the war? How was Inman's return also like a resurrection? How were the characters transformed by their struggles? Given these Lenten/resurrection and work/Sabbath analogies, what might be the meaning of the final meal years after the war?

3. "*Human work* proceeds directly from persons created in the image of God and called to prolong the work of creation by subduing the earth, both with and for one another" (*CCC*, no. 2427). If work stems from human dignity, the first principle of Christian social teaching, what other elements of this teaching (even from a negative perspective) are evident in the film? For example: 1) Subsidiarity: that no higher-level community should strip another community of their capacity to see, judge, and act on their own behalf; 2) that the common good be the determinant of economic social organization; 3) universal destination (or distribution) of goods because ownership of property is not an absolute right; 4) solidarity, the

alternative to globalization based on empathy for others; 5) an option for the poor from the social, economic, and cultural vantage point of the least among us and finally, 6) the integrity of creation. What might these principles of Christian social teaching as highlighted in this film (or others you have seen) have to do with the Sabbath and the honor of God? What does the Sabbath mean to you?

Prayer

Lord, when we are weary with our work, give us your grace of strength and encouragement and the promise of rest. Amen.

For Catechists

Catechism of the Catholic Church
The Lord's day, nos. 2174–2188
The cardinal virtues, no. 1807
The social doctrine of the Church, nos. 2419–2425
Blessed are the peacemakers, no. 2305

The Fourth Commandment

Introduction

Honor your father and mother./Do not disrespect parents or children.

It is often said that many Western cultures have lost the sense of family, especially of the extended family. Asian and African traditions have much stronger beliefs and practices about love, continuing care, and protection for all members of the family, young and old.

The busy-ness of the capitalist world requires so much time and energy that little time or energy remains for the care of aging relatives. People are living longer than they did a century ago. In general, people today live healthier lives well into their seventies and eighties, although many suffer from the debilitating aches and pains of age, from senility and Alzheimer's, and many of our elderly are homeless. Adult children lack the time and the skills to care for their parents, and the culture often devalues time spent with the elderly. Many adult children, though not all, feel that they meet their responsibilities to their aging parents and relatives by placing them in residential or nursing homes. The consequences for senior citizens and the elderly include isolation and loneliness as well as the risk of neglect and maltreatment from overworked, irresponsible, or uncaring staff members.

A social extension of the Fourth Commandment addresses the support and care that citizens in first-world countries owe to people in their own nations and to those in developing nations that suffer from the consequences of military and economic globalization. The social policies and structures of nations should work to provide the basic necessities to sustain family life.

For many adult children, the words: "Honor your father and mother" have enormous consequences, reaching far beyond the childlike utterances of the very young who confess to disobeying their moms and dads, grandparents, or caregivers. Unfortunately, otherwise mature adults get stuck on this overly simplistic understanding of the Fourth Commandment. With the new thrust in parishes toward inter-generational faith formation, there is hope for all to deepen their understanding of this commandment.

The challenge for adults with aging parents is to work out how to honor the commandment by valuing human life at all its stages. Care for the elderly is natural, and abandoning them physically and/or emotionally is not. Family mobility due to work, marriage, and travel, as well as loss of retirement benefits due to fraud and other reasons, can make elder care difficult for adult children and relatives. However, those cultures that believe that including and honoring the extended family is natural can enlighten those that consider this care a real burden or perceived inconvenience.

Divorce, remarriage, and the proliferation of blended families mean that the Fourth Commandment has grave implications for parents: *honor your children*. Indeed, much of the scope of the commandment needs to be focused on how parents can respect and care for their children. Raising children is not easy, especially when many children spend more time growing up among their peers or at school than they do with family members. The pressure and conflict of values presented by popular culture creates a huge challenge for the churches that seek to support parents. Additionally, parents' lack of knowledge about the stages of child development (alas, parenting does not come with a manual) as well as the conflicting values presented by government, legislation, business, education, entertainment and information media, advertising, and at times religion, can create a seemingly chaotic environment. Drugs, poverty, alcoholism, crime, gangs, war, and other social ills also challenge parents and caregivers.

Parents may feel exasperated and so, when their authority is questioned, they may respond by falling back on the saying, "Because I say so" or "Not in my house you don't." The challenge is to keep the door and communication open by articulating values and offering motivations for decisions, especially when a parent does not really understand what is going on with a child and the child is moody and hostile. In Jesus' much loved parable of the Prodigal Son (Luke 15), he describes the father as quite permissive. Not only does he allow his son to make mistakes, but also to fall into the depths of degradation. Yet he does not shut the door or disown his son. The son knows he can return to his father—and he does.

The revelations in the last decade about the amount of physical, sexual, emotional, and psychological abuse of children that occurs in the home (and churches) provide one of the greatest challenges of the Fourth Commandment. How can abused children honor their fathers and their mothers or other grown-ups when they are dishonored by them?

What was once considered a "nice" commandment concerned with doing or not doing what mommy or daddy says is now a commandment with demanding social consequences. The Fourth Commandment shows us the order of charity that God intended for the family, for respect for life, and for honor, affection, and gratitude for elders, teachers, and leaders. The rewards for observing this commandment are the spiritual and temporal fruits of peace and prosperity.

The films we have chosen for this commandment cover all the stages of life from childhood through old age. One of the limitations of these particular films is that they focus on the white male as the example of universal human experience. Of course, *Finding Nemo* is an anthropomorphic tale about fish, but the story, about a father and a son, is definitely told from the male point of view. *Ordinary People* is the angst-ridden family story of an upper-middle-class teenager suffering from depression, and *On Golden Pond* lets us see the aging Norman Thayer and his wife spend what is most likely their last summer together.

The Fourth Commandment

Genesis 37

1 John 4:14–19

Luke 2:41–52

Finding Nemo

U.S.A., 2003, 105 minutes

Actors (Voices): Albert Brooks, Ellen DeGeneres, Alexander Gould, Willem Dafoe, Allison Janney, Barry Humphries, Eric Bana, Bruce Spence, Geoffrey Rush, Bill Hunter, Austin Pendleton, Stephen Root, Elizabeth Perkins, Andrew Stanton

Writers: Andrew Stanton, Bob Peterson, David Reynolds

Director: Andrew Stanton, Lee Unkrich (co-director)

 *Finding Nemo*

Search, Find, and Let Go

SYNOPSIS

Happy clownfish parents-to-be Marlin (Albert Brooks) and Coral have just found a home in the Great Barrier Reef near Australia. When barracudas attack unexpectedly, they consume Coral and all but one of the couple's eggs.

That one little egg grows up to be a fish called Nemo (Alexander Gould). After Coral's death, Marlin becomes neurotic. He is afraid of the dangers of his environment and that something bad will happen to Nemo. On the way to Nemo's first day at school, Marlin lays down the safety rules for his son. But Nemo is adventurous. He defies his father's injunction and purposely swims beyond the end of the reef, where a diver catches him and makes it impossible for him to return home.

Marlin is frantic with worry and sets off to find and bring little Nemo home. Soon Marlin meets Dory (Ellen DeGeneres), a blue tang fish with a really short memory. She isn't all that practical, but her clowning around helps Marlin stay focused on the journey.

Nemo ends up in a fish tank in a dentist's office in Sydney. He makes friends with the other fish. When they learn that the dentist intends to give Nemo as a gift to his niece, Darla—who does not know how to take care of pets, and whom all the fish fear—they try to help Nemo excape.

Marlin and Dory encounter Bruce (Barry Humphries), a great white shark who "convinces" them to attend a meeting of "Fish-Eaters Anonymous." As part of their cure, the sharks chant, "Fish are friends—not food." Bruce falls off the wagon when he senses some dinner approaching. Marlin and Dory take the opportunity to escape and continue their search for Nemo.

Meanwhile, Nemo, with the help of pelicans, escapes into the Sydney Harbor. He learns from one of the birds that his father is looking for him.

Marlin and Dory part ways briefly. Finally, Marlin and Nemo reunite and meet up with Dory. They return to their home on the reef.

COMMENTARY

In recent years, Pixar Studios has received critical acclaim as well as huge box-office popularity with *Toy Story, A Bug's Life, Toy Story 2, Monsters, Inc.,* and *The Incredibles. Finding Nemo* continues this tradition and is a hugely enjoyable film for children and adults.

The animation is outstanding, not only because of the skillful creation of the fish characters with their varying sizes, shapes, and expressions, but also because the film enthusiastically suggests what life might be like under water. With their computer-generated images (CGIs), including the brightly colored barrier reef off the Australian coast and the ocean depths, Pixar Studios creates a fantasy world that is not too far from reality. The film's humor appeals to both adults and children, thus tempering any sentimentality that the plot might evoke. Pixar went on to further critical praise, an Oscar, and box-office success with *The Incredibles.* Their next movie was *Cars.*

The film's fascinating creatures feature a large cast of very talented voices. In all his films, Albert Brooks (*Lost in America, Mother, The Muse, The In-Laws*) plays a put-upon, lugubrious character distinguished by his ironic one-liners. He is perfect for Marlin. Ellen DeGeneres, with her zany comic style and deadpan patter, makes a delightful Dory. Geoffrey Rush is the Sydney pelican, Nigel. A trio of Australian talent voice the sharks: Barry Humphries (*An Audience with Dame Edna Everage*), Eric Bana (*Troy*), and Bruce Spence (Mad Max films). Alexander Gould brings just the right pathos and determination to Nemo's voice. A collection of eccentrics voiced by Willem Dafoe, Allison Janney, and a wide range of comic talent inhabit the dentist's fish tank.

Finding Nemo has strong family themes. Parents and children, most especially fathers and sons, will identify with this tale.

DIALOGUE WITH THE SCRIPTURES

Focus: While Marlin searches for his lost son, Nemo, he has to learn to be less protective so that Nemo can grow to maturity. The Gospel reminds us that Mary and Joseph searched for Jesus and had to learn how to let him go so that he could grow into the man he needed to be for his Father's mission.

The Fourth Commandment focuses on children's responsibility toward parents and, at the same time, fosters the strength of family life and the responsibilities of parents for children. At a time when so much parental violence and abuse of children is reported, the commandment is an important reminder of the loving care that parents are obliged to have for their children.

Nemo, the only surviving offspring of an attack on his family, grows up in the care of his widowed father, Marlin. Marlin is a loving father, but he is overprotective. This is a common temptation for parents whose love, driven by fear, can prevent their children from developing as they should on the social, human, and moral levels. Thus, children may not learn how to take responsibility or mature in respect for others and self. They may develop a sense of entitlement for attention and material objects and become very demanding. This can result in their never leaving home to lead happy, productive lives. Parents can either dominate their children or refuse to let them breathe. Parenting is not easy.

Genesis, chapter 37, offers the archetypal story of a fond, loving, but overprotective father. Jacob loves Joseph, the son of Rachel, very much. He spoils him and has given him the famous coat of many colors. Jacob's preferential love alienates Joseph's older brothers, the sons of Leah, especially when Joseph naively boasts of his dreams in which they symbolically bow in reverence before him. They are jealous and want to kill him, but Reuben persuades them to drop him into an empty cistern. Then Judah persuades them to sell Joseph into slavery instead. The story does indeed have a happy ending: Joseph reigns in Egypt, where he is reconciled with his brothers and reunited with his father. Despite its happy ending, it is a biblical cautionary tale of overprotective love.

Nemo takes a risk and moves beyond his father's control. He is a thoughtless child who is lost and taken where he would not have otherwise gone. The movie offers a wonderful portrait of a caring father, but Marlin has to learn to let Nemo become himself. While Marlin desperately searches for Nemo and is prepared to risk his own life for his son, he learns to be a better parent.

One of the best-known stories about parents losing a child is that of the boy Jesus lost in Jerusalem. Mary and Joseph had no idea where he was. They had allowed him the liberty of traveling in the caravan group with friends and relatives. But Jesus went beyond their control. Marlin's journey through the ocean is a reflection of the distraught parents' anxious and anguished three-day search for Jesus.

This story from Luke is unique in the Gospel narratives. It illustrates Jesus' maturing and the development of his sense of vocation. It is also the story of a boy at the time of his bar mitzvah assuming more adult responsibilities in terms of his place in adult Jewish religious society. Jesus' parents had something to learn as well: eventually, they would have to let go of their son. It is significant that Luke adds that the relationship between Jesus and his parents in the following eighteen years was characterized by harmony. This is the traditional model of the Holy Family. It shows the Fourth Commandment in practice. Jesus grows in physical, emotional, and psychological maturity: wisdom, age, and grace. Meanwhile, at their home in Nazareth, Mary kept reflecting on the meaning of her role as Jesus' mother and what the future would hold for her Son.

St. John's Gospel and his letters frequently refer to the relationship between Jesus, the Son, and his heavenly Father. In the First Letter of John, we hear how God is the most loving of fathers, a Father who did not cling to his Son but, for love of us and despite our sins, freely let his Son become one of us. God the Father sent Jesus to our world to show God's love for the world and for us.

God offers a wonderful image of a loving but not overprotective parent.

KEY SCENES AND THEMES

- The picture of happy family life with Marlin, his wife, and the little fish eggs; the sudden destruction of the family; Marlin left with only one egg; the overprotective Marlin learning that Nemo has gone too far from school and has been taken away.

- Marlin and his search, grieving for his son; learning the lessons about giving his son a chance to mature; his relationship with Dory.

- Nemo missing his father; his realizing that he had taken too much of a risk in swimming away from the school; finding himself in the fish tank with his new companions; their help in setting him free to be reunited with Marlin.

1. Often the myths and hero stories that emerged from the Mediterranean area began with the birth of a male child (the Greek Oedipus, the Hebrew Moses, and the Roman twins Romulus and Remus) who is left to die or fend for himself and then amazingly survives. The hero then sets out on a journey or quest as a way to grow, mature, and find meaning or love. A quest is a pursuit or a search for an ideal, a goal, and, in the case of *Finding Nemo*, a child. The film seems aimed at a young audience, yet the title, *Finding Nemo*, indicates that it's more the father's story than it is Nemo's. How is this so? How would you describe Marlin's quest? Nemo's? What role do the female characters play in the film?

FOR REFLECTION AND CONVERSATION

2. Most Hollywood films that deal with universal human experience are about men—fathers and sons (and therefore families)—or friendship between men. This storytelling tradition is as old as the Bible, Greek myth, Eastern traditions, and African tales. Some of the more recent films on this theme are: *Life as a House, Master and Commander: The Far Side of the World, The Shawshank Redemption, A River Runs Through It, Signs, October Sky, Finding*

Forrester, and almost all war movies. How do these films in particular show aspects and even deeper understandings of the Fourth Commandment? If the Fourth Commandment is about mutual respect between children and parents or elders, the relationships between brothers and sisters, and the relationships between children and grandparents, what basic idea or belief binds families or groups in society together?

3. Anthropomorphism attributes human characteristics to creatures and things that are not human. In *Finding Nemo,* what situations, gifts, and flaws did the characters demonstrate that were human in nature? How did the movie represent the female characters? Did you notice any less-than-perfect creatures in the film (Dory's limited mental abilities; Nemo's undersized fin)? Was Bruce, the great white shark, a symbol of evil, or was he only acting in accord with his nature when he ate fish? What does it mean for a human being to fulfill his or her true nature? What moral might the storytellers have been trying to teach by showing the "humanity" of the characters? Why might anthropomorphism be a useful technique for teaching life's lessons? What did you learn from *Finding Nemo?*

Prayer

Lord, amid the day-to-day tensions between parents and children, give them the grace of love and understanding. Amen.

For Catechists

Catechism of the Catholic Church
The nature of the family, nos. 2201–2203
The duties of children, nos. 2214–2220
The duties of parents, nos. 2221–2231

Henry Fonda and Katharine Hepburn in *On Golden Pond*.

On Golden Pond

U.S.A., 1981, 104 minutes

Actors: Henry Fonda, Katharine Hepburn, Jane Fonda, Doug McKeon, Dabney Coleman, Christopher Rydell

Writer: Ernest Thompson

Director: Mark Rydell

 *On Golden Pond*

Age and Care

Ethel (Katharine Hepburn) and Norman (Henry Fonda) Thayer arrive at their summer house on Golden Pond in Maine. The loons on the lake welcome them as they open the house after the long winter. Norman was a university professor, and now his memory is beginning to fail him. He is aware of it and so is Ethel, who is energetic, frank, and supportive.

SYNOPSIS

Their daughter, Chelsea (Jane Fonda), arrives with her new male friend to celebrate Norman's eightieth birthday. Her first marriage failed, and she seems happy to be with Bill Ray (Dabney Coleman), a dentist. They also bring thirteen-year-old Billy Ray (Doug McKeon) with them. Chelsea and Norm do not have a good relationship. She calls her father "Norman" instead of Dad.

After the birthday party, Chelsea and Bill Ray leave for a month in Europe, and young Billy Ray stays behind with Norman and Ethel. At first it seems that Billy Ray will be difficult, but Norman assumes a "grandfather" role, and soon they are friends. Norman teaches Billy Ray to fish for lake trout, and they keep trying to lure in Walter, the trout that Norman says always gets away. One day they have an accident, and Norman falls out of the boat. Billy Ray helps him to a big rock, and they hold on together until help comes.

Chelsea returns alone for Billy Ray since Bill Ray had to get back to Los Angeles. They were married in Brussels. Chelsea tells her mother she wants to be friends with her dad, but they end up arguing. Ethel tells her to grow up. Out in the cove, Norman and Billy Ray catch Walter at last. But they let him go. Chelsea has a talk with her father and calls him "Dad." She and Billy Ray leave for the West Coast, promising to return often.

As Ethel and Norman close down the house, he weakens and seems to be having a heart attack. Ethel thinks she is going to lose him. They talk about death. He recovers, and together they walk to the lake to hear the loons call out their farewell.

COMMENTARY

On Golden Pond received popular and critical acclaim when it was released in 1981. Jane Fonda accepted her father's Oscar for his role in the film, as he was too ill to go to the ceremony. Receiving the Oscar was the peak of Henry Fonda's career. With performances in *Young Mr. Lincoln, The Grapes of Wrath, My Darling Clementine,* and *Fort Apache,* he established himself as one of the screen's leading actors and became an American icon. He then moved to the stage for almost a decade, returning to movies in *Mister Roberts* and *War and Peace* in the 1950s. As Norman Thayer Jr. in *On Golden Pond,* Henry Fonda embodied perfectly the crusty old man with all the idiosyncrasies of advanced age. In her performance as his wife, Ethel, Katharine Hepburn won her fourth Oscar, having already won for *Morning Glory, Guess Who's Coming to Dinner,* and *The Lion in Winter.* Hepburn and Fonda's performances are well matched, and they seem an archetypal American couple.

Jane Fonda is effective as their daughter, Chelsea. The sequences involving Jane and Henry Fonda have echoes of their real-life clashes and reconciliations. Their scenes together are quite moving. Dabney Coleman, an excellent character actor (*The Guardian*), is very good in the role of Chelsea's friend, Bill Ray. Young Doug McKeon carries much of the second part of the film with Henry Fonda and highlights both the generation gap as well as the bonds between generations.

Ernest Thompson, who adapted his stage play for the screen, won an Oscar for the script, which was directed by Mark Rydell (*The Fox, Cinderella Liberty, The Rose, The River*). Dave Grusin's score blends attractively with the images to sustain the emotional balance of the film.

With its treatment of the themes of old age, generation gaps, and relationships, the film is an excellent piece of popular cinema. It was remade for television with Julie Andrews and Christopher Plummer in 2001, directed by author Ernest Thomson.

Focus: On Golden Pond *shows us aging parents who need love and care from their children. It leads us to biblical images of age and concern for our elders, like those of Jacob and his sons, of Paul and the Philippians, and, especially, of Jesus' care for Mary as he died on the cross.*

DIALOGUE WITH THE SCRIPTURES

The Fourth Commandment has traditionally been seen as an exhortation for children to be obedient to their parents. But obedience is not enough to fulfill the commandment. During the twentieth century, people began to live longer, and life expectancy in first-world countries continues to rise in the twenty-first century. Now another apt application of the Fourth Commandment is the care adult children take of their aging parents.

In the Old Testament, the patriarchs lived long lives. The story of the patriarch Jacob is a large feature in the Book of Genesis. He was the father of twelve sons who became the ancestors of the tribes of Israel. Tracing Jacob's story through Genesis, especially his love for his wives Leah and Rachel, we can see how he favors Rachel's sons, Joseph and Benjamin, more than the others. Jacob grieves at the (false) news of Joseph's death and then begins to favor Benjamin. One of the great scriptural sagas about a parent and children is the story of Jacob receiving the wonderful revelation that Joseph is still alive. The meeting between Jacob and Joseph after so many years is particularly poignant.

In considering *On Golden Pond* and the Fourth Commandment, we have the opportunity to examine the story of a long marriage as well as the strain that can develop between a father and his children. In Genesis, chapter 48, we read of the death of Jacob, his bequests, and his blessings for his children. The story of *On Golden Pond* shows us the need for reconciliation between children and parents and the obligation for children to care for their aging parents. The tension between Chelsea and Norman needs to be faced and healed. As Norman prepares for death and is in danger of death in the water with Billy, he reaches out to his daughter. She has to care for him.

Another image of age and care from the Scriptures comes from Paul. At the end of his Letter to the Philippians, he acknowledges how good the people of Philippi have been to him, and he expresses his gratitude. One of the appealing features of *On Golden Pond* is the picture of love between the aging Norman and Ethel. This love manifests itself in the smallest of things and in the understanding they have of one another despite irritations. They have moved from a life of activity to one of greater peace and serenity. The challenge for Chelsea is to appreciate this serenity, to become part of it, and to reciprocate her parents' love for her.

Perhaps the best scriptural image of a child's care for his mother is from the Gospel of John. While dying on the cross, Jesus sees his mother standing before him. He knows she will grow old without him. He fulfills the obligation to honor his mother by providing for her care, entrusting her to John, who "took her into his care" (Jn 19:27).

Norman and Ethel Thayer have become cinema icons of aging, love, and fidelity. They remind us of the continual need for adult children to honor their father and mother.

KEY SCENES AND THEMES

- Norman and Ethel together in the house, doing the chores, struggling with the stuck doors, going fishing; Norman on the phone and his crusty answers, buying gas at the garage; Norman driving the motor boat; his going off to pick strawberries, feeling lost and abandoned, and hurrying home.

- The bond between Norman and Billy; gradual communication, jargon, swearing, books, and fishing; the importance of the accident; Norman having the opportunity to mentor Billy and be an effective grandfather.

- Norman's experience of illness and the possibility of death; Norman and his fear; his greater dependence on Ethel; his life passing before him; his having the opportunity to celebrate his eightieth birthday and to be reconciled with Chelsea and his family.

FOR REFLECTION AND CONVERSATION

1. In *Finding Nemo,* we get a sense of the fear parents experience for their children's welfare; in *Ordinary People,* we get a glimpse of the darkness that exists in families; and in *On Golden Pond,* we come to the sunset of life when children become their parents' caretakers. In various cultures of the world, many generations form a family unit, and it is unthinkable to abandon one's parents. In the first world, how-

ever, the sick and the elderly are easily abandoned (resulting in homelessness) or shut away and forgotten (nursing homes). Why do you think this happens? It is a necessity now for people to prepare for their retirement, but fraud and other greedy business practices cheat many people out of the fruit of their life's labor. What is a pastoral response to this phenomenon?

2. "Intergenerational faith formation," a relatively new approach in faith communities and parishes, emphasizes bible study and other programs and events that bring families of all age groups together. What are some other ways to bridge the generations in families that will help us to fulfill our obligation to care for one another? What is the benefit to those who show care and concern for all the generations of their families? Talk about what *On Golden Pond* means to you from your own experience.

3. The Fourth Commandment and *On Golden Pond* deal with the blessings, struggles, forgiveness, and acceptance that exist in family life. Besides the obligations that family members bear, civil society also has obligations toward the family and the community. The responsibility of the State is to serve families and to uphold human dignity, beginning with the most vulnerable: the unborn, the sick, the elderly, and the dying. Civil authority must also "dispense justice humanely" (*CCC*, no. 2237) because "every society's judgments and conduct reflect a vision of [the human person] and his [or her] destiny" (cf. no. 2257). How does the light of the Gospel balance freedom and responsibility for soci-

eties and for individuals regarding the family? What can we contribute to society today in order to support the "institution" of the family and the families among us?

Prayer

Jesus, we thank you for showing us how to love and care for our parents even as you died on the cross. Amen.

For Catechists

Catechism of the Catholic Church
The duties of parents, nos. 2222, 2223, 2227, 2230
The duties of children, nos. 2214, 2215, 2216
Euthanasia, no. 2276
Respect for health, no. 2288
Safeguarding peace, nos. 2302–2306

The Fourth Commandment

Sirach 3:1–18

Ephesians 6:1–4

Luke 11:27–28

Ordinary People

U.S.A., 1980, 120 minutes

Actors: Donald Sutherland, Mary Tyler Moore, Timothy Hutton, Judd Hirsch, Dinah Manoff, Elizabeth McGovern, M. Emmet Walsh, Adam Baldwin

Writer: Alvin Sargent

Director: Robert Redford

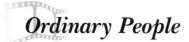 *Ordinary People*

Addicted to Perfection

SYNOPSIS

It is autumn in an upper-middle-class Chicago suburb. All seems well, and a choir sings, "In the silence of our souls, we contemplate your peace." A husband and wife, Calvin (Donald Sutherland) and Beth (Mary Tyler Moore), return home after seeing a play about marriage. They seem to be a loving couple. Their teenage son, Conrad (Timothy Hutton), pretends to be reading when his dad checks on him. But the boy has trouble sleeping. He has nightmares about his brother Buck's death—his drowning during a storm on a lake.

Conrad goes to see a psychiatrist, Dr. Berger (Judd Hirsch). Conrad had slit his wrists and spent four months in a mental hospital after his brother's death. He has now returned to school. He is on the swim team and sings in the choir, but he is still troubled. Conrad tells the doctor he wants to be in control of his life. Calvin is happy that Conrad is going to therapy, but Beth is not. She is humiliated and angry when Calvin tells a neighbor about Conrad. She is obsessively neat, and nothing is out of order in the house. She thinks about her dead son and cannot relate to Calvin, nor can he relate to her. They cannot communicate.

114

Conrad becomes friends with Jeannine, whom he meets at choir practice. One day at a restaurant, Conrad meets Karen (Elizabeth McGovern), who was in the hospital with him. She tells him, "Let's have the best year of our whole lives." She later kills herself, and Conrad is devastated. This precipitates a crisis, and Dr. Berger helps Conrad see that he feels guilty because he held on to the sinking boat and lived while his brother died. Meanwhile, Beth excludes Conrad more and more from her affections and refuses to change. One night she finds Calvin crying at the dining room table, and he asks her if she loves him. She cannot really answer. When he tells her he doesn't know if he loves her anymore, she packs her bags and leaves. Father and son embrace, ready to face the future as best they can.

In 1980, *Ordinary People* won an Oscar for Best Film and one for Best Director for Robert Redford in his directorial debut. The film has been rightly acclaimed for its perception about family dynamics and grief. Oscar-winner Alvin Sargent (*Julia*) adapted the best-selling novel by Judith Guest and, in so doing, wrote a compelling screenplay. *Ordinary People* is a movie of great sensitivity with excellent acting. Mary Tyler Moore, whose acting experience was in television comedy until her role in this movie, effaces her television image with the dramatic portrayal of the brittle, poised mother who, as one commentator noted, is "addicted to perfection." Donald Sutherland gives another marvelous performance as the warm, bewildered father. Judd Hirsch is a forceful, sympathetic psychiatrist.

COMMENTARY

But the film really belongs to Timothy Hutton. He won the Academy Award for Best Supporting Actor for his performance as the tormented surviving son.

Ordinary People is a valuable film that offers insight, encouragement, and hope amid depression. The year it was released also saw other films dealing with family relationships, especially *Tribute* with Jack Lemmon and Robby Benson and *The Great Santini* with Robert Duvall and Michael O'Keefe.

Robert Redford has always been a serious actor, as shown in his roles in *The Saga of Jeremiah Johnson, All the President's Men,* and *Brubaker,* as well as his tragic-comic character in *Butch Cassidy and the Sundance Kid.* This seriousness is even more evident in the movies that he directed: *The Milagro Beanfield War, A River Runs Through It, Quiz Show, The Horse Whisperer,* and *The Legend of Bagger Vance.*

DIALOGUE WITH THE SCRIPTURES

Focus: In the Gospel, Jesus indirectly praises his mother in response to the praise of the woman in the crowd. In Sirach, children are ordered to honor and obey their parents; the Pauline letter in the New Testament urges parents not to drive their children to resentment. How to balance these two directives is the conflicted situation of Ordinary People.

The reading from Ephesians refers to the Fourth Commandment and urges children to obedience. It sounds like the traditional and one-dimensionally interpreted exhortation that says children should be put in their place and stay there, or that children should be seen and not heard. But then the letter goes on to inform parents that the commandment entails obligations for them as well: they must never drive their children to resentment. This touches the nerve of *Ordinary People.* Beth, the demanding mother, puts so much pressure on her children that, when one of them dies, the surviving child attempts suicide and must take on the burden of survivor guilt, which he manifests through an enormous need for affirmation and affection.

The Letter to the Ephesians also places parental correction in its proper context; any correction and guidance should be patterned on God's dealing with people. God's unconditional love is the true definition of perfection.

As Beth walks out of the door of her home, her perfectionism constricts her. Beginning in the seventeenth century, the dictum to "strive for perfection" directed much of Western spirituality and behavior. The assumption was that if you tried hard enough, you could attain perfection, making you acceptable to God. This condition could be obtained—and maintained—through absolute adherence to religious, civil, and moral laws and cultural mores. Institutions—society, Church, and family—were and often are expected to be perfect as well. Though this spirituality was doomed to failure because it led to disillusionment and rejection, its traces can still be found in our culture today. *Ordinary People* shows powerfully, even desperately, that nothing on this earth is or can be "perfect."

Sirach offers much insight into parenting, though he uses the mother as the negative example. Once again, the passage assumes the superior role of parents and offers exhortations to children. It uses the language of blessing to describe the benefits for the child who honors his or her father and mother. However, in the middle of the poem, there is a startling verse, a contrast between a father's blessing and a mother's curse. It speaks to the situation of *Ordinary People:* "a father's blessing gives a family firm roots, but a mother's curse uproots the growing plant" (3:9). This puts an extraordinary burden on the child of a parent who cannot see how destructive his or her behavior and attitudes might be or who mistreats his or her children. Through his therapy, Conrad's challenge is to somehow reconcile with his mother and respond to his father's love. In so doing, he can become the person he is meant to be.

Jesus has a significant word to say about parenting. In Luke, a woman in the crowd is so overwhelmed by the power of his teaching that she cries out in praise of his mother. Jesus wants to make the point that, although he loves her, it is not simply because his mother conceived and gave birth to him that she deserves this praise. Rather, it is because she is a woman who heard God's word in her life, pondered it, and kept it. This is what truly made her a good mother.

Because *Ordinary People* is set in middle-class America with its façade of perfection, the film's prophetic witness is both alarming and challenging.

KEY SCENES AND THEMES

- Conrad and the sessions with the psychiatrist; the effort to talk and to remember; the flashbacks, especially of the accident, and the burden of his survivor guilt.

- Calvin talking with the psychiatrist and his feeling of liberation; his attempts to talk with Conrad, their bonding; Conrad's confrontation with him about how he communicates.

- Beth's running of the house; her order and efficiency; her treatment of Conrad; her judging and criticizing him, her inability to show him warmth and affection.

FOR REFLECTION AND CONVERSATION

1. By the 1980s, many more parents could face up to family problems than in the past, which is probably why both the novel and the film, *Ordinary People,* were so successful. People understood the moral of the story. In the film, Conrad says, "Mother thinks ordinary people don't have problems and should not run to experts, especially for any psychological therapy, if they do." Some members of today's audiences, however, might still agree that if a person just bucks up and takes control of his or her life, he or she will not need any outside help. Why might some people think that mental or emotional illnesses are flaws rather than a condition in need of healing?

How does the individualistic culture of the United States (and perhaps other countries) support this perspective? Have you known someone who needed spiritual, emotional, or psychological help but felt intimidated by a family culture that would not let him or her seek that help? Put yourself in the shoes of one of the characters in the film. What would you have done in his or her place?

2. *Ordinary People* invites audiences inside a family that has suffered a tragedy to look behind the affluent and respectable surface of upper-middle-class suburban life and discover the realities of suicide, parental expectations, inverted snobbery, and the need for self-awareness, understanding, tolerance, forgiveness, and reconciliation. Suicide is one of the top ten causes of death in the United States. Several biological, sociological, and psychological studies and surveys have led to convincing theories about why people take their lives. On July 8, 2004, the U.S. Senate passed a multimillion dollar bill to help states fund programs that will identify the early signs of depression, one of the causes that leads to teen and young adult suicide. What do you think are the causes of suicide? How can pastoral ministry to families help prevent the tragedy of suicide?

3. Beth is typical of many parents, especially those who would see themselves as ideal. They set high standards for the whole family; their goal is success, and they want to be perceived as perfect or at least as self-sufficient and strong. Beth is so busy keeping up the appearance of success that she cannot tolerate mistakes. This leads to brittleness and an inability to show affection, which makes it impossible to express

love. When a parent's expectations are unrealistically high, children can never attain them and consequently become a disappointment to that parent. Some leaders in faith communities think that parenting is the greatest pastoral need in Western countries today. Why might this be so? What is the link back to the Fourth Commandment? Compare different translations of Mt 5:48 and talk about what to "be perfect" means.

Prayer

Lord, we pray for families that struggle with relationships, high expectations, and parental control. Help us to see the need for love and respect of those whom we love, live, work, serve, and worship. Amen.

For Catechists

Catechism of the Catholic Church
The duties of children, nos. 2214, 2215, 2217, 2219
The duties of parents, nos. 2222–2224, 2227, 2228
Suicide, no. 2283

The Fifth Commandment

Introduction

You shall not kill./Respect life./Do not encourage violence.

We live in a violent age. Probably every generation has said this, but we who have lived through the twentieth century have seen two world wars, the beginning of the atomic era, and such genocides and massacres that we can say that our violent age has gone global. Although people the world over had hopes for the twenty-first century, it did not take long for terrorism and war to reach unbelievable proportions.

Some people find it difficult to reconcile the Decalogue's "You shall not kill" with the Pentateuch's law of retribution or lex talionis, the "an eye for an eye" dictum. Over the centuries, many proponents of war and of personal or communal vengeance through capital punishment have quoted this text to justify their actions. However, its real meaning is not retaliatory. Rather, it is an admonition that punishment should fit the crime and not go to excess. The teaching of Jesus takes us to a deeper understanding of peace over violence; he rejects the eye-for-an-eye theology and introduces a spirituality that encourages people to turn the other cheek. In recent times, public moral and legal disputes over issues such as abortion and capital punishment led the late Cardinal Joseph Bernardin of Chicago to introduce the "seamless garment" approach to life issues. He proposed that opposition to killing must be consistent and principled, protecting life not only from threats at its inception but also from enforced judicial death.

Bernardin's articulation of the life ethic requires a great deal of careful reflection. The issues are highly emotional and can become volatile. For example, some supporters of the right to life go over the edge, wreaking physical vengeance on abortionists and committing murder in God's name. Environmentalists sometimes use the same tactics to convince people to save the earth, but end in alienating them by their contradictory methods, such as burning vehicles and property. Activists who use violence to counteract violence and to change society and culture do not succeed in convincing people about the truth of their causes.

With the new advent of terrorism in New York, Washington, D.C., and Pennsylvania on September 11, 2001, people have to look again at the implications and questions associated with the long-term consequences of war. The traditional "just war" theory has had to be reexamined in the light of twenty-first century weapons and the fact that every country, whether it wants to or not, can be caught up in war. The *Catechism of the Catholic Church* is unequivocal about war:

> The strict conditions for *legitimate defense by military force* require rigorous consideration. The gravity of such a decision makes it subject to rigorous conditions of moral legitimacy... (no. 2309).

One of the targets for blame concerning the modern insensitivity to violence is the influence of the media. Contemporary media has given us new psychologies and new ways of developing self-identity and social responsibility—not all of which are positive and pro-human. As information and news entertain us and entertainment informs us, they very often normalize violence as a way to resolve problems.

The Fifth Commandment has something definite to say about how visual media—whether in the news or entertainment—presents graphic violence. This teaching says that we are to be educated and formed to the law of love, a process that includes peacemaking, communication, and negotiation. One of the debates in the media education community revolves around the belief that people have been "desensitized" to violence. The real issue, however, is that people have not been sensitized enough to peacemaking, communication, and negotiation as ways to resolve conflict.

Another issue regards the representation of violence in media and our understanding of the nature of storytelling and drama itself. In his *Poetics,* Aristotle said about the nature of drama and violence:

> Let us consider, therefore, the kinds of occurrences that seem terrible or pitiful. Actions of this sort must, of course, happen between persons who are either friends to one another or enemies or neither. Now if enemy harms enemy, there is nothing to excite pity either in his doing the deed or in his being on the point of doing it—nothing, that is, but the actual suffering; and the same is true if the parties are neither friends nor enemies. When, however, the tragic event occurs within the sphere of the natural affections—when, for instance, a brother kills or is on the point of killing his brother, or a son his father, or a mother her son, or a son his mother, or something equally drastic is done—that is the kind of event a poet must try for.

Even the Bible reflects the literary form of dramatic storytelling and deals with issues of power, sex, and money over and over again. Therefore, applying the Fifth Commandment to the media requires sensitivity to violence combined with a healthy appreciation for drama. Our sensitivities and consciences need to be "fine-tuned" when we choose what to listen to, watch, and read. And once we have chosen, we must be attentive to how we discern the meaning within the context of the presentation of the media stories we experience.

Violent crime is on the increase in many cities, and it is alarming. It is a fact that the local news media especially hype fear when reporting crimes. This creates a mentality where people rush immediately to advocate the easier "pseudo-solution" of stronger legislation, harsher penalties, and more severe jail sentences. The implications of the Fifth Commandment, however, are that we must seek the root causes of such crimes and violence and create solutions that give life, such as educational opportunities. These kinds of solutions can lead to a more realistic awareness in young people and their families of how poverty, racism, and drugs, as well as the availability of guns, contribute to our violence culture.

The breakdown of so many families, child endangerment, abuse, and the resulting lack of self-esteem in children have driven many young people away from home and on to the streets. This is all part of the violence that the commandment condemns and challenges us to remedy.

The specter of physical and sexual abuse, especially of children, has revealed that many respectable citizens in society and in churches have perpetrated violence with shocking consequences.

The Fifth Commandment is a command that touches every aspect of our lives.

The first two films we have chosen for the Fifth Commandment consider the racially based genocide of the Holocaust in *The Pianist* and the role of racism, killing, murder, and justice in *A Time to Kill*. *The Cider House Rules* deals explicitly with abortion.

Adrien Brody in *The Pianist*.

The Pianist

Poland, 2002, 149 minutes

Actors: Adrien Brody, Thomas Kretschmann, Frank Finlay, Maureen Lipman, Emilia Fox, Ed Stoppard

Writer: Ronald Harwood

Director: Roman Polanski

 *The Pianist*

Survival

One day in 1939 in Warsaw, Poland, a young pianist, Wladyslaw Szpilman (Adrien Brody), plays Chopin in a radio studio for live broadcast. The studio comes under attack, and the pianist continues to play even though the crew wants him to stop. Meanwhile, at home, his family begins to pack their belongings frantically so they can escape. They find ways to hide their money. The mother insists that they eat. Then they hear that Britain has declared war on Germany, and because Poland is no longer alone against the invader, the family decides not to flee.

SYNOPSIS

Meanwhile, the Jewish people have to wear a Star of David armband to identify themselves. Wladyslaw Szpilman continues to play in a café to earn money. Soon, the Nazis herd the Jews into one area of Warsaw and wall them into a ghetto.

Wladyslaw is offered a position in the Jewish police force. He refuses and joins other Jews working in German factories in the ghetto. The family stays together until 1942, when they are forced to go to a work camp. When his family is put on the train, Wladyslaw is saved by the Jewish police.

127

Wladyslaw survives by working to rebuild the ghetto walls. When the Jewish men discover that the trains are going to death camps, they plan an uprising; Wladyslaw helps bring guns into the ghetto, but he wants out. He sends a message to old friends and escapes. In 1943, the Jews stage the uprising, but it fails. Wladyslaw's friends hide him again, but the Nazis discover him. In August 1944, the Poles rise up against the Nazis, but the Nazis put down this rebellion, too. Wladyslaw returns to the ruined ghetto. He is sick, starving, and alone. He hides in the attic of a house with a piano, which he plays above the keyboard in silence. One of the last Nazi officers (Thomas Kretschmann) left in the city discovers him in the house and asks him to play. He is kind to Wladyslaw and gives him food and his coat before leaving as the Russians advance into Warsaw. At the end of the war, Wladyslaw plays Chopin again on the radio.

COMMENTARY

Director Roman Polanski was born in Poland in 1933, and his parents were interred in concentration camps during World War II. His mother died in one. Polanski escaped the Warsaw ghetto and roamed the countryside, living with various Catholic families. He was able to bring his own unique experience to the story of the famed pianist Wladyslaw Szpilman. Polanski is perhaps best known in the United States for *Rosemary's Baby* (1968) and *Chinatown* (1974). Though nominated for Oscars over the years, his first win was as Best Director for *The Pianist*.

Screen and television writer Ronald Harwood (*Cry, the Beloved Country*, 1995) wrote the script, which he based on Wladyslaw Szpilman's own account of his experiences in the novel *The Pianist* (2002). The book was released in its original form in Poland in 1946 under the title *Death of a City*. Harwood and Polanski collaborated again on a new dramatic version of *Oliver Twist*, released in 2005.

Adrien Brody seems to excel at portraying characters in frightening situations. He won the Oscar for Best Actor in a Leading Role for his portrayal of the young Holocaust survivor, Wladyslaw Szpilman. His recent work includes the role of the handicapped Noah Percy in M. Night Shyamalan's atmospheric thriller, *The Village* (2004), and John Maybury's drama of life, death, and afterlife, *The Jacket* (2005).

The sets and cinematography for *The Pianist* create a sense of threatening reality that other Holocaust films, such as *Schindler's List*, have matched in intensity. But the audience views this story only from Szpilman's point of view, which allows them to share in his struggle.

> *Focus:* The Pianist *portrays suffering and killing. Saul represents the longing of the human heart for peace. The Letter to the Ephesians and Jesus' Sermon on the Mount in Matthew's Gospel offer a vision in which quarrels cease before they lead to violence.*

DIALOGUE WITH THE SCRIPTURES

The Pianist is a powerful film in which director Roman Polanski shows the horror of war through the sufferings of ordinary people. He does not make grand statements, as did the opening scenes of *Saving Private Ryan*, nor does he take the audience into the bewildering jungle of the battlefield, as did *Apocalypse Now*. Through the eyes of one man, we experience the meaning of "You shall not kill" in the context of war. Though Polanski directed the film sixty years after the events, the story of Wladyslaw Szpilman and his family still touches nerves and hearts.

This emotional glimpse of suffering in Poland is all the more significant because, in the view of just war theorists, there was just cause for the war against Hitler and the Nazis. It was self-defense against the invasions and crimes of an aggressor. The actions of the Nazi war machine and the deaths of millions at their hands can never be justified.

They are horrible to behold in *The Pianist* and in other films about the Holocaust.

Music is the gift that Wladyslaw offers his fellow Jews when the Warsaw ghetto is established. For his own peace of soul, he plays music above the keyboard when he dares not play aloud. Then, toward the end of the film, his music soothes the soul of the German officer. The reading from First Samuel reminds us that music can be a medium for peace. Despite Saul's hostility toward and suspicions of David, the music that David plays soothes him. Saul is thus relieved of the enmity, or "evil spirit," that he feels.

Devout Polish Jews would have been able to understand their sufferings in the light of the passage from First Samuel. Christians are able to refer to Gospel texts to formulate their distinctive vision for peace, interpreting them in the light of the Jewish Scriptures. The Letter to the Ephesians offers the vision of the suffering Christ who experienced human violence in his own body to bring all people into the harmony of God's saving love. The sufferings of Holocaust victims are a constant reminder that these cruelties must never happen again to anyone. The blood of Jesus shed on the cross is a constant memory for Christians that Jesus offered himself as expiation for our sins, among them sins of anger, violence, racism, intolerance, and greed—the roots of unjust war.

All people of faith and good will agree with the commandment, "You shall not kill." In the Sermon on the Mount, Jesus, who had learned his spirituality from the Jewish Scriptures, gives his interpretation of the commandment. As a teacher, he meditates on its meaning and offers an exhortation to peace for every life situation. There should be no divisions between brothers and sisters; no insults and denigration of others; we are to break off clashes as soon as they begin. A reading of this text reminds us that every opportunity to negotiate for peace is of absolute importance and an integral part of living the commandment.

At the end of the film, Wladyslaw plays the piano for the German officer, and the German officer helps him to survive. Through these actions, we see an emotional reminder of the futility of war, and of the tragic uselessness of the loss of life left in its wake. We learn that peace, that state of respect for human dignity and the extended absence of conflict, aggression, and violence, is what is important.

KEY SCENES AND THEMES

- Wladyslaw playing the piano at the radio station; his family; their fear of the German invasion; their hope; the restrictions and armbands; their decision to stay because of the radio reports; the ghetto; the family's deportation to concentration camps.

- Wladyslaw staying behind, helped by the ghetto police; the forced labor; his decision to leave the ghetto; asking friends for safe haven; his existence in hiding and going without food; the hospital across the street; the ghetto uprising.

- Liberation; Wladyslaw's return to the ghetto; the empty house; playing the piano silently; finding the can of pickles; the German officer's help; the German officer pleading for recognition and help; Wladyslaw's return to the radio studio.

FOR REFLECTION AND CONVERSATION

1. *The Pianist* is above all a witness story about one man who had the blessing and inner strength to survive some of the most horrific and inhumane events in the world's history. Talk about Wladyslaw's survival. How did he manage to survive physically, emotionally, spiritually, and morally? How is God present in this film? Name one theme that emerges for you and relate it to the Fifth Commandment.

2. *The Pianist* begins and ends with music, and, at its bleakest moment, Wladyslaw must live in silence. As with all the arts, music is a universal language that transcends the barriers, both real and emotional, that people build between each other. In 1949, at the urging of the United Nations, a nongovernmental agency was formed to promote and insure the rights of musicians everywhere.

   The International Music Council aims at contributing to the development and strengthening of friendly working relations between all the musical cultures of the world on the basis of their absolute equality, mutual respect, and appreciation. It concerns itself with musical creativity, education, performance, broadcasting and promotion, research and documentation, the status of musicians and various other aspects of musical life (www.unesco.org/imc).

   How can music and the arts contribute to peace? How do these form a basis for dialogue and negotiation, the only way to peace?

3. The Fifth Commandment tells us: "You shall not kill." Yet many wars have been started or continued in the name of religion—or religion is brought into the rationalization for war—from the pagan Greek tragedies of Troy (as depicted in the 2004 film *Troy*), to the Crusades (as depicted in the 2005 film *Kingdom of Heaven*), to the recent war in Iraq. The Bible is filled with stories of war and war-like metaphors, and Christianity has hymns that liken evangelism with a military struggle, such as "Onward Christian Soldiers" and the United States' "The Battle Hymn of the Republic," which harmonize nationalistic patriotism and faith. How might all of

these factors contribute to a culture or state of war if citizens do not critically discern the question of war? James Hillman, in *A Terrible Love of War* (New York: Penguin Press, 2004), says:

> War defends civilization, not because a war is claimed to be a just war, or a justified war. The just cause lies not in the end— overcoming evil, repelling barbarians, protecting the innocent—but in the way the entry into war and the conduct of the war maintain the steadfast virtues....

How can ordinary citizens apply this ethic to the question of war? Who decides when a war is just? What is the burden of proof for conscientious citizens? How can citizens create peace?

Prayer

Jesus, you made peace for us with God by your death on the cross. Comfort all who suffer the ravages of war, and give individuals, families, and nations a sincere desire to live in peace. Amen.

For Catechists

Catechism of the Catholic Church
Peace, no. 2304
Avoiding war, nos. 2307–2317
Truth, beauty, and sacred art, nos. 2500–2501

THE FIFTH COMMANDMENT

Exodus 21:24–25; Leviticus 24:10–23;
Deuteronomy 19:21
Romans 12:14–21
Matthew 5:38–42

A Time to Kill

U.S.A., 1996, 143 minutes

Actors: Matthew McConaughey, Samuel L. Jackson, Sandra
Bullock, Kevin Spacey, Donald Sutherland, Keifer Sutherland,
Brenda Fricker, Charles S. Dutton, Patrick McGoohan

Writer: Akiva Goldsman

Director: Joel Schumacher

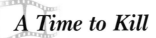

A Time to Kill

Eye for Eye, Life for Life

SYNOPSIS

A ten-year-old African-American girl named Toyna Hailey is walking home from the store in rural Mississippi near Canton. Two rednecks riding in a pickup truck see her, kidnap her, beat her, and rape her. They leave her for dead, but she finds her way home. Her siblings see her first, and her father runs to pick her up.

The rednecks are arrested for the crime. Carl Lee Hailey (Samuel L. Jackson), Tonya's father, chats with his rather inexperienced white lawyer friend, Jake Brigance (Matthew McConaughey), about a hypothetical instance regarding justice and the two accused perpetrators. On the day of their arraignment in court, Carl Lee shoots and kills the two men and injures a policeman. He is promptly arrested and asks his already debt-ridden friend, Jake, to represent him. Another friend, Harry Rex Vonner (Oliver Platt), Judge Omar Noose (Patrick McGoohan), and his own wife, Carla (Ashley Judd), tell Jake not to take the case, but he does anyway—partly because Carl Lee had intimated what he planned on doing and, though suspicious, Jake did nothing to stop him. Carl Lee later reveals that he only hired Jake because he is a white man. Jake's only supporter is his mentor, the drunken and disbarred attorney Lucien Wilbanks (Donald Sutherland).

A young Boston law student, Ellen Roark (Sandra Bullock), hears about the death-penalty case and goes south to assist in Carl Lee's defense. Meanwhile, the Ku Klux Klan plants a bomb under Jake's porch. He discovers it just in time. His wife and daughter flee to her parent's home. The husband of Jake's secretary is beaten and later dies. The KKK burns a cross in front of Jake's house, then they throw a Molotov cocktail into the house and burn it down. Later, the Klan kidnaps and beats Ellen.

The trial date nears. Jake delivers a powerful summation to the all-white jury, describing the beating and rape in great detail and then telling them: "Now imagine she's white." Jake poses the question to the court: is it possible for a black man to get a fair trial in America? The jury acquits Carl Lee, and he is freed. Jake and his family visit the Hailey's home, and their little girls play together.

COMMENTARY

A Time to Kill is based on the novel by John Grisham, his fifth novel to be made into a major motion picture. Akiva Goldsman (*The Da Vinci Code, Cinderella Man, A Beautiful Mind, Batman Forever*) adapted it for the screen, as he did for Grisham's *The Client* in 1994. Joel Schumacher, who also directed *The Client,* brings the same sensitivity to moral dilemmas and dexterity to this film. Both movies benefit from attorney John Grisham's ability to bring complex legal issues to popular attention.

Matthew McConaughey (*Lone Star, Contact, Amistad*) as lawyer Jake Brigance delivers an outstanding summation to the jury at the end of the film. Samuel L. Jackson's performance as Tonya's father, Carl Lee Hailey, is very believable and riveting in whatever emotion he displays— alternately enraged, manipulating, and loving. The other supporting parts in *A Time to Kill* are ably played by some of

Hollywood's A-list actors: Charles Dutton, Ashley Judd, Kevin Spacey, Sandra Bullock, Brenda Fricker, Donald Sutherland, Oliver Platt, and Kiefer Sutherland.

DIALOGUE WITH THE SCRIPTURES

Focus: Jesus said that the law of retribution—"an eye for an eye"—was the old teaching, now surpassed by his teaching about forgiveness. A Time to Kill shows us the force of hate and the need to go beyond vengeance to justice and forgiveness.

The Old Testament "eye for an eye," *lex talionis,* or "law of retribution," is often interpreted as permission for society, mobs, or individuals to take vengeance. It is frequently invoked when people perceive that justice will not be done according to the law—or their interpretation of it. However, "an eye for an eye" was originally instituted to guide the Israelites in meting out justice and preventing punishments that went beyond the offense. The propensity to go overboard with rabid vengeance rather than justice can be gauged from stories of vigilantism throughout history. One of the most notorious areas for mob lynching, in fact, is in the U.S. Southern states. There, the hanging of African Americans by the Ku Klux Klan in the name of God-fearing white Christianity continued until recent years. The most recently documented lynching by the KKK was that of Michael Donald, who was arbitrarily and randomly killed in retaliation for the killing of a white policeman in 1981.

The three versions of the *lex talionis* that are cited for our reflections in *A Time to Kill* are direct. However, the version in Leviticus offers a case study about how justice was to be handled according to the Law.

A Time to Kill also raises the issue of capital punishment in the context of the Fifth Commandment. Carl Henry took two lives. Should the State take his life? Has the State the right to take a life when other means of preventing that person from being a threat to society exist? It is important to remember that Jesus, who urged forgiveness and reconciliation, would himself become a victim of capital punishment on Good Friday. He was the innocent One who was nevertheless crucified publicly, executed between two criminals.

The Fifth Commandment specifies that there be no killing, but the Pentateuch indicates exceptions to the absolute ban. However, it is clear that the people of Israel had to remember the real meaning of the law as well as to learn a deeper and more spiritual approach as the centuries went by. The prophets, for instance, taught them that their God was one of tempered justice, love, compassion, and holiness. They, like us today, had to learn that their behavior must be more godlike.

These are the issues that *A Time to Kill* struggles with: racism, compassion for the injured and brutalized, and the consequences in modern society for taking the law into one's own hands. Carl Lee does this; the KKK does it, too.

The New Testament acknowledges the past. Jesus knew what was said "of old." Yet Jesus urges forgiveness rather than the retribution permitted by that law. He preached the heroism of forgiveness and turning the other cheek.

Paul beautifully sums up this vision of the positive side of the commandment—that we be people of peace rather than of violence—in his Letter to the Romans, who had a massive record of brutality and who, like ourselves, needed to be challenged by these ideals.

KEY SCENES AND THEMES

- Tonya walking down the road; her kidnapping and rape; the little girl finding her way home; her father's reaction; his talk with Jake; the two white men being taken to court; Carl Lee shooting them; his arrest.

- Carl Lee asking Jake to take the case and his explanation why; Jake's decision and the consequences for his family; the bomb and later the burning of the cross; Ellen's arrival; the Ku Klux Klan's activities.

- The trial and Jake's final summation to the jury; the jury's decision.

FOR REFLECTION
AND
CONVERSATION

1. *A Time to Kill* addresses a whole range of issues, including the use of intimidation and violence, personal endangerment for the sake of others, use of trials for political ends, racism, and the horror of child rape. The film also draws us emotionally and intellectually into the debate and misunderstanding of the "law of retribution." What does the term "retribution" really mean (the dispensing or receiving of reward or punishment)? In your opinion, was the film about retribution or vengeance? Why? Did Carl Lee seek retribution or vengeance? Is it ever right to seek justice outside the legal system of a society?

2. Talk about why Carl Lee hired Jake in the first place. Later, Carl Lee tells Jake that there is a war between white people and black people, that Jake can never be a friend to Carl Lee or truly understand what it is to be black. Why does Carl Lee say this? Is it possible for the dominant race and culture in a society to integrate with minorities? Can friendships between these "worlds" exist? Why? How? In his summation, Jake asks the all-white jury to shut their eyes and imagine the rape of the child. He then says, "Now, imagine that the child is white...." Was his argument aimed merely to winning? Or, given the context of racial inequality, racial profiling, and the long history of racial discrimination in the legal system and processes of the United States, was he really asking the jury to transcend the letter of the law and admit that the only way Tonya (and Carl Lee) would receive justice would be to think of the crime happening to a white child? But do the ends ever justify

the means? Can a black man get a fair trial in America? Why or why not?

3. The *Catechism of the Catholic Church* says, "By recalling the commandment, 'You shall not kill,' our Lord asked for peace of heart and denounced murderous anger and hatred as immoral" (no. 2302). How did the two "rednecks," Billy Ray and Pete, as well as members of the Ku Klux Klan (a terrorist organization founded in 1867 in Tennessee to thwart Reconstruction by whites and blacks after the Civil War), justify their behavior? If their behavior is judged to be objectively immoral, why is it not so to the members of the KKK? Why is racism so contrary to Jesus' law of love? Why does racism persist? What can we do as followers of Christ to create a culture of peace rather than one dominated by anger and hatred? How can entertainment and information media contribute to a culture of peace?

Prayer

Lord, make us instruments of your peace in our families, in society, and in our world. Amen.

For Catechists

Catechism of the Catholic Church
Intentional homicide, nos. 2268–2269
Respect for the souls of others: scandal, nos. 2284–2287
Respect for bodily integrity, nos. 2297, 2298

The Cider House Rules
U.S.A., 1999, 125 minutes
Actors: Tobey Maguire, Charlize Theron, Michael Caine,
Delroy Lindo, Jane Alexander, Kathy Baker
Writer: John Irving
Director: Lasse Hallström

The Cider House Rules

The Value of Human Life

SYNOPSIS

It is 1943, and Dr. Wilbur Larch (Michael Caine) runs St. Cloud's Orphanage in Maine. He assists in the birth of unwanted children and also performs abortions, though he knows this is illegal, so that women will not have to resort to back-alley abortions. He is also addicted to ether. He and his nurses care for the orphans with dedication and love. Dr. Larch trains one of them, Homer Wells (Tobey Maguire), as an Ob/Gyn assistant. Homer was adopted twice and returned to the orphanage both times, and Dr. Larch has become very fond of him. Homer is opposed to abortion.

One day, a young woman named Candy (Charlize Theron) arrives with her boyfriend, Captain Wally Worthington (Paul Rudd), for an abortion. Homer is attracted to their sense of freedom and decides to leave with them to see the world. He gets a job as a migrant worker at the Worthington orchard and enjoys his freedom. When Walter returns to the war front, Homer and Candy begin a relationship. After the apple crop is in, Homer works lobster boats for Candy's father.

Meanwhile, the board of the orphanage wants a new doctor to join the staff at St. Cloud's. Dr. Larch falsifies his own résumé and diplomas in favor of Homer and promotes him as the new doctor, though Homer has never even been to high school.

A year passes. When the migrant workers return, it is obvious that one young woman, Rose (Erykah Badu), is not well. Homer discovers that she is pregnant. Rose tells Candy that her own father, Arthur (Delroy Lindo), is the father of the baby. Homer offers to take Rose to the orphanage or to help her in any way he can. She refuses, and he performs an abortion for her.

They receive word that Wally's plane crashed and he is paralyzed from the waist down because of encephalitis B. Candy and Homer end their relationship. Rose runs away, and she knifes her father, thinking he is about to attack her again. Dr. Larch dies from an accidental overdose of ether. Homer decides to return to the institute to take the doctor's place.

COMMENTARY

John Irving (*The World According to Garp, The Hotel New Hampshire*) adapted his novel, *The Cider House Rules,* for the screen, recreating an idealistic image of a 1940s New England orphanage.

Tobey Maguire (*The Ice Storm, Pleasantville, Ride with the Devil, Wonder Boys, Spider-Man, Seabiscuit, Spider-Man 2*) plays the shy, earnest, devoted Homer, who has yet to discover a world beyond the orphanage. Michael Caine received a second Oscar for his performance as Dr. Larch.

The film captures the beauty of Maine with its changing seasons—the wintry scenes at the orphanage and the spring and summer orchards and the coast. Swedish director Lasse Halström is skilled in creating evocative movies against striking landscapes, such as *My Life As a Dog, What's Eating Gilbert Grape, Chocolat,* and *The Shipping News.*

The movie caused some controversy on its release because of its stance on abortion. The debate became more heated when the film received so many Oscar nominations, including Best Picture and Best Director, and when John Irving won for Best Adapted Screenplay. Pro-lifers protested the film.

The novel and the movie both raise serious questions about the social, ethical, and moral dilemmas surrounding abortion in the context of the 1940s as well as in our own times. It tells the troubled stories of women who choose abortion, dramatizes the dangers and the risks, and shows a concerned doctor and nurses. All of this combines to create a sympathetic view toward abortion, in contrast to Catholic teaching, which is unequivocally pro-life. Other movies that deal with abortion from a pro-abortion or pro-choice perspective are: *Roe v. Wade, If These Walls Could Talk,* and *Citizen Ruth.*

DIALOGUE WITH THE SCRIPTURES

Focus: The Cider House Rules *raises Fifth Commandment issues of the value of human life. Job says that God shaped and modeled him. Paul rejoices that the life of Jesus can always be seen in our bodies. The Gospel offers a guide for dealing with moral and legal dilemmas and a compassionate pastoral approach to them.*

The readings selected for dialogue with *The Cider House Rules* have very strong themes about life and the value of persons. The reading from Job on how God had shaped and modeled him, along with Psalm 22:10–11 ("You have been my guide since I was first formed, my security at my mother's breast. To you I was committed at birth, from my mother's womb you are my God") are two of the principal texts quoted in the *Catechism of the Catholic Church* in the section on abortion (no. 2270).

In his Second Letter to the Corinthians, Paul writes lyrically about the value of our being human, because the glory of God, who made us in the divine image and likeness, shines in us. We are earthenware jars holding God's treasure. At the same time, Paul stresses the strain of human struggles to choose what is right and the need for being like Christ in his suffering. Speaking of sin and grace, he says, "...death is at work in us, but life in you" (4:12).

The Cider House Rules takes great pains to show the humanity of those who care for the less fortunate, like orphans. It shows the plight of the victims of incest, the war-wounded, and workers on the margins of society. It is in this context that the film dramatizes the moral dilemma presented by abortion as an option to solve real problems for real people—but without any sense of transcendence beyond this world or objective morality. The stance of writer John Irving is obviously pro-choice. The movie does offer, however, an opportunity for reflection on the meaning of morality, the nature of the Fifth Commandment, and the pastoral care of those involved in abortion.

Jesus, as he walks through the cornfield and hears the Pharisees condemning his disciples for breaking the Sabbath, highlights the role of law, the degree of its importance in different aspects of life and behavior, and its relationship to people. Jesus says that the law about conduct on the Sabbath is at the service of people; the people do not exist to obey the laws of the Sabbath.

Natural law exists, and divine law has been revealed to us for the good of humanity. There is a hierarchy of values, however; not every moral choice has the same level of importance. Labor in service of others is very moral; labor for profit at the expense of others or human dignity or as a way to avoid personal commitments is problematic. But one issue is always maintained at a level of the highest importance: any direct attack on the lives of the unborn is always intrinsically wrong. The readings provide a perspective we can use to help deal with those caught up in serious moral dilemmas and choices.

- Dr. Larch delivering babies; mothers not wanting to see their babies; the young girl who attempted an abortion and died; Larch's attitude toward abortion and the children; Homer's view and those of the nurses; life in the orphanage; the children wanting to be adopted; those who remain; the meals, the movies, the goodnight in the dormitories; Dr. Larch's addiction.

- Candy and Wally and the reasons for their decision to have an abortion; the procedure and the after-effects; Homer's decision to leave the orphanage to find the freedom of the outside world; getting a job at the orchard and falling in love with Candy.

- Rose's situation, Homer's diagnosis; Candy talking to Rose and finding out about the incest; Homer's decision to do the abortion and his reasons; the abortion, Rose's father's death; Dr. Larch's death and Homer's return to the orphanage.

1. The movie dramatizes the oft-repeated case for abortion: better to have abortions done by a professional than by a back-alley practitioner. Candy, the pregnant girlfriend, and Rose, the victim of incest, give a human face to the situations in which women find themselves. The drama is concerned with the aspects of illegal operations in the context of 1943. Does the 1973 *Roe v. Wade* decision that legitimized abortions in the United States alter the moral issues surrounding abortion? Why or why not? Are abortions ever safe? The film fails to address the physical, psychological, and spiritual consequences of abortion; it merely states that the doctor provides what women want. What name is given to this kind of

morality? (Relativism and/or nihilism.) What is a Christian response to abortion providers and to the men and women involved, including mothers, fathers, and society as a whole? How do believers in the sanctity of human life from conception to natural death create a dialogue with those who believe that abortion is a right choice? How does the film *Vera Drake* compare to *The Cider House Rules?*

2. Premodern philosophies considered God as the Creator, center, and purpose of human life. People were considered children and servants of God. Modern philosophies, ushered in around the seventeenth century with the Age of the Enlightenment in Western civilization, trusted in science and technology to redeem people from poverty and suffering and to create an earthly paradise. People came to be considered machines, able to live without divine providence. Postmodern philosophy, which many consider to characterize our own era, does not believe in God, yet understands that we cannot save ourselves from our own folly. Thus its view of the human person is ambiguous—much like the view expressed in *The Cider House Rules.* How does Dr. Larch view the human person? How does he view unborn children? What was the meaning of his drug use? Does this film reflect contemporary society? Why or why not? How is the Christian view of the human person best expressed? What is the culture of life? What place does artificial contraception have in the culture of life? What does this culture of life involve, and what role does philosophy play in creating a consistent culture of life?

3. What were the "cider house rules"? What kind of morality was expressed by the migrant crew? What is

Gospel morality, and what are ethics? How are they the same or different? Think about each of the main characters in the film and their approach to morality and decision-making in their lives: Dr. Larch, Homer, Candy, Wally, Rose, Arthur, the nurses, Jack. How is freedom expressed in the film? Are any of the characters truly free? Who and why? Do you think that the prayers of the doctor, nurses, and Homer at the orphanage are sincere? How do believers communicate a culture of life in a culture that does not hold the same values? What is a pastoral approach to women considering abortion or to women who have had one? How are charity and truth, freedom and responsibility balanced in God's love?

Prayer

Jesus, you know the struggles in people's hearts and consciences as we suffer from our human weakness. Help us always to appreciate the value of human life. Amen.

For Catechists

Catechism of the Catholic Church
Abortion, nos. 2270–2275
The openness to fertility, nos. 1652–1654
The gifts and fruits of the Holy Spirit, nos. 1830–1832

The Sixth Commandment

Introduction

Do not commit adultery./Be loving and faithful./ Do not violate others.

The phrase used to describe the embellishment of an intelligence report by a British spin doctor to urge a decision to go to war in Iraq in 2003 was that he "sexed up" the documents. Although many commentators and the public could see no sense in using this inappropriate phrase, it stuck. And it could also be fair to say that during the second half of the twentieth century and into our own times, perspectives, attitudes, and behavior are considerably "sexed up."

Whether or not people are more sexually permissive now than in previous eras is debatable. Obviously, in the past, behavior was not tracked as it is now, nor did the media make it as visible. In our time, information and entertainment media exhibit and portray sexuality and sexual behavior in public, soft and hard pornography are available in epidemic proportions, and sexual crimes and scandal are more instantly publicized because of the electronic media. As a result, sexually explicit material can be available to children who are not developmentally able to deal with it psychologically, emotionally, or morally.

In terms of personal relationships, especially in marriage, the Sixth Commandment asserts that couples are to be loving and faithful and that betrayal through adultery is inherently wrong. Over the centuries, moral theologians and the official teaching of the Church have extended their interpretations of the Sixth Commandment to include all sexual sins. Because sins against this commandment often loom larger in people's consciousness than offenses against the other commandments, sex—rather than the all-encompassing view of the human person that Pope John Paul II has developed in his landmark teaching on the theology of the body—has become the main filter in some cultures for judging people's behavior.

The same holds true for some cultures' judgment of the media. The challenge for moviegoers and television viewers is to understand the presentation of sexuality within the context of a story. Money, sex, and power are the three main driving forces of human nature in need of redemption, and, alone or in combination, they form the dramatic or comedic premise for most media stories. Once again, we are called upon to discern "what" is presented and "how" it is presented and decide to watch the story or not. If we choose to watch it, then the Commandments can become our viewing lens for understanding the story.

In his ministry, Jesus was quite clear about the need for repentance for sexual infidelity and misconduct. He was also very forgiving. He forgave the prostitute who crashed the banquet of Simon the Pharisee (Lk 7:36ff.). And while Jesus insisted that the woman who was taken in adultery (Jn 8:53ff.) sin no more, he told the men who were ready to kill her that the one without sin should be the first to cast a stone.

From where does the negative focus on sexuality as a whole arise? History provides some perspective on this question. Perhaps it was St. Paul and his interpreters who steered the Christian conscience in the direction of focusing on sexual sins with the list of unacceptable sexual behavior in Romans 1:24–32 and Galatians 5:19. Some theologians blame the legacy of St. Augustine, who converted from the lascivious behavior of his youth, took a very severe attitude toward original sin and its consequences for human concupiscence, and made sexual sins a significant focus of his teaching and writing. In the seventeenth century, the

Flemish theologian Cornelius Jansen negatively interpreted an aspect of St. Augustine's teachings on predestination and grace. Although the Church judged his teachings heretical (1653), Jansen's influence on spirituality has extended to modern times and resulted in an intrinsically pessimistic view of human behavior, especially regarding sexuality. The influence of Puritanism in the United States, rather than offering an integrated view of the human person, has resulted in a dichotomy between our understanding of nature and grace and the individual and public understanding of human sexuality.

This historical attitude toward sexuality narrows the scope of the Sixth Commandment, but it is actually very broad. The commandment speaks against all violation of the human person and the environment that God has given to sustain life and dignity. Sexual language and imagery is aptly used to describe social exploitation of one kind or another. We speak of the rape of the land when it is abused or overused and the violation of people's rights when they are oppressed.

Sexual infidelity in marriage is a violation of the sacred covenant of marriage, human dignity, and the rights of both partners engaged in the sin, as well as their families—and families make up society. The history of invasions, wars, and occupying forces reminds us that sexual violation is all too prevalent by advancing or occupying forces as a way to subdue people. War displaces people, globalization creates famine, and the rise of the socially and morally unaccountable corporations can rob people of their livelihoods as well as contaminate land and waters. All of these are serious and significant violations of sacred covenants that lead to the breakdown of morality in society and diminish the value of the human person in cultures. If human rights are not respected and upheld on any level, then individuals may feel less responsible to respect the covenants in their own lives.

The positive dimension of the Sixth Commandment is that human beings live chastely and in respect for others and the earth. For married people, this means monogamy, mutual respect, and openness to having children; for everyone else, chastity means sexual abstinence, including from lust, masturbation, fornication, pornography, prostitution, and rape.

The first of the three films chosen to explore the Sixth Commandment is a coming-of-age movie, *Save the Last Dance,* that deals with teen friendship and romance and gives the audience a chance to consider the reality of premarital sex. The second film, *Lantana,* is a crime thriller about marital relationships and the social consequences of infidelity. Finally, *Unfaithful* is a direct treatment of adultery and its consequences.

THE SIXTH COMMANDMENT

Ruth 2–4

1 Corinthians 13:4–13

John 2:1–11

Save the Last Dance

U.S.A., 2001, 112 minutes

Actors: Julia Styles, Sean Patrick Thomas, Kerry Washington, Fredro Starr, Terry Kinney

Writers: Duane Adler, Cheryl Edwards

Director: Thomas Carter

Save the Last Dance

The Challenge of Chastity

As seventeen-year-old Sara (Julia Styles) rides the train to Chicago to live with her father (Terry Kinney), she recalls how her mother died. Sara, a ballet dancer, wanted her mother to attend her audition for the Juilliard School. As Sara danced for the audition, her mother was killed in a car accident. Sara blames herself for her mother's death and decides to give up ballet.

SYNOPSIS

Sara enrolls in an urban high school in a high crime area. She is one of the few white students there and is slow to make friends. She clashes with Derek (Sean Patrick Thomas) but likes his sister, Chenille (Kerry Washington), who is a single mom finishing high school. She wants her relationship with the baby's father to work. Chenille takes Sara to a hip-hop club one night, and Sara dances with Derek. He promises to teach her hip-hop moves.

They meet in an abandoned warehouse to dance. She tells Derek that she knows ballet, but she won't talk about it or her mother. When Derek is accepted into Georgetown University to study medicine, he takes Sara to a ballet performance. After, she confesses her guilt over her mother's death. He encourages her. He tells her that, in the past, he helped rob a store with his friend Malakai (Fredro Starr) but was not caught. When Derek takes Sara home, he and Sara fall into a passionate embrace.

They continue practicing dance together because Sara has another chance to audition for Juilliard. Derek teaches her how to blend hip-hop with ballet. Sarah clashes with Nikki (Bianca Lawson), Derek's old girlfriend. Chenille accuses Sara of being a white girl who wants to steal one of the young black men who has a future. Derek and Sara have become close, but Chenille's accusation leads Sara to break up with him. Although Sara's relationship with her father is stronger, she wants Derek to be at her audition. Malakai tempts Derek to side with him in some gang activity, but Derek decides to go to the audition instead. He arrives as Sara falters in her freestyle piece. He encourages her. She begins to dance again and is accepted into the Juilliard School.

COMMENTARY

Save the Last Dance, released in January 2001, was shot on location in Chicago and Lemont, Illinois. The teenfilm was directed by Thomas Carter, who also directed *Swing Kids* and *Coach Carter* and has numerous television series to his credit, including *Remington Steele, Miami Vice,* and *Hack.*

Save the Last Dance was nominated for several awards and won MTV awards, Teen Choice awards, and Young Hollywood awards for its cast. Julia Stiles is an up-and-coming actress who has already had roles in three remakes of Shakespearean plays: *10 Things I Hate about You* (*Taming of the Shrew*), *O* (*Othello*), and *Hamlet* (with Ethan Hawke). Her dancing and acting abilities contribute to her performance as the angst-driven Sara, and her talents blend very well with the performance of Derek by another up-and-coming actor, Sean Patrick Thomas (*The District*). The story and screenplay are by first-time writer Duane Adler, who credibly unites social themes with a coming-of-age story that uses the metaphor of dance to show growth and development. *Save the Last Dance* is one of the more thoughtful and entertaining of the recent spate of teen pictures.

> *Focus:* Save the Last Dance *takes us into the world of youth and the challenges of chastity while reminding us of the story of Ruth, the qualities of love, and Jesus celebrating a marriage at Cana.*

DIALOGUE WITH THE SCRIPTURES

One of the most romantic books of the Jewish Scriptures is the Book of Ruth. A short book, it focuses on a wonderful woman, a widow and daughter-in-law, who is being courted by a powerful, good man. She enters into marriage with him and, through it, becomes one of King David's ancestors, and one of the four women named in the genealogy of Jesus in Matthew's Gospel.

The story of Ruth is an optimistic story of fidelity, a story that is not often achieved in real life. Ruth's story stands as a strong example of the ideal of love and fidelity, demonstrating the positive side of the Sixth Commandment for those who might be tempted to adultery and sexual liaisons.

Ruth, from neighboring Moab, is an outsider to Israel. When her husband died, she could have stayed in her own country and lived a fulfilling life. Instead, she decided to move with her mother-in-law, Naomi, to strengthen her family loyalty. However, in a new place, she unexpectedly finds love, marriage, and children. In *Save the Last Dance,* we can find some parallels. Sara suffers bereavement when her mother is accidentally killed; she has to move to a new place to be with her father; she experiences some alienation; she finds a man who loves and supports her.

Critics pointed out that *Save the Last Dance* has some idealistic dimensions, especially the relationship between Sara and Derek. They are young, vulnerable, sensitive, creative, and gifted. And they are falling in love. Sara is white and an outsider in the Chicago world where she lives and goes to school. This is Derek's world, where the fact that he is a black youth with goals in life sets him apart among his peers. Sara and Derek share dancing and learn from each other, both about dancing and life. Their connection is a bond that transcends race and difference and leads to love.

Sara and Derek are not competitive in their love, but criticism comes from Derek's friends and Chenille and her friends. Caution comes from Sara's father. A story like this takes us to Paul's best-known text, the praise of love in First Corinthians. While Paul uses his words to praise spiritual love in the context of the Commandments, they also shed light on committed, faithful, married love that is patient, kind, never jealous, never boastful or conceited, never rude or selfish, does not take offense, and is never resentful. One could say that without this love, a marriage is also merely a gong booming or a cymbal clashing. Without love, husband and wife are and have nothing at all.

Paul's description of love images the kind of love that sustains society, the kind of love that makes the world go 'round and creates communion with God and others. It is to be celebrated. Jesus celebrated this love at the wedding feast of Cana. He did not offer a treatise on married love and fidelity. Rather, he went to a wedding with his friends, enjoyed it, and made sure, through a miracle, that the wine did not fail. His disciples later saw this celebration of marriage as an image of Jesus' sacramental love in the Eucharist.

Save the Last Dance reminds us of the gift of commitment and love while inviting us to talk about issues like teen chastity and abstinence before marriage when the film seems to indicate that Sara and Derek have a sexual encounter.

KEY SCENES AND THEMES

- Sara traveling to stay with her father; her mother's death; Sara's guilt; her changed living circumstances: new school, new friends, dislike for Derek; her decision not to dance.

- Derek, Chenille, and their world; the dance club; Derek and Sara becoming friends; teaching each other to dance; their blossoming and challenging relationship; Sara's relationship with her father.

- Derek and Malakai; Chenille and the father of her child; Derek's decision not to go with Malakai; Sara's audition for Juilliard and Derek's love and encouragement.

1. Although *Save the Last Dance* is a very watchable movie that provides us with material to reflect on the positive side of the Sixth Commandment, it also invites us to consider many other issues and consequences related to the commandment. For example, Chenille is a teen mom whose child has a deadbeat father (though he seems to mature as the film progresses); an unnamed man grabs Chenille, and she grabs him back to show what it feels like to be pawed; the dancing is very suggestive; it is strongly implied that Derek and Sara have sex, etc. How does the Sixth Commandment relate to these behaviors? What are the consequences of all of these? What is the social context? How does the film seem to normalize, yet question at the same time, premarital sexual behavior? Did you like the movie? Why or why not?

2. Speaking of the virtue and value of chastity's highest expression in the complete and lifelong mutual gift of a man and a woman to one another in marriage, the *Catechism of the Catholic Church* teaches: "Chastity means the successful integration of sexuality within the person.... The virtue of chastity therefore involves the integrity of the person and the integral-

ity of the gift" (no. 2337). What does this teaching mean to you? Why is human integrity, and therefore the dignity of the human person, always involved in the expression of human sexuality? What are the conditions for the faithful expression of human sexuality? Is sexual activity outside of marriage ever permissible? Why or why not? Basing yourself on the characters and situations in the film, what are the personal, spiritual, psychological, and social consequences of sexual activity outside of marriage? Is the film consistent in its view?

3. Grief is another dominant theme in this film, as well as perceived guilt for the death of a loved one. Friendship is yet another strong theme. How does Sara deal with these issues? What roles do Derek and Sara's father play over the course of the school year in her ability to accept her mother's death and take responsibility for her future? What is the nature of grief and forgiveness of self and others? Talk about Sara's struggle to make friends and to focus on her father and others rather than on her own grief. Why does she sometimes succeed yet more often stumble? What could she have done differently? What would you have done if you had been in Sara or Derek's place? What does the film say about racism in society and the nature of human relationships?

Prayer

Lord, you give us the fullness of love. May we learn to give ourselves completely to you and others in love as you did. Amen.

For Catechists

Catechism of the Catholic Church

"Male and female he created them....," nos. 2331–2336

The vocation to chastity, no. 2337

The integrity of the person, nos. 2338–2345

Charity and friendship, nos. 2346–2347

Chastity, no. 2348

Fornication, no. 2353

The gifts and fruits of the Holy Spirit, nos. 1830–1832

Lantana

Australia, 2001, 118 minutes

Actors: Anthony LaPaglia, Kerry Armstrong, Barbara Hershey, Geoffrey Rush, Vince Colosimo, Rachel Blake, Peter Phelps

Writer: Andrew Bovell

Director: Ray Lawrence

Lantana

In the Image of God

SYNOPSIS

Leon Zat (Anthony LaPaglia), a police detective in Sydney, Australia, is having an affair with Jane O'May (Rachel Blake), who is separated from her husband, Pete (Glenn Robbins). Jane lives next door to a happily married, working-class couple, Paula (Daniela Farinnacci) and Nik (Vince Colosimo), who have two children. Paula works, and while Nik stays home and cares for the kids, Jane flirts with him.

Leon's wife, Sonja (Kerry Armstrong), tells her therapist, Dr. Valerie Somers (Barbara Hershey), that she suspects her husband is having an affair, but that the real problem is that he does not tell her about it. A gay man, Michael (Peter Phelps), is also a patient. Valerie is married to John (Geoffrey Rush), and their union appears to have deteriorated since the murder of their daughter the year before. Valerie seems afraid of life and begins to suspect that her husband and Michael are involved because of the things Michael says in therapy.

One night, Valerie's car goes off the road and won't restart. She never arrives home. Nik is arrested on suspicion of murder because Jane, his neighbor, saw him throw a woman's shoe into the bushes across the road from their house. She calls the police, and Leon comes to the scene to find Jane, Paula, and Nik there. The shoe is identified as Valerie's. Leon questions Valerie's husband, John, asking about their marriage. Nik admits that he had given a ride to Valerie the night before. However, when he turned to take a short cut, she became frightened, jumped out of his moving truck, and fled into the thick brush. He followed her, but all he found was her shoe. He was afraid that he might be accused of wrongdoing, so he did not report the incident to the police.

Nik leads the police to the place, and the body is found deep in the brush. Everyone realizes that no one murdered Valerie; it was suspicion and fear that led to her death.

"Lantana" is a noxious weed that is colorful but encroaches on the countryside and destroys the natural fauna. Its use as the title of this film is a most interesting metaphor for the things that can threaten a marriage.

COMMENTARY

Lantana is an intriguing film, well written and tightly structured, a nonlinear, complex mosaic of characters and relationships. It won seven Australian Film Institute awards in 2001 for Best Film, Best Director, and Best Screenplay, as well as acting awards for Anthony LaPaglia, Kerry Armstrong, Rachael Blake, and Vince Colosimo.

The screenplay was written by noted Australian drama-tist Andrew Bovell, who based it on his own play. Bovell expands the action and opens it out so successfully that it does not seem at all theatrical. He is well served by the director, Ray Lawrence, in this, his second film—coming sixteen years after his movie, *Bliss*. He was then able to make a new film, *Jindabyne* (2005).

Lantana treats adult themes intelligently and emotional-ly and draws superb performances from its cast.

Focus: The Scripture readings, especially the Gospel, speak of the nature of man and woman, marriage, adultery, and

DIALOGUE WITH THE SCRIPTURES

divorce. Lantana *explores the lives of men and women who are married, but who risk everything because of infidelity, fear, and lack of trust.*

The creation accounts in Genesis offer a foundation for marital love and fidelity. Man and woman are made in the image and likeness of the creative and loving God. The man leaves his father and mother and joins himself to his wife, and they become one body. This is an image of the covenant between God and the people. The prophetic literature of the Bible explains the infidelity of God's people through images of adultery.

The Letter to the Ephesians (which, in the past, was often interpreted as a passage that sanctioned the domination of woman by man) appeals to an understanding of what the full maturity of commitment in marriage means. This passage was written for Christians in the Roman Empire, and it cuts across that patriarchal tradition that held that the husband was superior in all matters. The text can be used as a basis for understanding the loving and respectful adult maturity required on the part of both husband and wife for a marriage to work. The foundation for this commitment is reflected in the image of Jesus, who loves the Church, and Christians, who love one another and together make up the body of Christ.

As in the other Synoptics, the Gospel of Mark puts very strong words into Jesus' mouth regarding marriage, adultery, and divorce. Jesus appeals to the Scriptures and the teaching of Moses as the foundation for the strict fidelity he demands in the passage. He also speaks of human weakness and allowances that Moses made in particular situations (see Deut 24:1–4).

Over the centuries, the Church has developed an understanding of these texts and seeks to apply them rightly and with compassion. This means that the Church has had to look hard at the nature of consent given in marriage and acknowledge that many people were not mature enough at the time of their marriage to understand the true meaning of their commitment. Following canonical procedure, the marriage is then annulled, even if the couple had lived together and had children. Human frailty, fear, force exerted on one or other of the spouses, and arranged marriages are just some of the issues that complicate the situation.

The value of watching a film like *Lantana,* however, is not so much learning what may have made a marriage null and void, but what can destroy it and what can restore it.

In the final scene, when Paula is asked how she knew Nik was innocent, she replies, "Because he said he was." This is the dramatic highpoint of the film, because it shows that this working-class couple had a bond of trust that the other four couples did not have. Leon and Sonja can now move toward renewed love. Jane and Pete's marriage seems to have failed. It is too late for John and Valerie, but John can now live in peace.

KEY SCENES AND THEMES

- Leon Zat and his affair with Jane, the one- and two-night stands; his own self-image, his middle-aged crisis, and his using his affair to find a solution to his problems.

- Valerie and the book about the death of her child; Sonja talking to Valerie about her marriage, her suspicions of Leon's behavior, and her distress that he might not be truthful with her; Valerie's sympathetic listening; Valerie and Michael; Valerie's suspicions.

- John's confession to Leon that he had heard Valerie's message on the phone but had not responded; Leon reflecting on his behavior; John saying, "Sometimes love alone is not enough"; the investigation; Paula saying that she knew Nik was innocent because he told her he was.

1. This film is about the intertwining lives and relationships of four married couples, as well as that of a gay couple. Most of the characters are in the middle of an emotional midlife crisis and exhibit behavior based on fear and suspicion. This has been brought about by marital infidelity or, in the case of Valerie and John, the murder of a child. How do the Scripture situations and each of the relationships in the film compare? What does a person do when he or she fails, or when he or she becomes aware of his or her spouse's failure? Admit the betrayal? Cope with the pain? Break off adulterous relationships? Work toward reconciliation? Go for therapy or counseling? Pray? How does reconciliation come about when fear and suspicion seem to be inextricably part of the dynamic? Do couples think of the divine teaching on marriage in Scripture or the teaching of the Church (cf. *Catechism of the Catholic Church,* nos. 2331–2400) when things become difficult? Why or why not? How might a greater understanding of the sacrament of marriage help couples grow in fidelity?

2. The one couple that has a trusting relationship, Nik and Paula, is younger than the others. Do you think this makes a comparative difference in their relationship? How is Nik and Paula's marriage affected by the dysfunction of the other couples whose relationships intrude on theirs? Do you think that this incident will strengthen or weaken their marriage? Why? What are the social consequences of adultery?

3. "*Sexuality* affects all aspects of the human person in the unity of his[/her] body and soul. It especially concerns affectivity, the capacity to love and to procreate, and in a more general way the aptitude for

forming bonds of communion with others." If you analyze this quote from the *Catechism of the Catholic Church* (no. 2332) phrase by phrase, what do you think it means? Adultery occurs when a married person has a sexual relationship with another person outside of marriage. A *USA Today* poll taken in 1998 showed that in the United States, 24 percent of men and 14 percent of women have had sex outside of their marriages—and newer polls cite almost equal numbers. Some pastoral ministers say that adultery is one of the top challenges to the family in America today. How does adultery undermine the marriage in society? How does the film show the contrast between fear and suspicion and trust in a marriage?

Prayer

Lord, your love for us is boundless. Strengthen with your loving care those who struggle to remain faithful to their marriage covenant. Amen.

For Catechists

Catechism of the Catholic Church
"Male and female he created them....," nos. 2331–2336
Marriage in God's plan, nos. 1602–1605
Marriage under the regime of sin, nos. 1606–1608
The integrity of the person, nos. 2238–2345
The love of husband and wife, nos. 2360–2363
Conjugal fidelity, nos. 2364–2365
Adultery, nos. 2380–2381
Divorce, nos. 2382–2383
Truth, no. 2468

Diane Lane and Richard Gere in *Unfaithful*.

THE SIXTH COMMANDMENT

Hosea 2:1–25

1 Corinthians 6:15–20

John 8:1–7

Unfaithful

U.S.A., 2002, 124 minutes

Actors: Diane Lane, Richard Gere, Olivier Martinez,
Chad Lowe, Kate Burton, Margaret Colin,
Erik Per Sullivan

Writers: Alvin Sargent, William Broyles Jr.

Director: Adrian Lyne

Unfaithful

Who Is Innocent?

SYNOPSIS

The wind blows through a beautiful Westchester County home outside of New York City. Constance Sumner (Diane Lane), her husband Edward (Richard Gere), and their eleven-year-old son, Charlie (Erik Per Sullivan), are content as they go about their daily lives. As Edward leaves for work, Constance tells him she is going to the city later to arrange for a charity auction and to buy a birthday present for Charlie.

The wind blows stronger in the city, and Constance cannot get a cab to take her to the train station. While waving frantically for a taxi, she falls into a young man carrying an armload of books. She is cut, and he invites her to his apartment to dress her wound. An empty taxi approaches, but she chooses to go with Paul (Olivier Martinez).

Constance finds excuses to return to the city and visit the much younger man. They begin a passionate affair. Constance keeps saying she must stop, but she chooses to continue again and again. One day, two of Constance's friends, Tracy and Sally, see her near Paul's apartment. She lies about what she is doing there. They go for coffee, and, during their conversation, Tracy says that adultery is wrong; it always ends badly—for everyone.

Another day, Constance and Paul are at the café and Bill (Chad Lowe), who works for Edward, sees them together, kissing and laughing. When Edward fires Bill for disloyalty to the company that has been like a family to him, Bill yells back at him to look to his own family. Edward's gradually growing suspicions are confirmed when he hires a private detective who photographs Constance and Paul together.

Edward goes to visit Paul and, in his sorrow and rage, kills him and plans to dump his body in a landfill. Just before he leaves Paul's apartment, he checks his phone messages, and Constance has called, breaking off their affair.

Detectives come to question Constance and Edward, but they are evasive. Constance finds the pictures of her and Paul in Edward's coat and realizes what has happened. Guilt unites them, though Edward talks about turning himself in. Their future is as unclear as a windy, rainy, dark night.

COMMENTARY

Adrian Lyne has been associated with a number of movies that have explored sexuality, infidelity, and adultery, and many of them have been very frank in their depictions of sexual behavior. Some of them posed sexual moral dilemmas: *Nine 1/2 Weeks, Fatal Attraction, Indecent Proposal,* and *Lolita.* With *Unfaithful,* Lyne has shown greater restraint in portraying sexual scenes and placed more reliance on the perfor-mances and the power of the dialogue to convey the underlying emotions and issues. The movie is all the better for it.

The source for *Unfaithful* is a French film by a master of suspense and psychological thrillers, Claude Chabrol; it is based on his 1969 film, *La Femme infidèle* (*The Unfaithful Wife*). In it, Stéphane Audran portrays what the French call a "bourgeois" wife married to an older man, Michel Bouquet. Chabrol spent decades showing the darker side of the French middle class, using basic moral predicaments like adultery to challenge standards and values in French families and in society.

Because Lyne is so provocative in his filmmaking, the immediate reaction to *Unfaithful* was to view it as an exploitation piece. However, a careful viewing shows that Lyne is doing for American society at the beginning of the twenty-first century what Chabrol was doing for his French contemporaries. The ending is especially ambiguous, challenging audiences to think about what they would or would not do in similar circumstances.

An Oscar-nominated performance by Diane Lane as the unfaithful wife helps Lyne. Richard Gere is at his best as the aggrieved husband. Olivier Martinez (*The Horseman on the Roof, Before Night Falls, S.W.A.T.*) plays the lover. *Unfaithful* is a good example of Hollywood's ability to present moral issues and dilemmas for an adult audience.

DIALOGUE WITH THE SCRIPTURES

Focus: Hosea's wife and the woman in John, chapter 8, were both unfaithful. Their behavior is condemned, and they both experience repentance and forgiveness. In Unfaithful, *Constance repents, but too late to halt the consequences of her behavior.*

Unfaithful, as its title suggests, is a straightforward film about adultery. It looks at a marriage that is weaker than either the husband or wife have imagined. It shows the wife hesitating and then committing herself to an adulterous relationship while trying to keep marriage and family together. It also shows the suspicious husband learning the truth, as well as the unsuspected violence within him when he confronts his wife's lover.

The prophetic tradition of the Jewish Scriptures develops a significant use of the image of adultery to symbolize the people's rejection of God's covenant of love and fidelity and their seeking love elsewhere. This tradition begins with the experience of the prophet Hosea, whom God inspired to choose his wife, Gomer, from among the women serving as prostitutes at the temple of Baal. God loves his people no matter who they are or what they have done. Despite Hosea's love, Gomer leaves him, returns to her old ways, and is unfaithful. The prophets show how God always takes his people back with love, as Hosea did with Gomer. The unfaithful who return are beloved and forgiven. Hosea, chapter 2, may not be familiar reading to many people; it may prove difficult, but it tells a parallel story to *Unfaithful.* The prophet Hosea's experience of love, fidelity, and infidelity serve as a model for understanding God's *hesed,* his loving tenderness that flows out of a deep relationship—whether between us and God, husband or wife, or a societal connection. Out of sin and through the power of love can come repentance, forgiveness, kindness, loyalty, and graciousness.

In *Unfaithful,* Connie Sumner can be considered in the light of the story of the woman in the very act of committing adultery in John, chapter 8. Connie's husband has her followed by a detective. When he sees the photos of her with Paul Martel, he plans to confront Paul.

Jesus does not condone adultery. He affirms the commandment, urging the woman to sin no more. His message, however, goes beyond the transgression of adultery to its aftermath, to the woman's future. Not only does Jesus forgive, but he warns the male religious leaders who had righteously dragged the woman before him of becoming censorious, judgmental, and violent. He also points out their failure to admit their own wrongdoing. This is the challenge Edward Sumner faces so that he and Connie can have a future. Can he forgive her? After his own angry and righteous confrontation of Paul Martel—not to speak of his impulsive, unjust act of murder and his concealing his crime—must he forgive her?

Paul, writing to the Corinthians in chapter 6, offers some theological and spiritual grounding for the forbidding of adultery. Paul is angry at the permissive behavior of the Corinthians (particularly noted in chapter 5, where his strictures are forcefully worded). He appeals to the fact that we are all part of the body of Christ and that adultery and fornication are alien to our being one with Christ. Paul also appeals to the dignity of the body, calling it the temple of the Holy Spirit. His conclusion is that we should use our bodies only in ways that glorify God.

KEY SCENES AND THEMES

- Connie's first encounter with Paul and the taxi; visiting Paul in his apartment, his seductive behavior, her acquiescing and committing herself to the affair; the scene on the train as she returns home, the expressions on her face showing a whole range of emotions and the conflicting feelings that she had experienced; her friend's warning against adultery.

- Edward's suspicions of his wife's conduct confirmed by the photos; his visit to Paul; his emotional response to meeting Paul, to seeing and being in the place of his wife's adultery; his growing hurt and anger, and the violent attack resulting in Paul's death.

- The final decision for Connie and Edward: the possibility of giving themselves up to the police or of fleeing to Mexico; their consciences, their concern for their marriage, for their son; sitting at the traffic light outside the police station and the inconclusive but challenging ending of the movie.

FOR REFLECTION AND CONVERSATION

1. When a married man and/or a married woman engages in sexual intercourse with someone who is not his or her spouse, they are committing adultery. Adultery is as old as the books of the Bible that mention this sin by name at least forty times. "The Sixth Commandment and the New Testament forbid adultery absolutely" (*CCC*, no. 2380) because it is an

injustice and injury to the covenant of marriage. Adultery undermines the stability of marriage, the family, and the good of children. In what ways does adultery undermine a marriage? How did Constance's adultery undermine her marriage and family? Talk about Tracy's commentary on adultery and how it always ends disastrously for everyone. Do you agree, even if a person is never caught? Why or why not? Though polls show that more men than women engage in adultery (though more women do so now than before), this film, like the bible stories considered for our reflection, focuses on the woman's infidelity. Why do you think the Bible or Hollywood does this?

2. *Unfaithful* never tells us why Constance makes the choices she makes. Her name signifies "constancy," which means fortitude, fidelity, and loyalty, all of which she denies through her choices and actions. Recall the series of choices she makes (to go into the city even though the weather is bad; to go with Paul rather than take the taxi; to return to his apartment, etc.). What was the state of her conscience? Why do you think she gave in to temptation over and over again? What made her finally break off her affair? Were you surprised when Edward killed Paul? Why or why not? What was the state of his conscience by the end of the film?

3. The film is chock full of symbols that underpin its theme by showing how the choices a person makes can turn order into chaos. From the opening scenes, we see the laconic setting, the wind, the collection of glass "snow balls" from various cities, the camera, video camera, photographs, the train, water and

washing, the dry cleaner's, the sore on Constance's leg. In what ways did these visuals help you to make meaning of the film? In your moral imagination, rewrite the end of the film where the characters are in the car in the rain, in front of the police station, with the traffic light changing colors, but never turning green. What is their future? What is the right thing for them to do now? Can things ever be right for them? What will they do?

Prayer

Lord, we acknowledge our frequent infidelity to your love. Help us to repent and to thank you for your faithful love and healing forgiveness. Amen.

For Catechists

Catechism of the Catholic Church
"Male and female he created them....," nos. 2331–2336
The love of husband and wife, nos. 2360–2363
Conjugal fidelity, nos. 2364, 2365
Adultery, nos. 2380, 2381
Living in truth, no. 2470
Lies, nos. 2482–2487
Homicide, nos. 2268, 2269
Interior conversion, nos. 1430–1433

The Seventh Commandment

Introduction

You shall not steal./Be honest./Respect others' goods.

Here is a commandment honored more in the breach than in the observance. Dishonesty is prevalent at all levels, from corporate businesses through embezzlement and fraud to armed robbery, from street muggings to petty pilfering. Major fraud and confidence scams are continually exposed. While public opinion demands ever more openness from government and business, the individual consciences regarding honesty are frequently tainted.

In his story about the shrewd steward, Jesus praises the astuteness of the man who cuts deals with his master's creditors to ensure favor and employment after he gets sacked. Jesus indicates how fascinated we are by the designs and devices criminals come up with to swindle or to rob people, corporations, or the government. In fact, the caper-film genre is among the most popular with audiences, especially when intricate technology is used. Audiences enjoy the "Robin Hood Syndrome" expressed in film through plots in which characters rob the rich to give to the oppressed poor as well as those in which thieves get away with what they have stolen, for their own gain or just because they can, from oppressive government agencies or from other unscrupulous criminals. Audiences love it when the little guy wins out over the big guy, regardless of the moral complexities and the fact that the thieves had no right to the property to begin with. People will often say, "It's just entertainment!"

The consequence of this enjoyable glorification and normalization of intelligent robberies is it creates an attitude of "Why not? If *they* can get away with it, why not us, why not me?"

The virtue that is the backbone of honesty is personal, community, and social integrity. The honest person does not simply believe in balancing his or her checkbook. The honest person wants to create and maintain a sense of personal consistency, good principles, and ethical behavior. In an era of relative ethics and "feel-good" morality, integrity requires constant attention, openness, and authenticity.

Greed and stealing go together; we have had the spectacle of political dictators from Africa, Latin America, the Philippines, Iraq, the Caribbean, and some Eastern European countries stashing billions of dollars in secret Swiss or offshore accounts as if the money were their personal fortunes. They amass more than any individual or family could possibly need. Meanwhile, their people suffer from want and cannot meet their basic needs or improve the quality of their lives.

Recently, we have witnessed the spectacle of big business lying about assets and driving the market and utility companies, often with false inside information, until the companies collapse. People are overcharged and investors lose their savings. There are laws against this kind of large-scale dishonesty, but only a few people have been actually prosecuted or convicted. Corporations are powerful, and, because of their legal status, it is difficult to hold any one person responsible for their illegal activities.

There are other examples of the chronic dishonesty that plagues modern society: those who commit petty theft in the workplace; deliberate or pathological shoplifting; evasion of subway fares and other obligatory fees, taxes, and costs; falsifying accounts; credit card fraud, etc.

Jesus said that where our treasure is, there our hearts— our consciences—will be as well.

The films chosen for the Seventh Commandment deal with a choreographed heist in *The Italian Job,* the shady and devastating greed of stock traders in *Boiler Room,* and the personal story of a con artist against a thief in *Jackie Brown.*

Charlize Theron and Mark Wahlberg in *The Italian Job*.

Deuteronomy 25:13–16
1 Timothy 6:3–10, 17–19
Luke 23:39–43

The Italian Job
U.S.A., 2003, 111 minutes
Actors: Mark Wahlberg, Charlize Theron, Edward Norton, Donald Sutherland, Seth Green, Jason Statham, Mos Def, Franky G
Writers: Donna Powers, Wayne Powers
Director: F. Gary Gray

The Italian Job

Love of Gold

SYNOPSIS

John Bridger (Donald Sutherland) is a professional thief about to pull off the final heist of his career. He meets with Charlie Croker (Mark Wahlberg) in St. Mark's Square in Venice to finalize their plans, which include several other men. They use a speedboat to navigate Venice's canal system to arrive at the boat entrance of a "palazzo," and they proceed to steal $35 million in gold bullion from a safe.

Later, all those involved in the heist meet in the Alps to divide the gold and wish Bridger a happy retirement. But Steve (Edward Norton), their expert safecracker, outfoxes them with a heist of his own. He kills John and leaves the scene thinking the others have drowned. He escapes with all the gold.

John's daughter, Stella (Charlize Theron), works as an honest security technician in Philadelphia. A year after John's murder, Charlie visits her and tells her that he knows about her father's death and where Steve and the gold are; he needs her skills to steal it back. They go to Los Angeles and make their plans, which include the clever rigging of traffic lights to create an escape route.

Steve has been selling the gold anonymously, a little at a time, through a middleman, Yevhen (Boris Lee Krutonog). When Yevhen recognizes the gold as being from the Italian heist, Steve murders him. Then Yevhen's cousin, Mashkov (Olek Krupa), pursues Steve as well.

Stella goes on a date with Steve and blows her cover. Steve realizes that Charlie and his team are alive and after him, so he plans to move the remaining gold to Mexico. Charlie and his crew drive through subway tunnels in pursuit of the gold, using Mini Coopers and any other means of transportation they can find. Just when it seems Charlie has outwitted him, Steve appears on the scene, and they fight. Charlie leaves Mashkov to take care of Steve while he, Stella, and the rest of their team go off into the sunset.

COMMENTARY

Heist (or caper) movies form a kind of specialized sub-genre to crime movies. Heist movies are characterized by the incredible size of the haul; the cunning, talent, and skill of the perpetrator, alone or with others; the good-natured appeal of the characters; and the bravado the characters use to pull off the heist in a grand style. Some of the films from this genre are *The Lavender Hill Mob* (1951), which is on the Vatican's top forty-five film list under the category of "art," *Thunderbolt and Lightfoot* (1974), *The Thomas Crown Affair* (1968 and 1999), *Ocean's Eleven* (1960 and 2001), and *Matchstick Men* (2003). Even *Butch Cassidy and the Sundance Kid* (1969) qualifies, though this film was more a comedy-buddy movie about a crime spree and chase than about an actual heist.

Heist films are also characterized by the moral universe they create and then inhabit. There are rules, but they don't work in any consistent way because the moral premise on which they are constructed is flawed by the very criminal activity they are designed to enable. Why do they do it? Because they can.

The Italian Job is a remake of the 1969 film starring Michael Caine and follows a recent trend to recreate popular and successful heist movies in contemporary settings. Most critics agree that the current version is highly competent escapism, just right for the summer audience it was made to please.

Donald Sutherland plays John Bridger, the aging career criminal, and is convincing as the brains behind the crime, as is Edward Norton, who plays the con man who pulls a con on his own gang. Mark Wahlberg plays Charlie, who inherits John's mantle. He convinces Stella, played by Charlize Theron, to help the remainder of the gang get the gold back from Steve, giving the film its fairytale ending. What follows is clever mayhem, stylized revenge, and a colossal Los Angeles traffic jam. Direction is by F. Gary Gray (*The Negotiator, Be Cool*), and the screenplay is by Donna Powers and Wayne Powers, who adapted the original by Troy Kennedy-Martin.

DIALOGUE WITH THE SCRIPTURES

Focus: The teaching of the Scriptures from the First Letter of Paul to Timothy and Deuteronomy is that the love of money is the root of all evil. "You shall not steal" is a commandment that challenges us to be honest. From the cross, Jesus shows that those who steal can repent and be forgiven.

The reading from the First Letter of Paul to Timothy contains the oft-quoted statement that the love of money is the root of all evil. The words that precede it are wise as well: "Those who want to be rich are falling into temptation and a trap. They are letting themselves be captured by foolish and harmful desires which drag men down to ruin and destruction" (1 Tim 6:9). This is the kind of exhortation that goes back to the expressions of morality in Deuteronomy. Using the images of weights for measurements to illustrate his point, the sacred author goes on to say that anyone who is dishonest is an abomination to the Lord.

While honesty may be the best policy, it is dishonored in daily practice, in both large and small matters, by many people. Jails and courts around the world are filled with thieves, from the shoplifter and pickpocket to the heads of powerful corporations. It is clear that most people do not have a finely tuned conscience as regards pilfering, stealing, or fraud.

Robbery, such as we see in *The Italian Job,* is presented as an art form, a technical achievement that is to be admired. It is executed by the criminals because they are addicted to the "craft" and the "rush" of the danger as well as the money. As in most heist films, the amount stolen is enormous, yielding wealth beyond belief.

The text of the First Letter of Paul to Timothy is often misquoted as saying, "Money is the root of all evil." In fact, the correct text makes the deeper point that it is not just money or wealth in itself that is the root of evil. Rather, the problem lies in the heart's desires when they are focused on money, the out-of-control desire to amass things, or the illicit desire to possess—especially that which belongs to others.

The First Letter to Timothy talks about the consequences of greed and dishonesty: we will fall into traps, ruin, and destruction. It is also a common adage that there is no honor among thieves, and that they eventually will fall out. Soon after the gang affects the extraordinary escape through the canals of Venice into the Alpine snows, the path to ruin and destruction opens before them. The rest of the movie is the pursuit of the rogue betrayer and the recovery of the money that, by now, the men think of as rightly theirs.

Their values are, of course, the very opposite of those put forward in Deuteronomy and the First Letter to Timothy, especially when the latter exhorts the rich not to rely on so uncertain a thing as wealth, but to be generous, accumulating treasure for a good foundation for the future, for true life. The fact is, Charlie and his gang had no right to the gold in the first place.

What is Jesus' attitude toward thieves? To those who repent, it is more generous than might be imagined. While Jesus was on the cross, an unrepentant thief mocked him, but he promised paradise to the thief who asked for forgiveness.

KEY SCENES AND THEMES

- John and Charlie in St. Mark's Square; John talking to his daughter; this being his last job; his daughter's doubt; the heist and getaway.

- The meeting in the Alps to divide the gold; the gang's farewell; Steve's deception and John's death.

- The gang's survival; Charlie engaging Stella to help get the gold back; tracking Steve and planning the reverse heist; Steve outsmarting Charlie and the gang; the chase and the traffic jam; the final scene with Charlie and Steve; Charlie's vision for the future.

FOR REFLECTION AND CONVERSATION

1. While action takes center screen, especially during the scenes involving the spectacular Mini Cooper and subway chase through Los Angeles, moral issues begin to surface almost immediately in the film. Why did the thieves really carry out the Italian job in the first place? How much of the consequent pursuit is simply achievement, and how much is revenge? What will happen with the gold? Will they take it and run? What is the morality of thieves? In what kind of moral universe do they operate? What is the nature of their rules? Do the characters even realize that they have a moral dilemma? Why do you think people enjoy heist movies that stretch the limits of morality?

2. The Seventh Commandment forbids taking what does not belong to us and commands us to stewardship,

that is, taking care of the earthly goods God has given us and sharing them in justice and charity with others. What is the purpose of creation? For whom did God create the world? What explains the sense of entitlement that leads people to exploit the earth and others in order to accumulate and hoard great wealth or to become wealthy through deceit, fraud, and greed?

3. As with the other commandments that speak to human behavior in society, the dignity of the human person lies at the center of each of God's directives. The Seventh Commandment covers all areas of honesty, such as keeping promises and contracts, making reparation for injustices, gambling, and even the enslavement of other human beings. What kind of justice, if any, is achieved by the end of *The Italian Job?* A film like this helps us engage our moral imaginations and examine our consciences about how honest we are in small and large things. What would Charlie do at the end of the film if he were a person who could see beyond his own universe to how his actions and those of his gang affect others? Did Charlie show any compassion for Steve? We know this film is "just a movie," but what would be the right thing for Charlie and the others to do at the end of the film? Even if they are in no danger of being caught?

Prayer

Lord, on the cross you forgave the repentant thief. Help all of us to acknowledge the ways we are dishonest with others and ourselves and to trust in your forgiveness. Amen.

For Catechists

Catechism of the Catholic Church
"You shall not steal," no. 2401
Respect for persons and their goods, nos. 2407–2409
Restitution and reparation for injustice, no. 2412
Laws of social living, no. 2419

Boiler Room

U.S.A., 2000, 119 minutes

Actors: Giovanni Ribisi, Vin Diesel, Nia Long,
Tom Everett Scott, Ben Affleck

Writer: Ben Younger

Director: Ben Younger

 *Boiler Room*

Fraud and Deception

SYNOPSIS

Twenty-something Seth Davis (Giovanni Ribisi) is a college dropout who lives in New York. He runs a very successful casino from his home. His father (Ron Rifkin) is a federal judge who berates Seth for his illegal activities, quitting school, and putting his own judicial career in jeopardy. A gambling client brings a friend, Greg (Nicky Katt), to the casino one day. He is a stockbroker at the firm of J. T. Marlin on Long Island, and he invites Seth to become a trainee there. Seth thinks he can make a quick buck and please his father, so he agrees.

Seth goes through the training period so he can take the "Series Seven" test that will make him a broker with an SEC (U.S. Securities and Exchange Commission) license. The trainees are told that they are there only to make money. Seth has to bring in forty accounts for his group leader, Greg, before he can start to earn the big money on his own. He becomes interested in Abbie (Nia Long), the receptionist and Greg's former girlfriend. Greg warns him not to see Abbie, but they see each other anyway. Seth becomes friends with Chris (Vin Diesel), another senior broker.

Seth spends time with the partners and sees how ruthless they are. Meanwhile, he sees another worker shred documents and follows the owner, Michael (Tom Everett Scott), to another site where the company can move quickly if they are shut down. As Seth nears his quota, he talks Harry Reynard (Taylor Nichols), a young father about to buy a house, into spending all he has on worthless stock. The FBI approaches Abbie to turn in evidence against the company. Meanwhile, Seth tries to get his father to buy that same worthless stock, but his father agrees to help his son not to get caught instead. FBI agents have tapped their phones. They arrest Seth and then his father. They send Seth back to work for one day to get a copy of his computer hard drive. Seth gets Michael to sign off on selling Harry's stock so he can make his money back, and Seth warns Chris that the FBI is coming. Seth drives away as the bust begins.

COMMENTARY

Boiler Room seemed to have become lost on its first release. Its cast was not so well known in 2000, though some of them were just emerging as stars. The somewhat baby-faced Giovanni Ribisi had appeared in *The Gift, The Other Sister,* and rather unconvincingly as the action lead in *Gone in Sixty Seconds.* In succeeding years, he fared better in cameo roles (*Lost in Translation* and *Cold Mountain*) than as a leading man (*Heaven*). In *Boiler Room,* Ribisi has convincingly interpreted the role of a scheming moneymaker who desperately wants to please his father by succeeding in the business world.

Also appearing as a stockbroker is the now-famous action star Vin Diesel, whose films include *Saving Private Ryan, Pitch Black, The Fast and the Furious, xXx, A Man Apart,* and *The Pacifier.*

While Ben Affleck is the cast member with star power, he appears in only a few scenes, principally as the ruthless motivator of the young brokers who hypes their insatiable greed. In these scenes, Affleck shows how good an actor he can be—without relying on a more vapid presence as a romantic leading man (*Gigli*). His character is similar to that played by Alec Baldwin in *Glengarry Glen Ross.* In fact, *Boiler Room* seems to be a junior version of David Mamet's classic, dealing with American capitalism running rampant in small companies, destroying people's lives, and undermining moral fiber.

Particularly moving is Ron Rifkin's performance as Ribisi's father, a judge who has set impossibly high standards for his son and then compromises himself trying to save him.

The writer-director of *Boiler Room,* Ben Younger, reportedly spent time in a broker's firm to understand and get an accurate feel for the situation he was trying to dramatize.

DIALOGUE WITH THE SCRIPTURES

Focus: The words of Amos condemn the fraud committed by many modern corporations because their deceptive practices trample on the heads of ordinary people. Annas and Saphira suffer the consequences of their greed, as do the men in Boiler Room. *The virtue of the repentant Zacchaeus opens up the theme of restitution for theft.*

One of the most dismaying aspects of watching *Boiler Room* and the gung-ho enthusiasm of the scheming stockbrokers in training, who are out to make as much money as they can as fast as they can, is realizing they are economic and social leeches. Their fraudulent deals destroy people's lives for profit, and they don't care.

Fraud is one of the most pernicious crimes in modern society, and it is on the increase. The exposure of crooked dealings in so many large corporations and among rogue stock traders means that there is a constant need for the education, formation, and development of personal conscience from an early age. A 2003 film, *The Corporation,* highlights the psychopathic nature of corporations that have the legal status of individuals, but no conscience and no one to take moral responsibility for the company's policies.

"Do not steal" often sounds like stern advice intended only for individuals who are pilfering petty cash. It is, rather, an exhortation to honesty and fair dealing at every level of society.

Seth, the hero of *Boiler Room,* has run a successful illegal casino for college students. He is ripe for the world of J. T. Marlin, a company run by a young entrepreneur who floats stock for companies that do not exist and who skims profits. The recruits, that is, the young finance warriors, are indoctrinated with Wall Street's Gordon Gecko philosophy that "greed is good." The oracles of Amos, a dresser of sycamores and the Old Testament prophet of social justice, denounces behavior like theirs. Instead of condemning the inhumane atrocities committed by neighboring nations, he condemns the Israel of his time for the more common crime of fraudulent money dealings because "they trample on the heads of the weak." In chapter 6, Amos pictures the evildoers' lavish and indulgent lifestyle, something that *Boiler Room* does very effectively when it shows the brokers' hard drinking, arrogance, and their crude and callous attitudes. Amos also warns the Israelites that when they are judged, they will be the first to go into exile as punishment. *Boiler Room* ends with the FBI raiding the J. T. Marlin office, promising that these brokers will not be allowed to deal with the public again.

One of the main stories of fraud in the New Testament is that of the husband and wife, Annas and Saphira, in the Acts of the Apostles. It is a story with a drastic conclusion that warns the early Church against falsehood. The community had agreed to keep everything in common, but Annas and Saphira conspired to hold back part of their wealth. Thus, they lied to the community. Their deceit became public when the leaders confronted them and they were struck dead. There are echoes of such dire consequences in *Boiler*

Room. The authorities suddenly apprehend Abbie, the company secretary, and force her to spy on Seth and the other brokers. It is the death of her relationship with Seth. Seth appeals to his father for help. When his father tries to save him, he is implicated in Seth's schemes. Seth's life and livelihood are destroyed. The consequences of fraud are deadly.

The Gospels offer a story of hope for those involved in financial extortion and mismanagement who want to change their lives: the story of Zacchaeus. The message of Jesus moves the tax collector. A little man, he climbs a sycamore tree (note the connection to Amos) and goes out on a limb to see Jesus. Of all the people in the crowd who want to see him, Jesus singles out Zacchaeus and goes to his house for a meal. The key to Zacchaeus' change of heart is restitution. He publicly promises that he will repay fourfold whatever he has taken unjustly. This act of recompense is a sign of repentance and atonement.

Seth has a moral awakening when he realizes the harm he has done to his client, Harry. He sets things in motion to undo his crime and to make restitution before the FBI raids J. T. Marlin.

Boiler Room is a salutary parable illustrating contemporary breaches of the Seventh Commandment.

KEY SCENES AND THEMES

- Seth's gambling operation and recruitment by the J. T. Marlin Company; the motivational speeches by Jim Young, the bullying techniques, the appeal of quick and easy money, competitiveness, and greed; Young's treatment of the men.

- The relationship between Seth and his father, the memory of his breaking his leg and his father's hitting him; his father's explanation; Seth disappointing his father with the casino, with the corruption of J. T. Marlin; Seth implicating his father in his shady deal; their reconciliation.

- Seth's dealings with Harry, drawing him in, persuading him to spend more and to use his savings; after destroying Harry, Seth's refusal to talk to him on the phone; Seth's plans to make restitution to Harry and begging Chris to sign the document.

1. *Boiler Room* shows that there is hope for Seth and other thieves and dishonest people because Seth has a conscience and finally listens to it. Conscience is that inner place where every man, woman, and child is alone with God. It's where we struggle with the rightness or wrongness of the thoughts, words, actions—or omissions—we may be considering. At what points in the film does Seth engage his conscience? What are the obstacles to Seth's living by his conscience? Why does he finally choose to do the right thing? Is it for the sake of his conscience? How important is the family in the formation of a person's conscience?

FOR REFLECTION AND CONVERSATION

2. The positive aspect of this commandment is the beatitude, "How blest are the poor in spirit: the reign of God is theirs" (Mt 5:3). The ironic aspect of Seth's character is that he is poor in spirit; he wants success for the right reasons, and he goes about achieving a dubious kind of success the wrong way. Does Seth ever become aware that he is one of the "poor in spirit"? What does "poor in spirit" mean to you? How difficult is it to strive to be poor in spirit for the sake of the kingdom of heaven in a political economy such as that of the United States and other first-world countries?

3. One of the principles of Catholic social teaching that reflects another proactive and positive aspect of living the Seventh Commandment is that believers

and people of good will have a "preferential option for the poor." This means that as believers we are to strive to reduce excessive and sinful social and economic inequalities between peoples (cf. *CCC*, nos. 1937, 1938). How might restitution for fraud (as demonstrated by Zacchaeus and, more furtively, by Seth) be the beginning of justice for the poor? How can a person who has committed theft or fraud long ago make restitution now? How might a person who is caught up with the things of this earth be led to think of others first?

Prayer

Lord, Zacchaeus made generous restitution for his acts of fraud. When we have sinned against others, help us to make restitution in order to fulfill the Gospel teaching. Amen.

For Catechists

Catechism of the Catholic Church
"You shall not steal," no. 2401
Respect for persons and their goods, no. 2407
Theft, no. 2408
Financial speculation, no. 2409
Restitution, no. 2412
Catholic social teaching and profit, nos. 2422–2424
Right for economic initiative, no. 2429
Human work, no. 2427
Love for the poor, nos. 2443–2449

Jackie Brown

U.S.A., 1997, 148 minutes

Actors: Pam Grier, Samuel L. Jackson, Robert De Niro, Robert Forster, Michael Keaton, Bridget Fonda, Chris Tucker

Writer: Quentin Tarantino

Director: Quentin Tarantino

Jackie Brown

No Honor among Thieves

SYNOPSIS

Ordell Robbie (Samuel L. Jackdon) is an ex-con gun runner in metro Los Angeles who is prepping his ex-con friend, Louis, to get back in the game. One of his runners, Beaumont (Chris Tucker), is arrested, and Jackie (Pam Grier) posts bail for him with bondsman Max Cherry (Robert Forster). Then Ordell kills Beaumont to prevent him from making a deal with the Feds. Jackie Brown is a tired forty-four-year-old flight attendant for the shabbiest airline in America. She runs money to and from Mexico for Ordell's operation. Federal A.T.F. agents Ray (Michael Keaton) and Mark (Michael Bowen) stop her when she returns from a flight to Cabo San Lucas. They give her the option to turn in Ordell for gun running or to go to prison. Jackie is arrested, and Ordell posts bail again through Max Cherry. Max picks her up at the jail and falls for her right away.

Ordell has half a million dollars in Cabo San Lucas, Baja California. Jackie offers to bring the money to the states in installments so that the Feds can nail Ordell. She agrees to do a trial run with ten thousand dollars, passing it on to Ordell's friend so the Feds can follow him. The plan works, so she tells the Feds she is bringing in fifty thousand dollars—but there's another $450,000 at the bottom of the bag. Louis (Robert De Niro) and Melanie (Bridget Fonda), Ordell's surfer girlfriend, pick up the bag with the fifty grand. Louis gets angry at Melanie's taunting, and he kills her. Max Cherry picks up the bag with the $450,000 for him and Jackie to share. Ordell shoots Louis when he finds out what happened to Melanie. Ordell realizes that Jackie is behind the whole scheme. She notifies the Feds and lures him back to Max's office, where she tricks the Feds into killing Ordell. She wants Max to go with her to Spain, but he keeps his cut and stays in Los Angeles.

COMMENTARY

The name of Quentin Tarantino will always be associated with the film title *Pulp Fiction*. This 1994 movie won the Palme d'Or at Cannes, which serves as a European endorsement of style of moviemaking. *Pulp Fiction* lost out in the Oscars to *Forrest Gump* for Best Film, but Tarantino did win the Academy Award for Best Original Screenplay. A rash of tough crime thrillers followed, and Tarantino's name was used to describe this kind of hardboiled gangster movie characterized by violence. Tarantino made his initial mark with the robbery genre in *Reservoir Dogs* (inspired by Tsui Hark's 1987 Hong Kong thriller, *City on Fire*). Another quality of Tarantino's movies is the clever, flippant, and witty dialogue, much of it inconsequential chatter about hamburgers in Amsterdam or Madonna's songs, uttered in the midst of killing and mayhem.

Tarantino followed *Reservoir Dogs* and *Pulp Fiction* with *Jackie Brown*, but it took almost four years. It is much less thematically and explicitly violent than its predecessors, though very heavy on language. Tarantino adapted *Jackie Brown* from the novel *Rum Punch* by a master of classy pulp fiction, Elmore Leonard. Tarantino also assembled a great cast, including Pam Grier and Oscar-nominated Robert Forster. Both of these actors are throwbacks to the crime movies of the 1970s whose careers were revived by *Jackie Brown.* This film reflects a more intelligent and settled Tarantino, although his interpretation of the ambiguous world of crime, theft, and violence is still disturbing. His next movies, *Kill Bill: Vol. 1* and *Kill Bill: Vol. 2,* are ballet-like martial arts fests in two "volumes," released in 2003 and 2004.

> *Focus: The citations from Deuteronomy and James remind us of the scope of the consequences of stealing. The biblical condemnations of dishonesty, especially in Luke's parable and in sayings about the consequences of the love of money, are a challenge to Jackie Brown's scam.*

DIALOGUE WITH THE SCRIPTURES

One of the major difficulties in discussing so many of the robbery or heist films of recent decades is that they rely on the "Robin Hood Syndrome." Robin Hood robbed the rich to help the poor because, as legend has it, the rich were exploiting the poor. The modern "Robin Hood Syndrome" is not quite so straightforward. Contemporary thieves rob rich individuals or corporations who may be bending the law to their own purposes through money laundering, tax and retirement fund fraud, and business scams. Corporate thieves are the big-league players. Many of the very entertaining heist movies (or "capers" if we find the characters particularly entertaining and sympathetic) elicit our applause for "little" people who get the better of the big fraudsters. What does this mean for us as we consider the Seventh Commandment?

Jackie Brown is obviously a small-scale thief even though she finally gets away with a considerable amount of money. As the movie progresses, we realize how "worldly wise" she really is. She could have written the part about the shrewd steward, the central character in Jesus' parable about the dishonest servant. The steward is losing his position. Jesus does not tell us why the steward is losing his job, so we don't know if he has been caught for some criminal activity or if he is being unfairly replaced. What we do know is that he wants to take his revenge "in kind"; the steward makes his boss pay for his own financial loss. The steward approaches the master's creditors and colludes with them in altering their accounts. He does not want to do hard work. He is ashamed to beg. He will get his money by making deals and ingratiating himself with the "corporate bosses."

The startling thing is that Jesus praises the steward for being so clever. He then makes the point that the children of this world are sophisticated con artists, although many of them turn out to be pretty stupid. Jesus says, however, that these are not the standards for keeping the Commandments and being his disciples.

Jackie schemes and steals so she will not have to go to prison for her collaboration with Ordell or to escape from him. When we consider Ordell and his partner, Lewis, we are in the realm of the dishonesty described in the Genesis saga of Cain and Abel. Cain is possessive and greedy for God's approval. He deceives himself about how to gain God's favor and turns to violence. Cain has killed an innocent man, his brother, and God banishes him from his sight.

To cheat and manipulate accounts is thievery. In addition to protecting ill-gotten goods and fraudulent behavior, this kind of dishonesty begets violence. Ordell commits murder. Once Jackie Brown has her stolen money, she too resorts to violence to save herself. She sets up Ordell and shoots him. While the "Robin Hood Syndrome" can lead us to believe that stealing is "nice," *Jackie Brown* shows us that, ultimately, this is not so.

When we turn to the pages of the Letter of James, we see how Scripture holds dishonesty to be always sinful, in particular if it is for the sake of money. The letter describes, in a mixture of metaphors and realism, the greed, the inhuman treatment, the cheating, and the violence of the dishonest rich (although dishonesty is not reserved for the wealthy alone). These are the issues that movies like *Jackie Brown* or *Reservoir Dogs* raise. They are complex, certainly, but they challenge the discrepancy between our values and our actions.

- Jackie Brown's arrival at the airport and her long walk during the credits, allowing the audience to see her, start to know her, and gain sympathy for her; her being stopped by customs officials who check her bag and find the money; her going to jail.

- The three versions of Jackie Brown stealing Ordell's money; the complicated but smooth and successful scam that tricks Ordell and the police.

- The consequences for Jackie; her using both Max and the police to cover her killing of Ordell; Ordell as no longer a threat to her life or her use of the money; the contrast with Max, who refused the money and continued his job as a bail bondsman.

1. As we watch Jackie Brown shrewdly using Max to set up the drug dealer Ordell and rehearse her ploy for taking all his ill-gained money, we may even admire her cunning and cool sense of timing. She is stealing what is basically dirty money that doesn't belong to anyone anyway. Or does it? If it doesn't belong to her, to whom does it belong? Does that justify her actions? Can we praise her? What are the standards for her conscience and sense of honesty? How do these compare with ours? If you got extra money from an ATM machine, what would you do? Reconstruct the story to have a conscientious ending. Do you think it would have the same impact on the audience?

2. *Jackie Brown* is more plot-driven, character-driven, and linear than Tarantino's previous films, though the final robbery scam is shown from three points of view

that reveal more information each time. How does the convoluted presentation of the scam work for you? Is there any honor among thieves? Should there be? Is the film self-conscious, that is, more about its texture (how images, sound, and plot lines are constructed) than the moral dilemmas on which it is based and driven? Exactly what are these dilemmas? How do the characters deal with them? In what kind of moral universe does this film take place? What can the audience learn from a film like *Jackie Brown?* Why?

3. What evidence is there that conscience, that inner power to tell the difference between right and wrong, exists in any of the characters in *Jackie Brown?* On what do Jackie, Ordell, and Max Cherry in particular, base their choices? *Jackie Brown* is a con movie, so it is more about the "how" of the story than the "what." This creates a space for our moral imagination to enter into a dialogue with the story and test our own responses to the thoughts, choices, and action of the characters. What does your conscience say at this moment? Has art reflected life for some people, perhaps? What gets people into scams and messes like the ones in *Jackie Brown?* If Jackie had recalled the scriptures cited for this chapter, would they have made any difference in the face of her need to survive? Why or why not?

Prayer

Lord, we live in a dishonest culture of petty pilfering and large-scale fraud that often leads to violence. Help us to be honest and contribute to a more just and less violent world. Amen.

For Catechists

Catechism of the Catholic Church
"You shall not steal," no. 2401
Forbidding theft, no. 2408, 2409
Reparation for injustice, no. 2412
The demands of justice, no. 2419
Human misery and the preferential love for the poor,
    no. 2448

The Eighth Commandment

Introduction

You shall not bear false witness against your neighbor./Be truthful./Do not lie.

In a cynical world, when people say with great earnestness, "I give you my word," we may well be tempted to answer, "Thanks for nothing." It was not always like this. In fact, the Hebrew word for "word," in the sense of a promise, is a dynamic one that implies covenant, fidelity, and trust: *"brit."* The word holds out a promise and a pledge, like the ten words of the Lord, or the Ten Commandments. *"Brit"* held out an offer of covenant to the Israelites, and their acceptance of its obligations was what created the Israelite community. The power of God's *"brit"* in Genesis brought forth light, and in Psalm 33 we read: "By the word of the LORD the heavens were made" (Ps 33:6). In the New Testament, the Letter to the Hebrews says that "God's Word is living and effective, sharper than any two-edged sword" (Heb 4:12).

The promise and fidelity of God's "word," or covenant, is the key concept behind the Eighth Commandment. Lies to anyone undermine the foundations of our relationship with God and the covenant of love. Our word should be our bond, so, for our integrity's sake, we are to be truthful.

In the New Testament writings, *logos* is the Greek term for the "Word," who is Jesus, the fulfillment of the Father's promise through the prophets to send a Savior. Whether in the Hebrew Scriptures or the New Testament, whether as a verb or a noun, "word" is a term that is full of life, power, and promise.

196

In the Old Testament, "truth" meant something reliable, faithful, and constant.* In the New Testament, especially in the books attributed to John, there is an emphasis on the theme of "truth." We are all familiar with Jesus saying that he is the way, the truth, and the life (cf. Jn 14:6), and with his declaration that the truth will set us free (cf. Jn 8:32). Both the Old and New Testaments agree on the meaning of "truth," although in Western culture we tend to interpret this biblical idea as a rational concept rather than a state of being.

Fudging the truth or lying begins early in life. A child will lie to avoid punishment or to obtain something he or she wants. The moral formation of children must begin early so that they learn the value of telling the truth, even when it hurts, and that lies have consequences. It is more difficult yet when children and adults become habitual liars; their relationships with others and within society are not built on trust and will sooner or later collapse.

Many Catholics probably make sure their "list" for confession includes, "I told some lies" or "I told a lie four times." Some of these might be harmless fibs, or little white lies told in order not to hurt someone's feelings or to save ourselves from being hurt. But there are also the downright untruths we know do not match reality and for which there are serious consequences, even if no one ever finds out about them. Libel and malicious gossip fit into this category.

Trickier still is the notion of a mental reservation made in circumstances when a person is bound in conscience not to tell the entire truth or when someone has no right to know the truth. A mental reservation limits the sense of the speaker's words to a certain meaning. To make a complete reservation to the truth, however, ends up being a lie just the same. Unfortunately, a popular though mistaken

* *The Collegeville Pastoral Dictionary of Biblical Theology*, ed. Carroll Stuhlmueller (Collegeville, MN: Liturgical Press, 1996).

Catholic understanding of conscience and the Eighth Commandment approves the manipulation of the truth for self-preservation or personal gain as long as "it doesn't hurt anyone."

Hopefully, as we mature, we realize that deceptions and betrayals of love and friendship are deadly lies. When we look around us, read the news about politics, government, or religion, and see advertising, we know that lying is pervasive in our society. Companies juggle accounts and publish misleading reports. Politicians are not truthful when campaigning for election, often making promises they know they can never fulfill. Nations commit themselves to war on the basis of doctored intelligence dossiers for which no one takes responsibility. Society is riddled with deceit and with authority figures who will eventually pay a price for their deceit when people stop trusting them. Church leaders have been caught in their witting or unwitting cover-ups of abuse scandals. The media and paparazzi invade privacy, sometimes inventing gossip to sell papers and magazines or to bolster ratings.

In a world of instant communications, the Eighth Commandment has never been more relevant. To be authentic human beings, our word must be our bond. "The truth will set us free" is a modern call to integrity.

Liar, Liar uses comedy to highlight the consequences of parents making promises to their children that they do not keep and of lying in the workplace. *Veronica Guerin* is the true story of a journalist who is killed because she sought the truth about Dublin's drug world, and *Phone Booth* unmasks the secret life of a cocky young publicist.

THE EIGHTH COMMANDMENT

Sirach 5:11–17

James 3:1–12

Matthew 5:37; John 8:32

Liar, Liar

U.S.A., 1997, 82 minutes

Actors: Jim Carrey, Maura Tierney, Amanda Donohoe, Justin Cooper, Cary Elwes, Jennifer Tilly, Swoosie Kurtz, Mitch Ryan

Writers: Paul Guay, Stephen Mazur

Director: Tom Shadyac

Liar, Liar

Slips of the Tongue

In Los Angeles, a kindergarten teacher is surprised when five-year-old Max (Justin Cooper) says his dad, Fletcher Reede (Jim Carrey), is a "liar." She thinks that Max really means "lawyer." Actually, he is both.

SYNOPSIS

Fletcher is successful in court because he will do anything to win and bends the truth without scruples. He and his wife, Audrey (Maura Tierney), have divorced because he put work first. Fletcher's predatory boss knows he has no trouble lying and assigns him a sticky divorce case that is worth a lot of money to the firm. He accepts it because he wants to make partner.

Fletcher promises to be at his son's birthday party, and, as usual, he breaks his promise. Max makes a birthday wish that his dad won't tell a lie for twenty-four hours.

The next morning, Fletcher finds himself telling everyone "the truth" about how they look and what he thinks of them. He insults many people, and his faithful secretary quits. He goes to court, and though he tries to lie, he cannot. When he talks to Max, he discovers the birthday wish and begs him to un-wish it.

Audrey's boyfriend, Jerry (Cary Elwes), proposes to her. He is taking a job in Boston and invites Audrey and Max to come with him to look for a house. Fletcher learns his lesson about fatherhood at the end of the court case when he witnesses the relationship between the father and children in the divorce case he is handling. He begs Audrey not to go and promises to visit Max that night because he wants to explain his new outlook on parenting. But he is late, and they leave. At the airport, he races against the jet to prevent them from taking off. Audrey and Max decide not to go. A year later, the family is together for Max's sixth birthday.

COMMENTARY

Tom Shadyac is a Catholic director whose explicit spiritual sensibilities were not revealed until *Bruce Almighty* was released in 2003. However, hidden within screwball, physical comedy and, in this case, Jim Carrey's antics, very human themes of family and compassion have given rise to layered meanings in his films, such as found in *Liar, Liar, Patch Adams,* and *Dragonfly.* Shadyac believes in the power of comedy (and drama) to get people's attention. He received his early training when, at the age of twenty-three, he became the youngest staff writer ever for the late comedian Bob Hope.

Jim Carrey began his career in comedy doing stand-up in clubs in Ontario. *Liar, Liar* is his twenty-third motion picture, and he plays the professional and parental liar in an entertaining (though, to some, irritatingly) physical, manic way. Writing team Stephen Mazur and Paul Guay (*The Little Rascals*) have written an over-the-top but effective comedic commentary on the contemporary problem of (divorced) parents who make promises to their children that they don't keep.

Maura Tierney (*ER*), as the mother, and Justin Cooper, as the son, have to deal with Fletcher's lies, and their characters are poignant and believable.

Focus: Sirach and James warn us against the treachery of the tongue when we lie. Jesus urges us to speak the truth directly and clearly. Liar, Liar *illustrates the folly of a compulsive deceiver as well as the consequences of telling lies and telling the truth.*

DIALOGUE WITH THE SCRIPTURES

There is no mistaking what telling lies means in this funny Jim Carrey comedy. He falls afoul of all the biblical injunctions in Sirach, the Letter of James, and in the clear and succinct teaching of the Sermon on the Mount when Jesus tells us, "Say, 'Yes' when you mean 'Yes' and 'No' when you mean 'No.' Anything beyond that is from the evil one" (Mt 5:37).

The movie unequivocally reminds us just how often we lie and how we rationalize and persuade ourselves that what we are doing is all right. There are the small white lies that people tell to avoid hurting others. There are the small denials that people use as excuses or to protect themselves from uncomfortable situations and accusations. There are the more insidious lies people who are careless with the truth use to create different, even wrong, impressions. There are the malicious lies people tell when they deliberately set out to hurt others by not telling the truth or by telling untruths. Then there are the professional lies and misdirection that people employ in business, law, and in other walks of life in order to win or to make themselves appear better or more honest than they actually are. There is perjury, or lying under oath. A lie is falsehood told for the purpose of deceiving others. Lies of any kind or degree are never permissible, because lies offend justice, charity, and truth (see *CCC,* nos. 2483–2487).

Fletcher Reede may be a very successful lawyer, but he is a compulsive liar. In *Liar, Liar,* Jim Carrey's character tells all these kinds of lies or runs into people who do.

Sirach offers a sure guide to telling the truth: develop steady convictions, be sincere, be quick to listen, and be deliberate in reply by answering when there is understanding and keeping silent when there is not. The passage concludes with a poetic proverb, a popular form in Old Testament Wisdom literature: Both honor and dishonor come from talking; a man's tongue can be his downfall.

The citation from the Letter of James, chapter 3, has some even stronger words (quite striking in the Jerusalem Bible translation) on the mischief the tongue can do: "[The tongue] exists among our members as a whole universe of malice. The tongue defiles the entire body. Its flames encircle our course from birth, and its fire is kindled by hell...the tongue no man can tame. It is a restless evil, full of deadly poison" (Jas 3:6–8). It is easy to see why the commandment not to lie is so forceful.

In *Liar, Liar,* we experience the consequences of lying: the effect on a person's relationships and in society at large. Fletcher Reede has made his career by defending the indefensible; to succeed, he spins the incredible to look credible and tells lies so he can win his cases. He also lies so he can keep up his profession of lying for a living. Fletcher's lying is particularly harmful to his son, Max, when he promises to visit him even though he knows that he probably won't. When Max makes the birthday wish that his father will tell the truth for a single day, his wish is granted in ways that neither Fletcher nor we, the audience, could have anticipated.

In the most unfavorable professional circumstances for Fletcher, he cannot simulate or lie for a day. But the repercussions of being forced to tell the truth benefit not only himself, but also his son and his wife, Audrey.

However, the Eighth Commandment does not simply forbid lying. The positive aspect of the commandment is that one is to tell the truth. With his son's wish, Fletcher begins to utter his hidden thoughts and feelings and proclaim the truth even when he is not obligated to speak, such as giving his opinion about how other people look. Being a comedy, *Liar, Liar* provides plenty of laughs at Fletcher's expense when he is unable to control or conceal what he is really thinking.

The Eighth Commandment addresses the nature of our speech, which reveals the truth of our inner selves and demands honesty in dealing with ourselves and with others. Our speech is to correspond with our inner thoughts for the good of the human person, society, and our relationship with God. Jesus knew this when he said that the truth will set us free (Jn 8:32).

- Max at school talking about what his father does for a living; Fletcher's boss asking him to take a case and to win it by whatever means necessary and the reward of being made a partner; Fletcher not keeping his word to his son about visiting him.

- Audrey getting engaged to Jerry; Jerry trying to be like Fletcher; Fletcher missing the party; the birthday party and Max's wish.

- Fletcher telling "the truth" to everyone he meets; in court for the high-stakes custody trial, trying to lie but being unable to do so; redoing the birthday with Max so he can undo his wish; in court, seeing how the father acts with his two children; the final realization about how much telling the truth matters.

KEY SCENES AND THEMES

1. In the passage from Matthew selected for this film, Jesus tells us that our speech must correspond to our thoughts when taking an oath; we must say yes to mean yes and no to mean no. In the passage from John, Jesus tells the disciples that if they remain in his word, they will know the truth and that truth will set them free. Recall some other scriptural passages that address the issue of truthfulness and religious truth (1 Kings 22:16; Ps 5:9; Ps 51:6; Ps 96:13; Rom 1:25).

FOR REFLECTION AND CONVERSATION

What does "truth" mean in all these passages? What are the positive consequences for acknowledging and telling the truth? Is there any convergence—or distinction—in meaning between knowing and living the truth that will set us free? Why or why not? What is truth? What is truth for Fletcher Reede?

2. Fletcher and his wife are divorced and they have a son, Max. Fletcher has dalliances with the women he knows at the office. His boss uses her body to manipulate him and promote her own ambitions. She really does not respect Fletcher's reputation as a lawyer. Max wishes his father would stop lying and tell the truth. Fletcher lies and suborns people who have taken an oath to tell the truth. Talk about how many commandments *Liar, Liar* subtly addresses and how the Ten Commandments, especially the eighth, are positive norms that promote justice and peace for all people?

3. One of the fallouts of divorce is that the parents often share unequal custody of children. This means that one parent must promise to visit or is scheduled to have time with his or her children. Frequently, the parent fails to keep his or her promise and does not show up. Children suffer because they do not understand how anything, no matter how legitimate, can interfere with a parent's promise to them. How then might *Liar, Liar* be called a morality tale? What did Fletcher learn during the course of the film? What did you learn about keeping promises and covenants?

Prayer

Lord, you told us that the truth will make us free. Help us to discern what is right and always to speak the truth with integrity. Amen.

For Catechists

Catechism of the Catholic Church

"You shall not bear false witness against your neighbor,"
no. 2464

Truthfulness, nos. 2467–2470

Offenses against truth, nos. 2475–2486

Duty of reparation for lies, no. 2487

Children and the holiness of their parents, no. 2227

Caring for the physical and spiritual needs of children,
nos. 2224–2226

Cate Blanchett in *Veronica Guerin*.

Veronica Guerin
U.S.A./Ireland, 2003, 98 minutes
Actors: Cate Blanchett, Ciàran Hinds, Gerard McSorley,
Brenda Fricker
Writers: Mary Agnes Donoghue, Carol Doyle
Director: Joel Schumacher

Veronica Guerin

What Is Truth?

SYNOPSIS

In the mid-1990s, Veronica Guerin (Cate Blanchett) is a young wife, a mother of a young son, and a journalist in Dublin, Ireland. The sight of young children playing with discarded heroin needles in the projects is a catalyst for her to begin a journalistic war against drugs and organized crime.

Like a crusader, she goes after the drug lords one by one: Martin Cahill (Gerry O'Brien), Gerry Hutch (Alan Devine), and John Traynor (Ciàran Hinds), whom she considers a friend, but who is weak and eventually betrays her. She fearlessly seeks interviews and names names in her articles. She makes many enemies, but this does not seem to bother or deter her. Then she goes after the most dangerous drug lord of them all, John Gilligan (Gerard McSorley). When she visits his lush country home, she is viciously beaten and warned. Yet she persists in her crusade because she wants the police and government officials to take action. For a long time, it seems that no one is listening or paying attention.

Her family receives threats, and she is shot in the leg. On June 26, 1996, not long after she recovers, she is ambushed in her car, shot, and killed.

Immediately after making his small-budget film about truth and lies, *Phone Booth*, Joel Schumacher went to Ireland to film this story about the courageous Dublin journalist, Veronica Guerin. From 1998 to 2003, several films were made about crime in Dublin. They include two films about Martin Cahill, known as "The General." The first of these was John Boorman's *The General* (1998), with Brendan Gleason, and then Thaddeus O'Sullivan's *Ordinary Decent Criminal*, with Kevin Spacey. Joan Allen played Veronica Guerin previously in John Mackenzie's 2000 feature, *When the Sky Falls*.

Investigative journalism is always an interesting theme for crime movies because this subgenre is about risk taking and, often, heroism on the part of the journalist. The films begin with an aspect of corruption in society that is being covered up and needs exposing. These films take for granted that audiences really want the truth to come to light and that society will be better because of this.

The city of Dublin becomes a character in the movie. The beautiful aerial shots and action on location—in both squalid areas and affluent homes and properties—give credibility to the story. Cate Blanchett's vivid acting brings the caring and crusading Veronica Guerin to life. She won a Best Supporting Actress Oscar for *The Aviator* (2004). Academy Award-winner Brenda Fricker (*My Left Foot*) is her mother. Ciaràn Hinds is John Traynor, her limelight-seeking but treacherous informant, and Gerard McSorley is alarmingly sinister as John Gilligan, who was later imprisoned for his crimes.

Focus: Like Daniel, Veronica Guerin was a gifted investigator. Like Jesus, Veronica Guerin was born to tell the truth so that "the goodness and holiness of truth" could set people free and bring forth justice.

Veronica Guerin could make her own motto Jesus' words addressed to Pilate concerning truth. Truth, for both

Jesus and Veronica, was a pledge, a word full of promise and hope. The scenes of Veronica's mother in church and of her funeral cortege make us aware of Veronica Guerin's Irish Catholic heritage. She would have been very familiar with the passion accounts in the Gospels, and she had a powerful sense of vocation as an investigative journalist. Like Jesus, for this she was born, and for this she came into the world. She always wanted to find and to know the truth and to ask, like Pilate (though with more sincerity), "What is truth?" She wanted to communicate the answer to this question in her articles so that justice would be brought to the children of Dublin.

John's Gospel is the Gospel of truth; in fact, in the *Revised Standard Version* of the New Testament, "truth" is mentioned twenty-one times. Jesus was made flesh, full of grace and truth (1:17); Jesus himself is the way, the truth, and the life (Jn 14:6). The quest that Veronica Guerin undertook—and became a martyr for—was to unmask the criminals in Dublin who were destroying people, especially the young, with their drug dealing and violence. In her articles, which were widely read and gave people courage to come forward and testify against the criminals in court, she "testified to the truth" (Jn 5:33). The word "martyr" is derived from both the Latin and Greek word that literally means "witness." To die for truth is to be its ultimate witness.

The Book of Daniel has two investigative stories. In chapter 13, Daniel saved the life of the innocent Susanna with his "forensic" questioning of the two lustful elders who had falsely accused Susanna of adultery (see *Absolute Power,* pp. 62–68). Now we have another story of an investigation into fraud in Daniel 14. Here, Daniel exposes the priests of Bel who had set up what we might call a racket to deceive the devout public. Worshippers brought gifts to the temple of Bel, enriching the priests and their families. Every day the people also brought food that the priests claimed the "living god" consumed. The evening's offerings always disappeared by morning. Daniel was suspicious and, as we saw in the story of Susanna, used his flair for investigation. He secretly sifted ash on the temple's floor. When the temple was unsealed the next day, he was able to expose the fraud by pointing to the footprints of the priests and their families revealed in the ashes.

Veronica Guerin, through her persistence and intense desire to know the truth, followed in a long and solid tradition of the journalistic biblical exposé. Veronica's example integrated the themes of faith, family, and vocation on both personal and social levels. Truth is for all seasons.

While it is said that truth is important for its own sake, the consequences of the truth are also important, especially for the community. The legislative reform in Ireland following Veronica's death put pressure on the financial resources of the criminals and cleaned up Dublin's crime scene. The communal effect of speaking the truth is in Paul's Letter to the Ephesians, in which he addresses the transforming nature of "justice and holiness...born of truth" (Eph 4:24). Ephesians 6:14 is an epitaph for Veronica Guerin: "Stand fast, with the truth as the belt around your waist, justice as your breastplate."

KEY SCENES AND THEMES

- Veronica going into the Dublin slums and finding the addicts; the impact on her; her interview with the boy dealing drugs; joining with the protesters and parents for a drug-free Dublin.

- Veronica's confrontation of John in his home, trying to get an interview, trying to find out the truth; his brutality in beating her.

- The attack of Veronica in her home and being shot on Christmas Eve; her determination despite her fear to see her quest through; her mother, husband, and editor warning her; her assassination.

1. In addition to the Scripture citations for the film *Veronica Guerin,* the Beatitudes from Matthew 5 are particularly applicable to her life and vocation as an investigative journalist. She recognized the poor in spirit (the children) and those who mourned (the parents and families of the victims of the drug barons), she joined these victims as they hungered and thirsted for righteousness, and, though she agitated the criminal status quo in Dublin, she was a peacemaker. What do you think motivated her? What motivates anyone who follows a call so completely? What about her vocation as a wife and mother? How did all her callings fit together? Did Veronica do the right thing? Why or why not?

FOR REFLECTION AND CONVERSATION

2. Although the film does not show this, Veronica was killed two days before she was to address a conference in London on "Dying to Tell a Story: Journalists at Risk." Every January, the Committee to Protect Journalists (www.cpj.org) publishes a list of all the journalists from around the world who have been killed in the previous year. The CPJ reports that between 1994 and 2003, fifty-five journalists (including camera and sound crew and photographers) were killed in cross fire during war, and 264 were hunted down and "murdered in reprisal for their reporting." Only twenty-six of these 347 cases ever resulted in arrest and prosecution. Why is the freedom of the press so essential to democracy? While freedom of the press is highly valued, the press can also violate privacy, especially regarding celebrities. Talk about the ethics that govern the exercise of freedom of the press from the perspectives of journalists, societies, and governments. What role does the Eighth Commandment play in the

"Fourth Estate," that is, the media's role to act as a guardian of the public interest?

3. The dictionary defines addiction as the compulsive need for a habit-forming substance or the persistent, compulsive use of a substance known by the user to be harmful. Addiction is often applied to self-destructive behaviors as well. Why did the poor of Dublin, or any city or town for that matter, succumb to drugs? Whose responsibility is it to protect people from drugs? What are the drug lords addicted to? What role does conscience play in deciding to buy, take, sell, and distribute drugs? What are the consequences of drug trafficking and addiction in our country and throughout the world? What solutions can the faith community offer to help end the destructive dynamic of drug addiction and trafficking? Each of us can ask ourselves if we have ever abused drugs and engaged in "self-medicating" and why. What about the casual and recreational reference to or use of drugs on television, in film, and in music? How can media education (www. medialit.org) contribute to building a drug-free local and global culture and society?

Prayer

Lord Jesus, full of grace and truth, you have promised the consolation of the truth. Also give us its courage. Amen.

For Catechists

Catechism of the Catholic Church
"You shall not bear false witness against your neighbor,"
  no. 2464

Offenses against the truth, nos. 2475–2486

The duty of reparation for sins against truth, no. 2487

The use of social communications media, 2493–2495, 2497–2499

The sacrament of Matrimony, nos. 1604, 1605

The vocation to follow Christ, no. 1694

Phone Booth

U.S.A., 2002, 82 minutes

Actors: Colin Farrell, Kiefer Sutherland, Forest Whitaker, Radha Mitchell, Katie Holmes

Writer: Larry Cohen

Director: Joel Schumacher

Phone Booth

Live by the Truth

SYNOPSIS

Stu Shepard (Colin Farrell) is a cocky young publicist. His clothes, his mobile phone, and his deals for clients define who he is. He tries to impress his trainee, Adam, and is infatuated with an aspiring actress, Pam (Katie Holmes). He loves his wife, Kelly (Radha Mitchell), but this does not stop him from going into the only old-fashioned phone booth left in Manhattan every day, slipping off his wedding ring, and calling Pam.

One day, as Stu removes his ring to call Pam, a man tries to deliver a pizza to him in the booth. Stu rudely sends him away. When the phone rings in the booth, Stu answers it. A man (Kiefer Sutherland) tells Stu it is not in his best interest to hang up. Stu is then caught in a terrorizing conversation with the caller, who boasts that he has executed several men morally guilty of cruelty, greed, or deception who would not confess to their sins and failings. The caller proves he is serious when he shoots Leon, a pimp who is trying to force Stu to leave the phone booth so his prostitutes can use it. The police converge, a crowd gathers, and television crews turn up. At first, everyone thinks Stu is Leon's

214

killer, and the caller/sniper threatens Stu with death if he hangs up or lets the police know what is actually happening.

The caller/sniper enjoys tormenting Stu in this cat-and-mouse game. He forces him to do dangerous things such as reaching for a gun hidden in the ceiling of the phone booth. When Kelly arrives on the scene, the caller insists that Stu publicly tell her the truth about his infidelities, which Stu does.

Captain Ramey (Forest Whitaker), who heads the police effort, slowly figures out what is happening. He, too, is humiliated when the sniper/caller insists that Stu confront him with secret truths about his life. But the captain remains steady, willing to hear the truth. Eventually, the sniper's threats and lies overwhelm Stu, who makes a full confession of his deceit-filled life to everyone watching. He leaves the booth, arms extended, willing to be killed. The police shoot him with a rubber bullet to misdirect the sniper. The media records every word and action for the evening news.

Stu and the captain figure out the caller/sniper's location. When the police arrive, they find a man in a hotel room whom they recognize as the pizza delivery man who had visited Stu in the phone booth. He has apparently committed suicide by shooting himself. They assume that he was the caller/sniper. A medic gives Stu an injection for pain as he waits in the ambulance. As Stu begins to feel the drug's effect, the real caller/sniper passes by and urges Stu to maintain his newfound honesty.

COMMENTARY

During the 1930s, Patrick Hamilton (author of *Gaslight*) wrote a radio play about a man who was pursued by an unseen assailant from telephone booth to telephone booth until he was shamed into admitting the truth about his life. Seventy years later, the concept reached the screen with this film written by Larry Cohen and directed by Joel Schumacher. Cohen became successful in the 1970s and 1980s by writing and directing a succession of small-budget horror films such as *It's Alive!, The Stuff,* and *Q: The Winged Serpent.* Joel Schumacher directed some of the biggest hits of the 1990s, including *Falling Down,* two Batman films, and two adaptations of John Grisham novels, *A Time to Kill* and *The Client.* He also directed the movie version of Andrew Lloyd Webber's *The Phantom of the Opera* in 2004. However, he has also made a number of small-budget dramas like *Flawless* and his Vietnam movie, *Tigerland. Phone Booth* was made in ten days with a minimal budget and has a very brief running time, but Schumacher's flair ensures that this is an impressive and tense drama.

Colin Farrell emerged as a popular leading man in Schumacher's *Tigerland,* and his popularity was reinforced by *Hart's War, Minority Report, Daredevil, The Recruit,* and *S.W.A.T.* He appeared in five films in 2003, and had the lead role in the 2004 epic *Alexander,* directed and written by Oliver Stone. Farrell suits the part of Stu perfectly. Kiefer Sutherland provides the sinister voice of the judgmental sniper, and Forest Whitaker (*The Crying Game*) is the careful and sympathetic police chief. Schumacher is something of a razzle-dazzle director, and he uses this style to pump up audience tension and excitement by pacing Stu's growing exasperation, the hectic pulse of Manhattan, and the circus atmosphere provided by the crowd of onlookers and the media.

Katie Holmes (*Dawson's Creek, The Gift, The Singing Detective, Batman Begins*) appears as Stu's unwitting girlfriend, and Radha Mitchell (*High Art, Pitch Black, Melinda and Melinda*) as his wife.

DIALOGUE WITH THE SCRIPTURES

Focus: Like Stu Shepard, men and women can be tempted by worldly ambition, and they can become deceitful. When they are forced to face their sinfulness like Adam and Eve, who disobeyed God in the garden, or Peter, who denied Jesus, the acknowledgement of their sin breaks through their shame, and the truth sets them free.

Satan is often called the Great Deceiver, a title that takes us back to Genesis. In the garden, Adam and Eve, as representatives of the fallen human race, are tempted with lies that lead them to disregard the word of God and to choose to try to become greater than they could ever be. When the voice of God confronts them, they realize what they have done. Their eyes are opened, and they see that they are naked before God. They are ashamed.

Phone Booth can be seen as a contemporary allegory of this Genesis story. Stu Shepard is a man from humble circumstances in Brooklyn. He has fallen for the modern lie: that if you dress in designer clothes, talk incessantly on your mobile phone, promote yourself in the most profitable way, twist the truth, make inflated promises, flatter, and lie, you can fool yourself into believing that you are really someone. Stu believes that he has become like a god and that any rules of right and wrong do not apply to his dealings with people, even his wife. When he is assailed by a godlike voice in the phone booth, even though the voice is from a Satan-like character, he is stripped of all pretensions and forced to acknowledge his moral nakedness.

In this nakedness, Stu finds redemption. He is forced to make life-and-death choices and cut a swathe through his web of lies. A sinister voice forces Stu to acknowledge who he really is. When Stu finally tells the truth about himself, he is at first ashamed, but then freed. His confession moves his wife. The police chief offers sympathy, even admiration. Satisfied that Stu has acknowledged his sins, the caller/sniper lets him live. Stu is at the beginning of the journey to maturity that Paul describes so beautifully in the reading from Ephesians; he is no longer a child, nor is he "tossed here and there, carried about by every wind of doctrine that originates in human trickery and skill in proposing error" (Eph 4:14).

Stu's plight in *Phone Booth* can also be seen as an allegory of Peter's moral fall and repentance during the passion of

Jesus. At the Last Supper, he boasted to Jesus that he would be unswervingly faithful, but that promise proved empty within a few hours. Stu, the "big man" and full of hot air, walks along the Manhattan streets followed by his naive apprentice. As he is about to call his girlfriend, he removes his wedding ring and effectively denies his marriage. After Peter denied the Lord three times, Jesus looked at him. Peter's conscience woke; he was grief stricken and wept bitterly. While Stu's accuser cross-examines and torments him, he sees the faces of his wife and girlfriend in the crowd. It is Stu's turn to weep as he acknowledges the truth of his deceit and infidelity.

Jesus forgave Peter and asked him to acknowledge his love for him. The sniper asks Stu to confess his guilt publicly for those in the street and the television audience. Stu confesses fully because he is shamed and does not want to hurt those he loves more than he already has. He confesses not because his life is threatened, but because he has learned the value of truth. Forgiven, Peter received a commission of community and moral leadership among Jesus' disciples. Stu is now ready to live a decent life, a life of integrity. His confession and a greater appreciation of the truth have set him free.

KEY SCENES AND THEMES

- Stu's long walk down the New York street with the eager Adam in tow; Stu's flashy clothes, the phone calls, the promises, the deals, talking with celebrities, and wanting to be famous; going into the phone booth to call Pam, taking off his ring, making promises to Pam.

- The interaction in the phone booth between Stu and the caller/sniper: the game playing, the deadly truth confirmed by the shooting of the pimp, the voice challenging Stu about all the details of his life; Stu's superficiality, his deception in his work and relationships; Stu gradually breaking down and admitting the truth; the cruel and unrelenting caller/sniper.

- The build-up to Stu's confession; his desperation facing the likelihood of death and his finding the moral courage to confess everything publicly; Captain Ramey's compassion; Kelly's forgiveness; the caller/sniper allowing him to live.

1. As *Phone Booth* opens, we see the cosmos, and a voiceover reminds us about the role of telecommunications in modern life, from satellites to streets crowded with people using mobile phones. The old-fashioned phone booth is disappearing, but Stu Shepard, a publicist with an inflated ego, uses the only traditional phone booth left in Manhattan to deceive his wife and flirt with an aspiring actress. Suddenly, the phone booth is Stu's prison as a disembodied voice becomes an unseen judge and jury. The voice threatens Stu physically with a rifle, psychologically through emotional games, and morally by forcing him to tell his wife and the public the truth about himself. Talk about the phone booth as a metaphor for the role that technology plays in human relationships. Does technology bring us closer to others, distance us from others, or a little of both? Why? Why does Stu use the phone booth instead of his mobile phone? Are there really any secrets out there? In the end, what are the consequences of deceit?

FOR REFLECTION AND CONVERSATION

2. The *Catechism of the Catholic Church* addresses the use of the means of social communication or the media in the section on the Eighth Commandment (nos. 2493–2499). All information provided by the media is to be at the service of the common good, and all communication is to meet the demands of justice and charity. How does *Phone Booth* comment on the news media in modern life? How can we compare

the use of the telephone between individuals and the communication that occurs in the use of mass media? How does the element of justice enter into this difference? How does the need for communication and truth transcend all dimensions of human existence? In what ways have you noticed a disregard for truth in public life as well as moments when people stood up for the truth?

3. In addition to the Scripture citations noted on page 214, there are many other verses and stories that refer to offenses against truth, respect for truth, and living in truth (Deut 5:20, Prov 8:7; Jn 17:17; Mt 18:16). Often, as in the story of David and Bathsheba in First Samuel 11–12, sinning against one commandment means sinning against others as well. Have you ever noticed this in your own life? How many commandments did the film *Phone Booth* actually deal with? If you could name one good idea from the film that inspires a change in your life, what would it be?

Prayer

Lord, we deceive ourselves every day. In your light, may we see our sinfulness, acknowledge it, and confess it so that your truth may set us free. Amen.

For Catechists

Catechism of the Catholic Church
Living in truth, nos. 2465–2470
Offences against truth, nos. 2475–2487
Respect for the truth, nos. 2488–2492
The use of the social communications media, nos. 2493–2499
Repentance, nos. 1430–1433

The Ninth Commandment

Introduction

You shall not covet your neighbor's wife./Be faithful./Do not lust after another.

The archetypal story of the abuse of this commandment is the story of King David's desire to possess Bathsheba, the wife of his officer, Uriah. David's act of covetousness had drastic consequences. His voyeurism led to his unlawful desire and subsequent adultery. The whole story is told so graphically that if shown in a film it would probably receive an "R" rating.

David's adultery led to lies and false protestations of friendship for Uriah. Uriah was a man of virtue whose loyalty to King David was profound, thus he abstained from sexual relations with his wife while on duty. Because Bathsheba's pregnancy could not be attributed to Uriah, David committed callous, premeditated murder by commanding that Uriah be placed at the frontline of battle so that he would most certainly be killed.

David repented, and he had much for which to repent. If David's act of covetousness were not already bad enough, the subsequent lies and violence only made matters worse.

Jesus spoke against lusting after a woman in the heart (Mt 5:28). In 1976, President Jimmy Carter said in an interview that was quickly published around the world:

> I try not to commit a deliberate sin. I recognize that I'm going to do it anyhow, because I'm human and I'm tempted. And Christ set some almost impossible standards for us. Christ said, "I tell you that anyone who looks on a woman with lust has in his heart already committed adultery."
>
> I've looked on a lot of women with lust. I've committed adultery in my heart many times. This is something that

> God recognizes I will do—and I have done it—and God
> forgives me for it.

Carter's confession, while reminding us that temptation itself is not a sin, nevertheless shows us how a good man can be tempted, something that is possible for all of us.

As noted in the introduction to the Sixth Commandment, sexual sin seems to dominate the Catholic conscience, often at the expense of giving serious adult attention to the other commandments. The Ninth Commandment emphasizes purity of heart.

The Reformation tradition combines the Ninth Commandment with the Tenth Commandment. Some theologians feel that this grouping yokes the idea of women to that of possessions, consequently reinforcing a male-dominant perspective that demeans women in popular consciousness. The Catholic tradition has two distinct commandments for coveting and envy: "the Ninth Commandment forbids carnal concupiscence; the tenth forbids coveting another's goods" (*CCC*, no. 2514). The Genesis account of creation reminds us that God created male and female—both in the image and likeness of God.

The Ninth Commandment is a healthy reminder that neither men nor women are mere objects of desire or lust, but children of God. Additionally, the implications of this commandment are strongly feminist and offer a positive response to historical patriarchal traditions that consider women secondary citizens in the world and the Church, both in life and in cinema stories.

The Ninth Commandment also demands that we learn and live the beatitude, "Blessed are the single-hearted for they shall see God." (Mt 5:8). Obedience to this commandment makes us mindful of other virtues such as chastity, purity of intention, internal and external vision, and modesty.

It is very significant that the *Catechism of the Catholic Church* requires a *"purification of the social climate,"* and says that, as a result, purity of heart brings, "...freedom from widespread eroticism and avoids entertainment inclined to voyeurism and illusion" (no. 2525) such as pornography. The *Catechism* also says that "...*moral permissiveness* rests on an erroneous conception of human freedom" (no. 2526) and that moral education of young people can be reasonably expected to include respect for truth, qualities of the heart, and the nature of the moral and spiritual dignity of man (no. 2526).

It is very interesting to note that these elements can form a viewing lens with which to exercise the moral imagination when considering cinema stories.

The three films we have chosen to explore for the Ninth Commandment begin with *The First Wives Club,* a humorous tale of spurned wives who find a way to turn revenge for their husbands' adultery and abandonment into something positive. *The English Patient* is the painful and tragic story of an illicit wartime love affair. *American Beauty* captures all the sad elements of infidelity in the Ninth Commandment with an emphasis on the consequences when purity of vision is lost.

THE NINTH COMMANDMENT

Sirach 23:16–27; 21:11–21

1 John 2:15–17

John 15:1–6, 9–12

The First Wives Club

U.S.A., 1996, 103 minutes

Actors: Goldie Hawn, Bette Midler, Diane Keaton,
Maggie Smith, Stockard Channing, Sarah Jessica Parker,
Marcia Gay Harden, Elizabeth Berkely, Stephen Collins,
Dan Hedaya, Victor Garber, Eileen Heckart, Philip Bosco,
Bronson Pinchot, Rob Reiner, James Naughton, Ivana Trump

Writer: Robert Harling

Director: Hugh Wilson

The First Wives Club

Payback

SYNOPSIS

In 1969, four college roommates, Annie, Brenda, Elise, and Cynthia, prepare for graduation. Cynthia gives each girl a pearl necklace, and they promise eternal friendship. About twenty-five years later, Cynthia (Stockard Channing), lonely and depressed, writes notes to each of her friends, who have not kept in touch. She then commits suicide because her husband has left her for a younger woman. The other three friends meet again at the funeral and resolve to stick together.

Elise (Goldie Hawn) is an actress whose husband, Bill (Victor Garber), is suing her for divorce, half their assets, and alimony, while he dallies with a younger actress. Annie (Diane Keaton) and her husband, Aaron (Stephen Collins), an advertising executive, live separately, but go to couples' therapy. When he asks for a divorce, Annie discovers that he and her therapist have been involved. Brenda's (Bette Midler) husband, Mortie (Dan Hedaya), has left her for a younger woman (Sarah Jessica Parker) as well. After this introduction to the lives of the characters, the women receive the letters Cynthia sent them and form The First Wives Club.

The women start to renovate a building Elise owns as a base of operations from which to carry out vengeance on their cheating husbands. Elise finds a way to sell everything out from under Bill, leaving him with a dollar; Annie has her lesbian daughter infiltrate Aaron's advertising company so that Annie can buy out the partners secretly and become Aaron's boss; Brenda obtains Mortie's old business records that show he started his company with stolen property and help from the mob. Soon, however, Annie, Elise, and Brenda realize that revenge is empty, so their motivation changes to justice. They even turn on each other before they come to understand that they can transform their situation into something good in memory of Cynthia. They then decide to use their building as a crisis center for women in her memory, using funds extricated from their mostly unwilling husbands. At the grand opening of the center, Brenda and Mortie reconcile. Annie becomes a businesswoman, and Elise continues her career as an actress.

COMMENTARY

The First Wives Club is based on a first novel written by Olivia Goldsmith and published in 1992. The book sold more than one million copies, and the film grossed more than $150 million at the box office and made the cover of *TIME* magazine (October 1996). As one critic wrote, the book touched the soul of women's issues because it dealt with the superficiality of the contemporary lives of men. Ironically, Goldsmith died in January 2004 from complications from a facelift.

The screenplay is by Robert Harling, who also wrote the play and script for *Steel Magnolias, Soapdish,* and, more recently, the well-intentioned though somewhat disappointing romantic comedy about marriage, *Laws of Attraction.* Direction is by Emmy and Humanitas award-winning Hugh Wilson (*Dudley Do-Right, Guarding Tess*).

The success of *The First Wives Club* is most certainly due to the comedic ensemble cast of the three principle characters, who are played by Academy Award winners Goldie Hawn and Diane Keaton, and Emmy winner Bette Midler. They play the fading movie star, the doormat wife, and the frumpy hausfrau with just the right amount of exaggeration, lending credibility and sympathy to wives who are left behind by husbands in pursuit of younger women. The film seems to deal with the issue of adultery and divorce superficially because it makes us laugh, but the statistics on these issues in the United States alone are not a laughing matter.

DIALOGUE WITH THE SCRIPTURES

Focus: The Scriptures strongly condemn husbands who stray from their commitment and betray their wives, as we read in Sirach and the First Letter of John. The husbands of The First Wives Club *deserve their condemnation, for they have broken the bonds of love that are imaged by the union of the vine with the branches as described by Jesus in John's Gospel.*

The First Wives Club is a comedy, but its underlying themes are dark. They deal with the callous and self-centered behavior of husbands who break their commitment to their wives by lying, cheating, and coveting other women. The husbands in the film look outside their marriage covenant for love and companionship. When their behavior is exposed, they experience humiliation and, thankfully, some repentance.

The men in *The First Wives Club* illustrate the secular reality and lack of values that the reading from the First Letter of John addresses. These professional men love the material world; they are not only unfaithful, but they are also ambitious and greedy because they opt for "carnal allurements, enticements for the eye, the life of empty show" (2:16). John reminds us that this behavior is ungodly. He also tells us that "the world" and "its seductions" are coming to an end.

Catholic biblical tradition places the Old Testament's Wisdom literature after the Pentateuch and historical books and before the prophetic books. The wisdom books do not have the dramatic immediacy of prophetic imagery and teachings, but, through the literary forms of poetry, aphorism, and proverb, they do show extraordinary amount of insight into fidelity and infidelity. It should be noted that the wisdom literature reflects the society in which it was produced—a patriarchal society that focused on men and their rights rather than on the rights of women. These books (Job, Psalms, Proverbs, Ecclesiastes, Song of Songs, Wisdom, and Sirach) sometimes sound strongly sexist. This places on us the responsibility to interpret the patriarchal passages according to the biblical truth that men and women are equal. Sirach 23:16–21 challenges unfaithful men about their behavior, while Sirach 23:22–26 speaks to unfaithful women.

The man who commits incest or adultery is roundly condemned. He might think that no one sees because darkness conceals what he does, but Sirach warns that the eyes of the Lord are extremely bright and see into the most secret places. The scribe's final words summarize the consequences to the covetous husbands portrayed in the movie: "Such a man will be punished in the streets of the city; when he least expects it, he will be apprehended" (23:21).

For the movie to make its point through comedy, the husbands are presented as fools. Sirach, who might have enjoyed the movie's tone, uses a satiric tone in all of chapter 21 when he speaks about the difference between fools and men of culture. For example, he says, "A fool's mind is like a broken jar—no knowledge at all can it hold.... A fool raises his voice in laughter, but a prudent man at the most smiles gently" (21:14, 20). As the men in *The First Wives Club* lose all that they possess, they illustrate Sirach's aphorism: "Like a house in ruin is wisdom to a fool; the stupid man knows it only as inscrutable words" (21:18).

The positive side of the Ninth Commandment encourages and celebrates fidelity in marriage. When we look at Jesus' Last Supper discourses in the Gospel of John, we find that they are full of images of love and fidelity. One of the most powerful of these images is long hallowed in the writings of the prophets (Is 5:1–7; Jer 2:21; Ez 15:2–7, 17:5–10, 19:10): the union of the branches with the vine is like the union of God with his people, an image that is also found in the New Testament. In John 15, this analogy is made more specific because the image signifies the love between Jesus and his friends. Jesus then goes on to explain how committed is his love when he speaks about resting and remaining in that love, making his and our joy complete.

No one can show greater love than by laying down his or her life for a loved one. Jesus did this completely in his life, passion, death, and resurrection. We have not been asked to go out and literally to look for ways to die for others, but we are obligated in faith to lay our lives down day by day in loving, faithful commitment. This is the basis of marriage and enduring covenanted love. The women in the film have a sense of this, and they realize that if their marriages are to bear any fruit at all, they must turn away from vindictiveness and do something positive for others, literally at their husbands' expense. The men have the most lessons to learn.

KEY SCENES AND THEMES

- The girls graduating from college and Cynthia's gift; their promise to each other; Cynthia's suicide; the funeral and the reunion; each woman's regret for not being there for Cynthia; their worries about their marriages, aging, and fading beauty.

- The three husbands and their infidelity; the women discovering their husband's activities and plans; the women's decision to take vengeance.

• The women carrying out their plan and realizing that vengeance is not enough; making their husbands contribute to the counseling center they have started for women who have been dumped by their husbands.

1. Women's issues are the focus of *The First Wives Club.* These issues range from their husbands' infidelity to the consequences of adultery, suicide, theft, and fraud, and their effects on the family: the husbands and wives, and on children in particular. The film also looks at the cult of youth that plagues both the film's men and women in different ways. Talk about how the women and men differ in dealing with the threat of aging. Have you ever known anyone who, like the characters, was obsessed with growing older and responded like the men and women in the film? What do you think about marital fidelity, and how do you respond to scriptural wisdom about it? Why is marriage sacred? What is it about our culture that normalizes adultery and fornication? What are the strongest challenges to chastity in modern living?

FOR REFLECTION AND CONVERSATION

2. While there are many films that deal with male bonding (e.g., road trip and buddy movies), by comparison, there are few that deal honestly and sensitively with female bonding and friendship. What is the symbol of the covenant between friends in this film (the necklaces)? What is the symbol of the covenant between the husbands and wives? Why don't the men take their marriage commitments seriously? What unites the women in the film? What characteristics define the marriage covenant in *The First Wives Club* and other films about women, marriage, and family, such as *Steel Magnolias* or *Moonstruck?*

3. The response of the women to their husbands' adultery, desertion, or request for divorce is to take vengeance on them. Why do the women realize that revenge is not a lasting or satisfying solution? Why do they found the center? Aside from the fact that it probably wouldn't be as funny, why won't the men and women acknowledge one another's responsibility for the success or failure of their marriages? The film does not refer explicitly to the practice of faith or spirituality in a marriage, yet how do they help nurture a marriage? Granting that the film deals with the superficial and worldly aspects of contemporary married life, how could the film have been rewritten in a satisfying way to show that these characters were more substantial than the comedy permitted, that they were capable of more? What about the film's younger women, whom the men chase after? What does the story imply about them? What did the movie mean to you?

Prayer

Lord, we pray that the covenant of love between husbands and wives be strengthened in the love of Jesus, who loved us and laid down his life for us. Amen.

For Catechists

Catechism of the Catholic Church
Lust, nos. 2514–2516
The battle for purity, nos. 2520–2527
Unity of marriage, nos. 1643–1645
Fidelity of conjugal love, nos. 1646–1651

The English Patient

U.K., 1996, 162 minutes

Actors: Ralph Fiennes, Kristin Scott Thomas, Juliette Binoche,
Willem Dafoe, Naveen Andrews, Colin Firth, Kevin Whately,
Julian Wadham, Jürgen Prochnow

Writer: Anthony Minghella

Director: Anthony Minghella

The English Patient

Passion and Tragedy

A man and a woman are flying over the Egyptian desert at the beginning of World War II. The small plane is shot down and crashes. The woman is dead, the pilot is burned beyond recognition, and Bedouins save him and tend to his wounds. He ends up in Italy in 1944 with Allied forces that are liberating the country. They question him and cannot figure out if he is English or a German spy. He is actually a Hungarian, Count Laszlo de Almásy (Ralph Fiennes), who had gone to school in England. He travels north with the army. When her friend is killed, Hana (Juliet Binoche), a French-Canadian nurse, decides to stay at an abandoned monastery and take care of the man until the war is over. She and Kip (Naveen Andrews), a Sikh who clears mines with the British army, begin an affair.

An English-speaking Canadian, David Caravaggio (Willem Dafoe), arrives at the monastery. He has heard about the man who carries a copy of *The Histories of Herodotus* (fifth century) and knows the words to every song he ever heard. Caravaggio believes the man a traitor and wants to kill him.

Almásy was a member of the Royal Geographic Society. His task was to make maps of northern Africa for the British in the late 1930s. A photographer/pilot, Geoffrey (Colin Firth), and his wife, Katharine (Kristin Scott Thomas), an artist, joined Almásy's expedition. Katharine and Almásy fell in love. Geoffrey discovered they were having an affair during a trip to Cairo. Later, when his expedition was cancelled, Geoffrey volunteered to fetch Almásy from the desert, and he took Katharine along. He tried to crash the plane into Almásy, but was himself killed. Almásy promised the injured Katharine he would return with help. The British refused to give him a plane because they thought he was a German, and they sent him to Cairo in a prison car. He escaped and was captured by the Germans. He bartered his maps for a plane to rescue Katharine. Caravaggio was among the many who were caught and tortured because the Germans had the maps. Almásy found Katharine dead. As he flew her body from the desert, the plane was shot down.

The war ends. Back at the monastery, Hana and Kip end their affair. Caravaggio leaves. Almásy pleads silently with Hana to directly end his life with an overdose of morphine. She does.

COMMENTARY

Director and screenwriter Anthony Minghella adapted *The English Patient* from Michael Ondaatje's 1992 Booker Prize-winning novel. Minghella also wrote and directed some of the Inspector Morse telemovies as well as the very popular *Truly Madly Deeply*, *The Talented Mr. Ripley*, and *Cold Mountain*.

Visually, the film is extraordinarily beautiful, with its African desert locations and the monastery in Tuscany. The principal setting is Italy at the end of World War II.

Americans obviously took the film to heart—it won nine Oscars in 1996, including Best Film and Best Director. Although the story and the passionate feelings profoundly moved many U.S. critics and viewers, elsewhere the response was mixed. There are many wonderful sequences in the film, beginning with the opening in the desert, the plane crash, and the visual portrait of the hideously burned man. A memorable sequence involves an engineer lifting Hana up a high wall to view the frescoes in a Tuscan church.

Author Michael Ondaatje's novel is a meditation on life issues. Not only is it a story of betrayal and passion, it also raises the issue of assisted suicide (when someone helps another person's own act of self-destruction, and euthanasia or "mercy killing," when someone directly kills another, with or without that person's consent). Filmmaker Anthony Minghella has adapted the novel by creating a narrative, finding moving images that correspond to the poetry of the written word. Its style is nonlinear, mosaic-like storytelling, freely flowing back and forth in time, with the pieces finally coming together at the end to shape a complete story of passion, betrayal, war, and possibilities for redemption.

Focus: The English Patient *parallels the classic Ninth Commandment biblical story of David, Bathsheba, and Uriah very clearly. The Gospel and the Pauline writings speak of the positive aspects of purity of heart that exclude sexual betrayal.*

DIALOGUE WITH THE SCRIPTURES

The best-known Old Testament story that illustrates the Ninth Commandment is that of David's adultery with Bathsheba, the wife of one of David's soldiers, Uriah, as recounted in the Second Book of Samuel. To cover up his sin and Bathsheba's pregnancy, David commands her husband Uriah to be put in the frontline of battle so that he will be killed and David's criminal behavior concealed. The prophet Nathan acts as David's accuser and conscience when he speaks God's word directly to the king. He tells David a parable about a rich farmer who slaughters a poor farmer's only sheep to entertain a guest. When David responds indignantly, moved by this story of injustice,

Nathan points to him: "You are the man." The message against coveting and taking a neighbor's wife in lust is absolutely clear.

The English Patient stirred its audience with the illicit romance between Count Almásy and Katharine, the wife of his colleague, Geoffrey Clifton. The sweep of their unlawful passion and their attractiveness invited audiences to feel intense sympathy for them, despite their transgressions. Like Uriah, Geoffrey Clifton was a basically decent, nondescript man who was rather stolid in his love for his wife. Unlike Uriah, he becomes fully aware of their affair, but instead of Almásy killing him (as David killed Uriah), Clifton kills himself. His injured wife, Katharine, is saved by Almásy, only to be abandoned by the fates of war and to die alone in a cave.

There is glamour in the romance, but the consequences of infidelity are deadly, as seen in both the biblical story and the film.

Jesus speaks of honesty and integrity in the Gospel. The Pharisees were preoccupied with surface rituals of cleanliness and decorum rather than the actual condition of their souls, and Jesus condemns their double standard. He points out that appearances are not the criteria for moral judgment; instead, it is what comes out of the heart that makes a person unclean or immoral. His examples include adultery and fornication. Katharine has time to reflect on this as she dies alone. Almásy has time to reflect on this as his life gradually ebbs away as he suffers from his horrific burns. He starts to remember his life, begins his confession to Caravaggio, and eventually requests assistance in hastening his own death.

The Letter to the Colossians is almost a hymn to the pure and ideal life of the Christian who follows Jesus' teaching. It praises the person so graced with integrity of heart and conscience that he or she seems to be the living example, extolled by Paul, of the Sixth and Ninth Commandments. To live an "earthly" or secularized life without standards rooted in human dignity is to die. A secular life without transcendent values is one that explicitly includes the possibility and reality of fornication, impurity, and illicit passion.

- Katharine's deceiving Geoffrey and her meeting Almásy; her fainting, deceiving people at the Christmas party; Geoffrey dressed as Santa Claus; the affair.

- Geoffrey crashing the plane, his death and Katharine's injuries; Katharine in the cave; Almásy going to get help, but being arrested instead; Katharine alone in the cave and facing her death.

- Almásy's burned body and face; being cared for by the Canadians and especially by Hana; being questioned by Caravaggio, his time for remembering his past, coming to terms with it, and making a confession; his plea to die.

KEY SCENES AND THEMES

1. The screenplay introduces a story from the Greek historian Herodotus (c. 484–425 B.C.), who is called the Father of History. He traveled extensively and spent a long time in war-time Egypt when the Athenians occupied the country. Almásy was a cartographer and a Hungarian count who also traveled extensively and stayed for a protracted time in Egypt, which is occupied first by the British and then by the Nazis during World War II. Almásy carries Herodatus' *The History* with him as if it were a bible. Unlike *The English Patient*, Herodotus' historical account of the Persian war and invasion of Greece is straightforward. Like the writer and filmmaker of *The English Patient*, he is a romantic and given to

FOR REFLECTION AND CONVERSATION

describing rather than analyzing scenes and action. Herodotus tells the story of a king, a marriage, a betrayal, and a killing, a literary and cultural variation on the story of David and Bathsheba and a parallel to *The English Patient.* What other stories or films about illicit passion mirror the story of Almásy and Katharine, David and Bathsheba? How has romanticism as a "philosophy" (a simplified definition of "romanticism" is understanding and deciding by feelings rather than reasoning) influenced present-day storytelling and the way people make moral decisions? Why did Almásy carry the book with him all the time? What are the symbols of memory in the film? What do they mean?

2. In theology, covetousness, or concupiscence, refers to intense desires that are stronger than our reason. This is a disorder attributed to original sin that creates a constant tension or pull between the flesh and the spirit. What hope, then, does the Ninth Commandment offer us for overcoming this tension, especially regarding deliberate impure thoughts and imaginings, immodesty, and sexual immorality? How can the practice of the virtues of temperance, modesty, chastity, and purity of heart help us to walk according to the Spirit? What is the effect of sinning against the Ninth Commandment for society? What can we learn from these tales of "grand passion" and their consequences as seen in the film, the Bible, and the history of the Greeks?

3. "If we think of theology as rooted in story," writes Theresa Sanders in *Celluloid Saints: Images of Sanctity in Film* (Macon, GA: Mercer University Press, 2002), "it should come as no surprise that some of the most

profoundly theological works of the past century have been movies." If we define theology with St. Anselm of Canterbury as "faith seeking understanding," is it possible for believers to find God's presence in *The English Patient*? Would you agree that *The English Patient* could be considered a theological work? Were you able to enter into the film with your moral imagination in order to understand the characters' situations, their dilemmas, and the consequences resulting from their immoral choices, from adultery to the act of assisted suicide at the end? Why or why not? Or better yet, how?

Prayer

Lord, grant us hearts that are pure, honest, and sincere, and help us to remember your commandments as we follow you day by day. Amen.

For Catechists

Catechism of the Catholic Church
Lust, nos. 2514–2516
Purification of the heart, nos. 2517–2519
Truth and lies, no. 2464
Moral permissiveness and human freedom, no. 2526

Kevin Spacey and Annette Bening in *American Beauty*.

THE NINTH COMMANDMENT

Song of Songs 8:6–7

1 Corinthians 7:1–5

Matthew 5:27–30

American Beauty

U.S.A., 1999, 116 minutes

Actors: Kevin Spacey, Annette Bening, Thora Birch, Mena Suvari, Peter Gallagher, Wes Bentley, Chris Cooper, Allison Janney

Writer: Alan Ball

Director: Sam Mendes

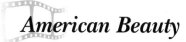

American Beauty

The Quality of Beauty

Forty-three-year-old Lester Burnham (Kevin Spacey) speaks from beyond the grave to narrate the last year of his life as if in the present. He writes for a magazine, his wife, Carolyn (Annette Bening), sells real estate, and Jane (Thora Birch), their only child, is sixteen, angry, insecure, and confused. His wife and daughter think he is a gigantic loser. Lester feels sedated. He doesn't know how he lost his life, but he is determined to get it back. Lester's job is threatened.

SYNOPSIS

New neighbors, the Fitts, move in. The father, Frank (Chris Cooper), is a homophobic former Marine with a gun collection. The mother (Allison Janney) keeps house in a daze of insecurity. The son, Ricky (Wes Bentley), is eighteen. He just spent two years in an institution for drug abuse. He videotapes whatever he thinks is extraordinary. The Burnham family is superficial, and the Fitts family is repressed.

Carolyn has a meltdown after a bad day at work. When Lester sees Angela (Mena Suvari), Jane's friend, he is immediately infatuated with her beauty. He flirts with her.

Ricky Fitts works as a waiter at a business function. He meets Lester there and offers him marijuana, which Lester accepts. Ricky tells his dad that he gets money from catering jobs, but he is actually a drug dealer. Lester overhears Angela telling Jane that he would be hot if he exercised. He starts to do so immediately. He loses his job but blackmails the company into a generous severance package. He then takes a low-end job at a fast-food restaurant. Meanwhile, Carolyn has an affair with her real estate competitor, Buddy (Peter Gallagher), who tells her that the way to release stress is to go to the firing range. She buys a gun.

Lester and Carolyn argue and are miserable. One day, she and Buddy stop for food at the drive-through, and Lester sees them kissing in the car. Frank suspects Ricky and Lester of being sexually involved and kicks his son out of the house. Frank then goes to see Lester and kisses him. Lester kindly says he has it all wrong. Lester goes in the house to find Angela, they kiss and begin to move toward sex, but stop when he finds out she is a virgin. Carolyn is on her way home determined to shoot Lester. Meanwhile, Frank shoots him. Carolyn hides her purse with the gun in it and then mourns for Lester.

COMMENTARY

American Beauty is a dark, satirical reflection on the suburban dysfunction in the realms of middle-class America. It is a film reminiscent of *The Ice Storm,* but it focuses more on the tragic absurdity in the lives of the characters.

American Beauty is a film that irritates. Its very raw revelation about how what lies behind the façade of a picture-perfect house with a white picket fence and American Beauty roses growing in the front yard is something we'd rather not gaze upon. This kind of life seems anything but funny, but the film's irony works.

American Beauty is British stage director Sam Mendes' first feature-film production. The film won five Oscars, and, in a rare move for a first-time film director, an Oscar was awarded to Mendes for his brilliant work. His next film was *Road to Perdition*. Kevin Spacey also started his career on the stage and won his first Oscar as Best Supporting Actor for *The Usual Suspects*. Spacey won the Best Actor Oscar for his personification of Lester Burnham in *American Beauty*. Annette Bening, another stage-turned-screen actor, was nominated for an Oscar for her role as the strung-out wife. The screenplay is by Alan Ball, who also created, writes, and produces the HBO hit program, *Six Feet Under*.

Focus: In American Beauty, *a marriage has collapsed. The husband and wife look elsewhere for the kind of happiness and satisfaction described in the Song of Songs, but it eludes them. Their struggles echo the sayings of Jesus in the Sermon on the Mount and Paul's reflections to the Corinthians.*

DIALOGUE WITH THE SCRIPTURES

When *American Beauty* won the Oscar for Best Film of 1999, it was the beginning of a new century, a new millennium. *American Beauty*, however, did not reflect any optimism for this new era. Rather, it seemed to sum up so much of twentieth-century American life: emptiness, false complacency, dissatisfaction, and envy eating away at the comfortable middle class, with the lurking possibility of violence. Central to this dissatisfaction was the illicit lustful covetousness—between consenting adults and between an adult and a teenager—and infidelity.

Lester Burnham is in his forties. He has allowed himself to be trapped in a suburban malaise that keeps him in routine inertia at home and in his job. As the movie opens, he tells us that he will be dead within a year, and what we are seeing turns out to be his last chance at life and happiness. To a large extent, he achieves a numb, suburban kind of happiness symbolized by a plastic shopping bag blown about by the wind among the leaves in patterns and rhythms of beauty. Ricky shows Jane this scene because it represents what passes for beauty in his world. By the time Lester might appreciate this kind of beauty, it is too late.

The sexual choices that Lester and his wife make are those that Paul reflects on in his First Letter to the Corinthians. Paul writes of both the positive and negative realities of marriage. He knows that in the world there is sexual struggle, so, in biblical and theological tradition, he urges marital fidelity and mutual love and respect. He also acknowledges the many temptations faced by married couples and how easy it is to lose self-control.

Though still living together, the Burnhams are estranged. Lester is self-absorbed, locked into his world of advertising and domestic acquiescence. Perhaps he could have achieved more in his life, but he got lost along its superficial edges. He then succumbs to what Jesus prohibits in the Sermon on the Mount: he looks at a young girl with lust. Jesus says that when a man does this, he has already committed adultery in his heart. Lester notices the beauty of his daughter's friend Angela and begins to create a fantasy life with her images. Lester crosses the moral line by proposing a sexual relationship with a high school girl, but his infatuation begins to "liberate him" in other ways: he defies his young boss, goes back to the music and pot smoking of the '70s, and gets a job in a burger joint. He loses the pressures of expectations. But to what end? The screenplay has Lester killed before he can completely face the issues treated in First Corinthians and Matthew 5. However, he shows some level of self-awareness and decency when he cuts short his liaison with Angela—discovering that she is a virgin brings him to his senses.

Carolyn Burnham is more blatant about the way she covets another man; she actually engages in an affair. The banality of Carolyn and Buddy's conversations, as well as their unexpected discovery by Lester at the drive-through, mock both fidelity and infidelity.

Were the filmmakers saying that at the end of the twentieth century the United States had lost its ideals and its grasp on moral values and that most people's lives were lived in personal futility? Perhaps. Any reflection, however, on the breaking of the Ninth Commandment in fact or "in the heart" needs to highlight the positive values that the commandment proposes as well. In chapters 6 and 7 of First Corinthians, Paul speaks of the body as being the temple of the Spirit of God and urges his readers to lives of love and purity. He writes to them with a sense of urgency that the Second Coming is close at hand, using rhetoric similar to that of the Y2K threat and apocalyptic language prevalent at the end of the twentieth century. As contemporary readers and viewers, we need something more long lasting than fear to motivate us. The famous poetic verses from the Song of Songs describe love as a seal on the heart, a force as strong as death with flames of blazing fire. These words offer us a powerful ideal to contemplate in our prayer and in our life choices.

KEY SCENES AND THEMES

- The family setting, the neighborhood; leaving the house for school and work; Carolyn getting the house ready to sell and her emotional outburst; Carolyn and Lester's conversation as they drive to the basketball game; the first time Lester sees Angela and his infatuation; Ricky videotaping Jane; the Fitts and Burnham families at breakfast; Angela, Jane, and Ricky at school.

- Lester and Carolyn at the party and meeting Buddy; Lester meeting Ricky, and Ricky selling him dope; Angela flirting with Lester, his fantasies and decision to exercise; Ricky videotaping Lester; the drug test; Ricky writing Jane's name in flames; Ricky's drug stash and money; Caroline's affair; the video of the plastic bag in the wind; the Nazi plate.

• Lester and Carolyn's argument over the lost job; Lester signaling Ricky about drugs; Frank searching Ricky's room; his confrontation of Ricky and kicking him out of the house; Carolyn and Buddy in the car at the fast-food restaurant; Frank seeing Ricky and Lester in the garage; Carolyn's journey home and the gun; Lester and Angela; Frank visiting and kissing Lester; Frank's humiliation; Lester's death; the reactions of everyone at the house.

FOR REFLECTION AND CONVERSATION

1. This is a film that is full of the characters' pithy statements about their philosophy on life. Angela's philosophy is very simple: "I don't think that there's anything worse than being ordinary," and "everything that is meant to happen will eventually happen." Jane's philosophy is even more basic. She tells her dad, "You can't all of a sudden be my best friend, just because you've got a problem." Carolyn's world view can be summed up by Buddy's motto: "In order to be successful, one must project an image of success at all times." Ricky says, "When you see something like that [a homeless woman who has frozen to death] it's like God's looking right at you, just for a second, and if you're careful you can look right back." Jane asks Ricky, "What do you see?" And his answer is, "Beauty." Lester knows that a benevolent force wanted him never to be afraid. He needs to remember that, because sometimes there is so much beauty in the world, he can't take it. Do you think these characters have any sense of faith to begin with? Do the Burnhams' and Fitts' marriages reflect any understanding of the commandments or teachings of Jesus? Why or why not? What is your philosophy of life, marriage, and commitment?

2. At the end of the film, Lester asks the audience if we remember the saying, "'Today is the first day of the rest of your life.' Well, that's true for every day except one—the day that you die." What is the meaning of life according to Lester and each of the characters (Carolyn, Jane, Angela, Ricky, Mr. and Mrs. Fitts, Buddy)? What motivates them? What are the family and cultural systems or dynamics that seem to imprison them and keep them from acting freely? What does the film say about the potentialities, freedoms, and responsibilities of the human person? What do the commandments, especially the ninth, have to say to the characters in *American Beauty*? Why are all the main characters white and upper middle class? Are the problems and issues that the characters in the film face, especially about sexual and family issues, different for other classes and races in America? Of the characters, who gains insight, grows, and changes? How? What questions does the film ask of the viewers?

3. Everything in the film, from the songs (e.g., *American Girl, The Seeker*) to the symbols (guns, the family photo, the video camera, the red door, the white house, the picket fence, the tree-lined street, windows, mirrors, cars, the plastic bag, the roses), works together with the characters to create meaning. Nothing in the film is accidental, including the names of the characters. What kind of mood did the images of suburban life, adolescence, midlife, sexuality, sexual attraction, sexual orientation, and the potential sexual activity between an adult and a high school student create for you? Does the Ninth Commandment mean anything in the context of

the film? Was the film about psychology or spirituality—or something else? Talk about your responses to these questions. What did the film mean for you? Why?

Prayer

Lord, as we struggle with our daily lives and experience depression and temptation, give us the courage to do what is right and the grace to remain faithful to you. Amen.

For Catechists

Catechism of the Catholic Church
Lust, nos. 2514–2516
Purification of the heart, nos. 2517–2519
Moral permissiveness and human freedom, no. 2526
Passions and the moral life, nos. 1767–1770

The Tenth Commandment

Introduction

Do not covet your neighbor's goods./Be content with what you have.

"Depictions of the business world," wrote journalist Jamie Wolf in 2001 (*PWC Global*), "like most things in the movies, tend to be more glamorous, more sinister, sexier, and generally larger (or smaller, more hellish and oppressive) than they are in life. We look to them less for documentary truth than as a way of fixing the meaning and place of business in our cultural mythology." Current events, however, prove that movies can capture the "truth" of corporate life, if not the exact facts.

The "meaning of business" put forth by Hollywood—in movies including *The Godfather* in the 1970s, *Wall Street* in the 1980s, *Glengarry Glen Ross* in the '90s, and *Boiler Room* and the documentary *The Corporation* in the twenty-first century—draws a cinematic landscape of corporate greed, economics, capitalism, and globalization that is morally chilling. If we enter into these films with our moral imagination, it is easy to analyze the experience of people of good will challenged to live the courage of their individual moral convictions in the workplace. Thus, the moral analysis of such movies shows the tension between the temptation to greed and the exercise of character and virtue.

Following the Decalogue in Ex 20, chapters 21–23 contain strong, casuistic injunctions about how the Israelites are to relate to one another. Chapter 22 deals with the coveting of other people's property, the punishment to be meted out to a thief or to someone who damages the property of another, and how restitution is to be made. Although the rural details were important in the nomadic phase of Israel's existence, it is easy enough to get the point: coveting another's property, stealing it, and damaging it are against God's Commandments and require punishment and restitution within the community. We see covetousness in a cruel and abhorrent form in the story of Naboth, the innocent owner of a vineyard killed by Jezebel because King Ahab coveted his vineyard.

In the Gospels, Jesus spoke about the virtue of poverty when he addressed the issue of possessions. He gave unusually stern warnings to those who put their hands to the plough to follow him, but then looked back on their former life. He said that foxes have holes and the birds of the air their nests, but the Son of Man has nowhere to lay his head. He advised the rich young man to give away his goods and become a disciple. The man turned away and was sad, for he was a man of great wealth. Jesus was not an advocate of the "greed is good" maxim made famous by Gordon Gekko in the 1987 movie *Wall Street*. Rather, he gave us an example of what it means to "have enough" and to share what we do have with the poor.

Most of us live between the extremes of greed and detachment. In the human person, there is a perennial and persistent temptation to want more than we need. This reality highlights some of the great ills of our time: the growing gap between the rich and the poor, the increase of crass materialism urged on by commercialism that creates false needs through advertising, a spiraling abuse of the earth's ecosystem by deforestation, the creation of artificial famines because of politics, and the formation of mountains of trash full of unrecyclable materials.

Many people feel the need to "keep up with the Joneses" by getting the latest, the trendiest, or the most fashionable car, appliance, or home-theater system available. Capitalism without guidance contributes to this blindness toward one's neighbor (at home or in other countries) and a lack of stewardship for the earth. Planned obsolescence (when one model expires and it is economically advantageous to replace it with a newer model), a product of the industrial and high-tech eras, is just one consequence of capitalism run amok.

A great challenge faces us as people of faith and good will. In our culture of greed, the Ten Commandments compel us to consider our responsibility to poor nations that have huge debts and inhuman working conditions brought about by multinational corporations that pay workers barely enough to exist. Emerging economic rationalism exalts the individual and the corporation at the expense of the poor and the earth. Looking at cinema stories about business can help us realize our responsibilities to our brothers and sisters.

The twentieth century saw material experiments in radical socialism in the Communist countries where the individual lived and died at the government's behest. These cultures collapsed and almost instantly embraced the opposite socioeconomic system: the unbridled capitalism fueled by consumerism, the system of the first world. The saying that any American citizen can grow up to be the president of the United States—with sufficient campaign funds—can be summed up in the title of the popular television quiz show, *Who Wants to Be a Millionaire?* This show sprang up in dozens of countries around the world almost immediately. Everyone wants to be a millionaire.

The Tenth Commandment reminds us that individual, corporate, or national greed is not good. Goods are necessary and beneficial, but, as human beings, we are bound to a moral balance between freedom and responsibility. The Tenth Commandment implies that if we do not covet, monopolies will not exist. The virtue of the commandment is sharing, and the teaching of the commandment is that we cannot take it (money or things) with us when we die.

Cuba Gooding Jr. and Tom Cruise in *Jerry Maguire*.

Jerry Maguire

U.S.A., 1996, 133 minutes

Actors: Tom Cruise, Cuba Gooding Jr., Renée Zellweger,
Kelly Preston, Jay Mohr, Jerry O'Connell,
Jonathan Lipnicki, Eric Stoltz

Writer: Cameron Crowe

Director: Cameron Crowe

 *Jerry Maguire*

"Show me the Money"

SYNOPSIS

Jerry Maguire (Tom Cruise) is a sports agent who has gradually become aware of how inhumane he and the sports promotion business have become. His conscience bothers him, and he wonders if he is "just another shark in a suit?" One sleepless night, he writes a mission statement called "The Things We Think and Do Not Say: The Future of Our Business." He distributes a copy of this scathing exposé to everyone in the office the next morning.

All of his colleagues applaud him, but, when he is fired at lunch, no one wants to be near him. As he collects his things, he challenges someone who shares his newfound ideals to come with him. A twenty-six-year-old single mother and widow, Dorothy Boyd (Renée Zellweger), is inspired by his "memo" and goes with Jerry to set up a new business. But only one client, an unexceptional Arizona Cardinals wide receiver named Rod Tidwell (Cuba Gooding Jr.), decides to keep Jerry as his agent. Jerry's fiancé breaks off their engagement.

Jerry struggles to keep star football player Frank Cushman, but, like Jerry's other former clients, he decides to go where he can get the best commercial endorsements.

Jerry gets discouraged, and Dorothy tries to keep up his spirits. She falls in love with him, and though he is merely attracted to her, he genuinely loves her young son, Ray. Dorothy's sister, Laurel (Bonnie Hunt), who runs a group for divorced women, warns her not to accept Jerry's proposal, but she does anyway.

Things go well for a while, but Dorothy realizes soon enough that this was a sympathy marriage. She tells Jerry to take a business trip and call it what it is: a "nice, long break." Jerry goes on the road to support the charismatic but temperamental Rod, who is always yelling, "Show me the money!" Just when things couldn't be worse, Rod is knocked unconscious during a game. But when he gets up and makes an amazing touchdown, Jerry realizes then that he needs and wants Dorothy to be with him because he loves her. He goes to find her and Ray.

COMMENTARY

Jerry Maguire was written and directed by Cameron Crowe, whose other credits include *Vanilla Sky, Almost Famous,* for which he won an Oscar for Best Screenplay, and *Elizabethtown.* Cuba Gooding Jr. won the Oscar for Best Supporting Actor for his portrayal of Rod Tidwell in *Jerry Maguire,* which was nominated for Best Picture and Best Screenplay as well. Crowe's very first script, the now classic *Fast Times at Ridgemont High,* launched the careers of many of today's most popular actors, including Sean Penn, Jennifer Jason Leigh, Forest Whitaker, Eric Stoltz, Nicolas Cage, and Anthony Edwards.

The inspiration for *Jerry Maguire* is said to have come from a photo Crowe saw one day of a football player and his agent. The script took over five years to develop. His wife, Nancy Wilson, wrote the theme song, "We Meet Again."

Jerry Maguire is Tom Cruise's twentieth film, and he remains one of the industry's most bankable actors. He is quite believable as the angst-ridden, commitment-shy sports agent, but Cuba Gooding Jr. as the bombastic Rod, Renée Zellweger as thoughtful and sweet Dorothy, Jonathan Lipnicki as the spiky-haired Ray, and Bonnie Hunt as the wry and wise older sister Laurel, helped to create a pleasing ensemble rather than a one-actor picture. *Jerry Maguire* is entertaining, but it is also a bold commentary on business ethics and the fleeting nature of celebrity.

Focus: The sports agency world of Jerry Maguire *says, "show us the money." Jesus warns that we cannot be slaves of money and serve God.*

DIALOGUE WITH THE SCRIPTURES

Deuteronomy 15 teaches the Israelites about "The Sabbatical Year." This year is neither a reason to take time off from work nor a warning to workaholics to slow down. It is about the issues of money, not exacting payments from one's neighbor, and a concern for the poor. It offers a stimulating challenge on how to observe the Tenth Commandment.

There is one line that comes immediately to everyone's lips when the film *Jerry Maguire* is mentioned: "Show me the money." Cuba Gooding's rendition of this sentence has become a classic. So much of the film is about wanting money: Jerry's producing the money, seeing the money, and getting the money. Most of the characters, at some stage, with the exception of Dorothy, are covetous of the others' money or the money that might be theirs someday. Since this is the world of celebrity sports endorsements, the players and their agents want the big money that has become associated with their astronomical fees and substantial percentages. The big money for agents and sports stars is in promotion, advertising endorsements, sponsorships, and, ultimately, profits gleaned from the people who purchase the merchandise associated with sports. This phenomenon is a reality of the contemporary capitalist-oriented world.

No one can argue against men and women earning good money for work and/or services rendered. It is the inflated payment to inflated egos and the consumerism of the commercial world of celebrity endorsements that do not square with the Scriptures: the ideals of Deuteronomy, the story of the early Christian community sharing their goods in the Acts of the Apostles, and the sayings of Jesus about money and the impossibility of serving two masters.

Jerry Maguire opens with the hotshot, conscience-troubled Jerry having a dream that inspires him to write a mission statement for his company. It is a fine mission statement that, if put into practice, would make the agency a model of fair play and justice. As Jerry Maguire produces copies for distribution, his colleagues applaud him in public but whisper behind his back that he will last only another week.

The movie is the story of Jerry Maguire's struggle to do the right thing by his players while being caught up in the continuous hype of big profits.

Cuba Gooding's Rod Tidwell, a struggling pro-football player, believes this hype and that he is entitled to the money that it promises. He has to come to terms with the precarious nature of professional football, with its dangers and physical injury. He succumbs to the temptation of serving the master that is mammon. But his willingness to trust Jerry and the sequences with his wife are a counterbalance to the greed syndrome in which he is caught up.

It is the same with Jerry. He knows that success as a sports agent can be a nine-day wonder and is always a gamble. What Jerry must learn is that Dorothy and Ray's love for him and their willingness to make a deep commitment to him, whether or not his future is financially successful, is the most important thing he could ever hope for.

In the aftermath of Jesus' death and resurrection, the disciples who knew him well established a community in

Jerusalem that honored people rather than achievement. Everyone was treated equally and with respect. The sharing of material goods was one of the basic principles on which the community was based.

Luke 16 is the primary Gospel teaching regarding money issues. It begins with a story about the fraudulent steward and ends with the parable of the rich man and Lazarus. It is a warning for those who are self-centered as well as the unmerciful rich. In between are sayings of Jesus about "dishonest wealth" and about honesty and trust. They culminate in his warning that we cannot be slaves both of God and of money.

The Pharisees who "loved money" mocked Jesus by responding to his words with laughter; it was the same kind of derision that greeted Jerry Maguire's mission statement. It was the hollow laughter of those who have sold their souls for money.

KEY SCENES AND THEMES

- Jerry encouraging the injured player to return to work and the derision of the injured player's son; Jerry hearing the words of his mentor and crafting the mission statement; the reaction of his colleagues; Jerry getting fired; challenging people to accompany him.

- Dorothy's belief and trust; Jerry's fiancé breaking up with him; Jerry's growing relationship with Dorothy and Ray; Laurel's women's group and her warnings to Dorothy; Jerry trying to get more clients and representing Rod.

- Jerry and Rod trying to make things work; Rod's relationship with his wife and family; Jerry and Dorothy's marriage and separation; Rod's success on the field and Jerry's realization that he needs Dorothy and Ray more than success.

FOR REFLECTION AND CONVERSATION

1. Jesus knew that "the worldly take more initiative than the other-worldly when it comes to dealing with their own kind" (Lk 16:8). Talk about the "values" of the sports management company in the film and contrast them to Jesus' teaching on ambition and wealth. What epiphany caused Jerry to write the mission statement? How did he grow and change over the course of the film?

2. "The Tenth Commandment concerns the intentions of the heart; with the ninth, it summarizes all the precepts of the Law" (*CCC*, no. 2534). Both these commandments deal with the desires of the heart and can help us to channel them toward our personal good and the common good. What virtues and values (generosity, love, hope, "enoughness," care, justice, stewardship, etc.) in the film express the common good, and which character personifies them? What virtues do the main characters eventually identify with and why? How are the consequences of disordered desires for money, sex, and power countered by Jesus' example and teaching about poverty, chastity, and obedience in the Gospels? What do these evangelical counsels mean to you personally? How can they extend to your place in and relationship to the world?

3. The voice of wisdom and conscience in the film is that of Jerry's mentor, Dicky Fox. Which of his sayings impressed you the most, and how did his voice influence Jerry's choices and behavior? Conscience is that inner sense of what is right and wrong in one's conduct, the motive that impels a person to right action. The Christian spiritual life includes a daily examen of conscience on both a general and a

particular level. The general examen is an overview of one's moral behavior during the day. The particular examen invites a person to look at his or her tendencies regarding moral misbehavior, such as lust, greed, anger, the admonitions of the Ten Commandments, the encouragement of the Beatitudes, and so forth. The fruit of this examen is self-knowledge and, through prayer, the ability to act differently tomorrow, to make amends, to start again on the road to fulfilling one's true destiny as a child of God and member of the human family. Do I make a daily examen of conscience? Why or why not? How did Jerry grow in self-awareness about his moral behavior? How was he able to continue growing as a mature man?

Prayer

Lord, teach us to be satisfied, not greedy, givers, not hoarders. Help us to be grateful for your blessings and generous to those who are more in need than ourselves. Amen.

For Catechists

Catechism of the Catholic Church
Greed and avarice, nos. 2534, 2536
Envy, nos. 2538–2539
Poverty of heart, nos. 2544–2546

The Business of Strangers

U.S.A., 2001, 80 minutes

Actors: Stockard Channing, Julia Stiles, Fred Weller

Writer: Patrick Stettner

Director: Patrick Stettner

The Business of Strangers

Envy, Power, and Control

SYNOPSIS

Julie Styron (Stockard Channing) is a polished, uptight, high-powered executive for a software development company. She is on her way to make an important presentation with the help of a technical assistant from the main office, Paula Murphy (Julia Stiles). Styron has to go it alone, however, because Murphy comes late—on purpose. Styron is furious, fires her, and then heads for the hotel.

Julie Styron has demanded that her associate Nick Harris (Fred Weller) meet her at the hotel for a brief meeting. When he arrives, Styron finds out she has been shut out of an important board meeting. She fears for her job. The topic of their meeting falls by the wayside. Soon she gets a call and discovers that she has been made CEO of the company. She is pleased, almost happy. Nick leaves to make his flight.

Styron notices Paula in the bar. Her flight was cancelled. Julie has a change of heart and rehires her. They have a drink, and Styron gets Paula a room. Though beautiful, Paula has tattoos and an attitude that makes her hard to like. The two women overcome their mutual animosity and go running, swimming, and then to the sauna together.

258

They find Nick in the bar. His flight was also cancelled. Later, they leave him and return to Styron's room and continue drinking. Paula says she knows Nick and that he raped a friend of hers. Styron, in a drunken haze, is outraged and demands that they do something, but Paula refuses. When Nick shows up at the room, Styron wants to send him away, but Paula decides to welcome him. Styron is confused. Paula puts several pills she has stolen from Styron in his drink. When he passes out, the women move him to a storage area in the hotel. They write all over his body and mistreat him badly. Styron thinks that it was really Paula who was raped and realizes that she is seriously disturbed. Paula really does not know Nick. They make sure Nick is still alive and return to the room to sleep. In the morning, Styron watches as Paula steals money from her purse and leaves. She gets dressed and goes to the airport as if nothing were amiss. Nick joins her there, unable to remember what happened. Across the airport lounge, they both watch Paula, who is in a world of her own.

COMMENTARY

The Business of Strangers seems as if it could have been written for the stage, however, it is an original screenplay written and directed by Patrick Stettner. The skillful performance of the burnt-out executive by Stockard Channing, who has had a long stage and screen career from *Grease* to *Six Degrees of Separation,* is effective. Young film actress Julia Stiles (*Save the Last Dance, Hamlet, Mona Lisa Smile, The Bourne Identity,* and *The Bourne Supremacy*) is convincing and frightening as the angry young woman who may or may not be telling the truth about anything in her life. The performances of both actresses ensure that the perspective of some women relating to the world of business dominates the film. Fred Weller (*The Shape of Things*) plays the only major masculine role. He is a corporate headhunter who becomes the target of the women's calumny and hatred toward men in general.

**DIALOGUE WITH
THE SCRIPTURES**

Focus: Paula's lying tongue, of which the Letter of James speaks, manipulates Julie Styron, a self-made business-woman. In the Jezebel-like scenario of the film, Julie has the opportunity to look at her values and to find where her heart and her treasure are.

The colorful narrative of Jezebel's coveting Naboth's vineyard in First Kings is one of the most vivid illustrations of sin against the Tenth Commandment in the Old Testament. The exhortations in the First Letter to Timothy, which discusses the ruin and destruction caused by the love of money, the root of all evils, echoes the greed that propels envy into murder. James' catalogue of the evils of those who lack religion or, as in the case of the characters in *The Business of Strangers,* who make position and prestige their religion, are all illustrated in the movie: envy, rivalry, insults, evil suspicions, mutual frictions, and so forth.

Julie and Paula, who cross paths in *The Business of Strangers,* are not quite as ruthless as Jezebel, but close enough. Each one of them has her violent moments: Julia, when she fires Paula in anger, and Paula, wanting and getting retribution for Nick's alleged rape. They are matched when they game play, humiliate, and batter Nick.

In comparison to Jezebel, who sets up the murder of Naboth so her husband, Ahab, can take possession of the dead man's vineyard, the interaction of Julie Styron and Paula is subtler. The screenwriter sets up relationships so that the characters can take control of the situation socially and at work. Though Julie might think she has control over Paula, the disturbed Paula deceives and outwits her. Paula also acts as a catalyst for Julie to reconsider what her friendless, work-centered life really amounts to.

When talking about her life, Julie Styron illustrates an important aspect of the Tenth Commandment. She asks what happens when you have achieved all that you have struggled for and possess all that you have coveted, all that you have desired? Julie is a self-made businesswoman in a tough man's world. She has chosen not to have children. She is divorced. She spends a great deal of her time at airports, exercising in gyms, or frequenting bars in hotels en route to a flurry of business appointments. The fulfillment of her ambitions has resulted in a growing inner emptiness.

For Jezebel, the fulfillment of all her ambitions also eventually results in emptiness. The Lord spoke a curse through the prophet Elijah, saying that dogs would devour Jezebel. On the other hand, after her bewildering experience of befriending Paula and their bizarre treatment of the unconscious Nick, Julie has a chance, like Ahab, to do some soul-searching and to change her life. Stockard Channing's final look at the camera offers a glimmer of a smile and hope.

This is the message of Jesus in the Sermon on the Mount when he talks about building up our treasure in heaven. He knows that the goods of this world can deteriorate, that market prices can go down, and that thieves can steal possessions. Julie realizes that Paula has the capacity to rob Julie of her self-respect and to put her in danger of being apprehended, losing her job, and perhaps going to prison. Jesus urges us to look beyond our greed, envy, coveting, and possessiveness to the consequences for self and others. He urges us to store up values in our lives that can help us to withstand any disaster.

The hearts of those who succumb to temptations against the Tenth Commandment remain with their great but ephemeral temporal treasure. These people run the risk of completely losing themselves, their hearts, and everyone they truly love.

The hearts of those who choose a life of virtue and values are with God, who is, in fact, their treasure.

KEY SCENES AND THEMES

- Julie Styron's presentation to the company; Paula arriving late, the company closing the presentation, and Julie firing Paula.

- Paula's story about Nick and the rape; her leading Julie to having feelings of anger and revenge against Nick; their subsequent humiliation of him.

- Julie and Nick discuss whether he was ever in Boston; Julie's realization that Paula invented her story; Paula looking at Julie silhouetted against the window; Julie wondering about her future and looking at the audience with the slightest of smiles.

FOR REFLECTION AND CONVERSATION

1. *The Business of Strangers* takes us into the world of corporate business through the experiences of two women. While *Glengarry Glen Ross, Boiler Room,* and *Wall Street* are also concerned with the competitiveness, ambition, and greed of the business world, they took place in and revealed a man's world of boardrooms and market floors. The macho ethos of achievement at all costs defined the behavior of the characters. Except for a few moments of an information technology presentation, *The Business of Strangers* does not take us into boardrooms. The rest of the movie takes place in a hotel where the three central characters are stranded, waiting for delayed flights. How does the film create a world characterized by a feminine ethos of relationships that include power and control? Do you think the film's scenario is credible? What is really going on? Is it real or some kind of a dream, a nightmare? How does Paula describe the difference between a man's world and a woman's world? A man's world is usually marked, or stereotyped, by drinking, swearing, and talking about sex. Does the film seem more dis-

turbing because the key characters are women behaving badly? Is the film trying to equalize the playing field or to expose a double standard? Why or why not?

2. In July 2004, the Vatican issued a letter, *The Collaboration of Men and Women in the Church and in the World*. It says:

> women learn to love inasmuch as they are unconditionally loved, they learn respect for others inasmuch as they are respected, they learn to know the face of God inasmuch as they receive a first revelation of it from a father and a mother full of attention in their regard. Whenever these fundamental experiences are lacking, society as a whole suffers violence and becomes in turn the progenitor of more violence. It means also that women should be present in the world of work and in the organization of society and that women should have access to positions of responsibility which allow them to inspire the policies of nations and to promote innovative solutions to economic and social problems (no. 13).

How does this paragraph inform our experience and understanding of the relationships between men and women in the workplace and our interpretation of The Business of Strangers? Does it apply? Does this quote support or put down women in the workplace? Why or why not?

3. There are different kinds of feminism expressed in contemporary society. One kind is based on the equal sharing of power in which women seek to become exactly like men in both negative and positive aspects. The Christian idea of feminism is relational and expressed in the truth that God created men and women equal in humanity and dignity. What happens, however, when envy, ambition, aggression, money, sex, and power become part of

the relationship between men and women? What are your thoughts on how the Tenth Commandment and the film relate to these characteristics? Statistics show that the rate of men abusing women and children is growing at an alarming rate. How do you resolve and express the quality of relationships between men and women in such a culture?

Prayer

Lord, touch our hearts so that we may recognize you as our true treasure. Amen.

For Catechists

Catechism of the Catholic Church
The disorder of covetous desires, nos. 2535–2540
The desires of the spirit, nos. 2541-2543
Poverty of heart, nos. 2544–2547
The Beatitudes, nos. 1716–1717
Kidnapping, no. 2297

THE TENTH COMMANDMENT

2 Samuel 12:1–12

2 Corinthians 9:6–14

Matthew 25:14–30

Glengarry Glen Ross

U.S.A., 1992, 97 minutes

Actors: Al Pacino, Jack Lemmon, Ed Harris, Alan Arkin,
Kevin Spacey, Jonathan Pryce, Alec Baldwin

Writer: David Mamet

Director: James Foley

Glengarry Glen Ross

The Violence of Greed

SYNOPSIS

Four real estate salesmen, Shelley (Jack Lemmon), Dave (Ed Harris), Ricky (Al Pacino), and George (Alan Arkin), are in a restaurant in a New York suburb. They are whining about the evening strategy meeting that they are supposed to attend at the offices of Premiere Properties across the street. Except for Ricky, they all go. Ricky stays to close a deal with a man he met at the bar, James (Jonathan Pryce). Ricky manages to get a check and a signed contract from him.

Blake (Alec Baldwin), the representative from the main office, delivers a brutal, humiliating, dehumanizing speech to the men and tells them that they must always be closing [a deal] or that they are worth nothing. He proposes a contest: the first prize is a Cadillac, the second prize is a set of steak knives, and the third prize is to be fired. Blake holds out a batch of cards with new leads on them about a development project, but he will only give them to "closers." He outlines the sales protocol: attention, interest, decision, action! So the men are left with old leads, that is, forms people filled out months before to ask for information about the real estate development project.

Shelley makes a deal with the office manager, John (Kevin Spacey), to share profits on any closings he makes. Shelley leaves to follow up old leads and is unsuccessful. His daughter is in the hospital, and he needs to find money to continue to pay for her treatment. George and Dave devise a scheme to rob the office that very night, take the batch of new leads, and sell them to a colleague, who is now in business for himself.

There is a robbery that night. The contracts from the day before, the batch of new leads, and the phones have all been taken. The police interrogate the four salesmen. James comes in to get his check back because his wife doesn't want to go through with the property purchase. Shelley confesses that he robbed the office. They are all verbally abusive to one another and blame each other. But they press on, always salesmen.

COMMENTARY

Playwright and screenwriter David Mamet won the Pulitzer Prize for Drama in 1984 for his play *Glengarry Glen Ross*. It was made into a film in 1992. The dialogue in Mamet's films is measured and deliberate, and in none more so than *Glengarry Glen Ross*. The film does not mask the fact that it is a filmed play, much like *The Big Kahuna* or *On Golden Pond*. The film still delivers blistering insights into the cutthroat world of corporate business and the consequences for salesmen who are not always "closing" a deal.

The mostly male cast is superb, made up of many Academy Award-winning or nominated actors including the venom-spewing hatchet man sent from downtown played by Alec Baldwin, the con man you hope you'll never meet played by Al Pacino, the bitter Ed Harris, and Jack Lemmon's despair-ridden, sad figure of masculine failure.

Direction is by James Foley, who also directed *The Chamber* (1996) and co-directed Madonna's *The Immaculate*

Collection, which includes, among others, the music video, *Papa Don't Preach* (1990).

> *Focus: The greed of David merits the condemnation of Nathan.* Glengarry Glen Ross *recreates the cutthroat world of salesmen whose ethos is the same competitiveness, greed, and envy that the Tenth Commandment condemns. Jesus exhorts us to the opposite in his parable of judgment.*

DIALOGUE WITH THE SCRIPTURES

In Oliver Stone's *Wall Street* (1987), inside trader Gordon Gekko promoted the slogan "Greed is good," and it became a byword for the era. *Glengarry Glen Ross* was written about the same time, and it brought to the screen a vision of the corporate world of real estate salesmen and the conflict between need and greed. The Tenth Commandment refers to covetousness, envy, and greed, that is, disordered desires; *Glengarry Glen Ross,* with its frank, blunt, and crude dialogue, is a drama about a worldview characterized by those same drives. One reviewer wrote that *Glengarry Glen Ross* "speaks forcefully about decency being snuffed out by desire, good men taking wrong turns despite their best efforts, and the stench of the American dream gone mad."* The verbal violence and the disrespect for persons present in the film support this analysis.

The speeches that David Mamet continually puts into the mouths of his characters are manifestos of the corporate failure to acknowledge and live by the values of justice, humility, poverty, and true happiness proposed by the Tenth Commandment.

David's condemnation by the prophet Nathan in the Second Book of Samuel illustrates this failure (already discussed in *The English Patient*). Nathan told David a parable about a rich man who had flocks in abundance, but who

---

* Kilmaney Fane Saunders, ed., *Radio Times Guide to Films* (London: BBC Worldwide Limited, 2000).

took the ewe lamb from a poor neighbor and made a meal of it for his visitors. David was indignant at hearing of such a covetous and greedy injustice, and he condemned the man in the story. "You are the man," says Nathan. The men in *Glengarry Glen Ross* are presented in a far more complex way, but the final impression they make on the audience is one of disgust at their lies, tactics, cajoling, and merciless treatment of naive clients. The salesmen and their bosses are trapped by the culture of "greed is good." Nathan declares that restitution should be made to the poor man of the parable. At this stage of their lives, with their desperation to close sales, to be top salesman of the month, and to win the prize car for being top salesman, the salesmen have no awareness of the need for restitution to the people they have conned. Blake's motivational speech is full of abuse and humiliation; it is the "gospel" they work by.

Paul, writing to the Corinthians, knew about hard work with gains and profit. He knew that thin sowing would only produce thin reaping. He sounds as if he were about to develop something of a work and profit ethic. But he offers a radical alternative. He spoke of service to the community. His keynote word is the opposite of greed—it is generosity. He saw generosity as a blessing, a spirituality of possessions that are not meant to be accumulated for one's self, but for the service of others. This spirituality of generosity is "glorifying God for...obedient faith in the Gospel of Christ."

Jesus offers us a parable of the kingdom on this same theme. It is one that the real estate salesmen might have adopted as their own if they knew or thought about it. The parable tells about a man who, before going on a long trip, calls in his three servants and entrusts five talents (a unit of money) to the first, two to the second, and one to the third. When he returns, he sounds like the head of a corporation when he calls his servants to make an account of what they have done with the money. Even his method of dealing with the man who buried his talent sounds like capitalist policy. He complains that the servant did not earn interest on the money he buried instead of investing. So the man gives the servant's money to the one who had five and managed to earn another five. The man, or CEO, commends the astuteness of his servants who make a profit. Recall that in Luke 16, Jesus commends the worldly prudence of the steward who secures his future by "cooking" the books of his master's debtors after he has been dismissed. Although the heart of the parable's lesson centers on being ready for the coming of the kingdom, its juxtaposition with *Glengarry Glen Ross* creates the opportunity to reflect on the worship of money that Jesus warns against as well.

While Jesus talks of making monetary profits, he also says that the key to successful business transactions is faithful commitment. It is not profit for greed or for profit's sake, but a conscientious and committed service that should underlie all dealings with money and goods.

The key scriptural ideas of generosity, fidelity, and commitment challenge a culture that defies the Tenth Commandment and offers wealth as the goal of life.

KEY SCENES AND THEMES

- Blake's speech in the real estate office about bad leads, bad strategy, and the need to always be closing; the various reactions of the salesmen; Shelley's need for help; begging for leads on the Glengarry properties.

- Ricky and the man at the bar; schmoozing with him; conning him; lies and desperation; Shelley trying to sell door-to-door in the rain; the break-in and cover-up.

- The interviews by the police; the reaction of the office manager; Shelley accepting responsibility for the break-in; the salesmen continuing as before and verbally abusing one another.

1. *Glengarry Glen Ross* is arguably one of the most violent films ever made because of the brutality of the language and the steel-edged, venomous, dehumanizing way in which it is delivered—all for the sake of making a sale. How did the film make you feel? How is the language and tone a sign of the inner reality of Blake, his bosses, and the salesmen? What could have broken the out-of-control capitalist cycle that these middle-class American men were caught up in? Is it possible to give capitalism a conscience? If so, how?

2. It is a fact that most people struggle to survive even though the wealth of individuals and average per capita income in the United States and other countries continue to grow. But economic, agricultural, and manufacturing globalization creates many more victims than it helps because it moves forth relentlessly without conscience, oversight, transparency, or guidance by a consensus of nations. Talk about what the principles of Catholic social teaching (discussed under *Cold Mountain* as well) bring to the debate about the profit of a few through globalization. Discuss: 1) the inherent dignity of the human person; 2) subsidiarity: that no higher level community should strip another community of their capacity to see, judge, and act on their own behalf; 3) the idea that the common good be the determinant of economic social organization; 4) the universal destination (or distribution) of goods based on the idea that ownership of property is not an absolute right; 5) solidarity, the alternative to globalization based on empathy for others; 6) an option for the poor from the social, economic, and cultural vantage point of the least among us; and, finally, 7) the integrity of creation.

3. One critic called Shelley's character a "chronic loser." Do you agree with this assessment? He is a man nearing retirement with a sick daughter to care for. What are his options? In an era in which many corporations are using or losing the retirement funds of their employees, how does a person who may have spent his or her whole life trying to live the Commandments and is now nearing retirement face the future? In the economic free-trade zones in developing countries, how do sweatshop workers cope with unjustly low wages and terrible working conditions so that multinational corporations can profit? What is the lasting response of a believer in these circumstances?

Prayer

Lord, you understand the desperation of those who struggle to make ends meet, who are consumed by the desire to do better with their lives, but are trapped by material needs or their disordered desires for more. Help them to trust you more and to trust in your providence. Amen.

For Catechists

Catechism of the Catholic Church
Greed and avarice, nos. 2534, 2536
Human dignity, nos. 1701–1704
The Beatitudes, nos. 1716, 1717
Conscience, nos. 1776–1778
Economic activity and social justice, no. 2426
Human work, nos. 2427, 2430, 2432, 2434
Unemployment, no. 2436
The right to economic initiative, no. 2429

Appendices

Contents by Movie Title

Movie Title	Commandment	Scripture	Page
Princess Caraboo	1	Gn 3:1–13; Rom 13:8–10; Mt 20:20–21	Page 21
Save the Last Dance	6	Ru 2–4; 1 Cor 13:4–13; Jn 2:1–11	Page 151
Simone	1	Ex 32:11–14; Ps 113; Acts 14:8–18; Lk 12:16–21	Page 29
Ten Commandments, The	All	Ex 20:1–17; Dt 5:1–6:13; Rom 12:8–10; Mk 10:17–22	Page 1
Time to Kill, A	5	Ex 21:24–25; Lv 24:10–23; Dt 19:21; Rom 12:14–21; Mt 5:38–42	Page 134
Tuesdays with Morrie	3	Ex 31:12–17; Heb 12:22–25; Mk 2:23–3:6	Page 72
Unfaithful	6	Hos 2:1–25; 1 Cor 6:15–20; Jn 8:1–7	Page 165
Veronica Guerin	8	Dn 14:1–22; Eph 4:22–25; 6:14; Jn 18:33–38	Page 207
Witness	3	Zep 3:11–13; Rv 21:1–8; Mt 11:25–30	Page 78

Contents by Scripture Passages			
Scripture	**Movie Title**	**Commandment**	**Page**
Gn 1:27; 2:22–23	*Lantana*	6	Page 158
Gn 3:1–7	*Phone Booth*	8	Page 214
Gn 3:1–13	*Princess Caraboo*	1	Page 21
Gn 4:3–16	*Jackie Brown*	7	Page 189
Gn 37	*Finding Nemo*	4	Page 98
Gn 48:1–12	*On Golden Pond*	4	Page 107
Ex 17:8–16	*Glory*	2	Page 53
Ex 20:1–17	*Ten Commandments, The*	All	Page 1
Ex 21:24–25	*Time to Kill, A*	5	Page 134
Ex 31:12–17	*Tuesdays with Morrie*	3	Page 72
Ex 32:11–14	*Simone*	1	Page 29
Lv 24:10–23	*Time to Kill, A*	5	Page 134
Dt 25:13–16	*Italian Job, The*	7	Page 175
Ru 2–4	*Save the Last Dance*	6	Page 151
1 Sm 16:19–23	*Pianist, The*	5	Page 127
2 Sm 11:2–12, 25	*English Patient, The*	9	Page 231
2 Sm 12:1–12	*Glengarry Glen Ross*	10	Page 265
1 Kgs 21:11–29	*Business of Strangers, The*	10	Page 258
Jb 1:1–2:10	*Bruce Almighty*	2	Page 45
Jb 10:8–12	*Cider House Rules, The*	5	Page 140

Scripture	Movie Title	Commandment	Page
Ps 113	*Simone*	1	Page 29
Prv 12:12–28	*Client, The*	All	Page 11
Sg 8:6–7	*American Beauty*	9	Page 239
Sir 3:1–18	*Ordinary People*	4	Page 114
Sir 5:11–17	*Liar, Liar*	8	Page 199
Sir 23:16–27, 21:11–21	*First Wives Club, The*	9	Page 224
Is 2:1–5	*Cold Mountain*	3	Page 87
Dn 13:1–64	*Absolute Power*	2	Page 62
Dn 14:1–22	*Veronica Guerin*	8	Page 207
Hos 2:1–25	*Unfaithful*	6	Page 165
Amos 2:6–7; 6:1–7	*Boiler Room*	7	Page 182
Zep 3:11–13	*Witness*	3	Page 78
Mt 5:21–26, 39	*Pianist, The*	5	Page 127
Mt 5:27–30	*American Beauty*	9	Page 239
Mt 5:37	*Liar, Liar*	8	Page 199
Mt 5:38–42	*Time to Kill, A*	5	Page 134
Mt 6:19–21; 22:15–22	*Business of Strangers, The*	10	Page 258
Mt 11:25–30	*Witness*	3	Page 78
Mt 13:44–46	*Cold Mountain*	3	Page 87

Scripture	Movie Title	Commandment	Page
Mt 15:10–20	*English Patient, The*	9	Page 231
Mt 20:20–21	*Princess Caraboo*	1	Page 21
Mt 20:24–28	*Absolute Power*	2	Page 62
Mt 25:14–30	*Glengarry Glen Ross*	10	Page 265
Mk 2:23–28	*Cider House Rules, The*	5	Page 140
Mk 2:23–3:6	*Tuesdays with Morrie*	3	Page 72
Mk 9:14–29	*Gift, The*	1	Page 36
Mk 10:2–12	*Lantana*	6	Page 158
Mk 10:17–22	*Ten Commandments, The*	All	Page 1
Lk 2:41–52	*Finding Nemo*	4	Page 98
Lk 11:27–28	*Ordinary People*	4	Page 114
Lk 12:16–21	*Simone*	1	Page 29
Lk 14:30–33	*Glory*	2	Page 53
Lk 16:1-8	*Jackie Brown*	7	Page 189
Lk 16:9–15	*Jerry Maguire*	10	Page 251
Lk 18:9–14	*Bruce Almighty*	2	Page 45
Lk 19:1–10	*Boiler Room*	7	Page 182
Lk 23:39–43	*Italian Job, The*	7	Page 175
Jn 2:1–11	*Save the Last Dance*	6	Page 151
Jn 8:1–7	*Unfaithful*	6	Page 165
Jn 8:32	*Liar, Liar*	8	Page 199

Scripture	Movie Title	Commandment	Page
Jn 14:21–24	*Client, The*	All	Page 11
Jn 15:1–6, 9–12	*First Wives Club, The*	9	Page 224
Jn 18:33–38	*Veronica Guerin*	8	Page 207
Jn 18:25–27; 21:15–17	*Phone Booth*	8	Page 214
Jn 19:25–27	*On Golden Pond*	4	Page 107
Acts 4:32–35	*Jerry Maguire*	10	Page 251
Acts 5:1–11	*Boiler Room*	7	Page 182
Acts 14:8–18	*Simone*	1	Page 29
Acts 17:23–31	*Gift, The*	1	Page 36
Rom 12:8–10	*Ten Commandments, The*	All	Page 1
Rom 12:14–21	*Time to Kill, A*	5	Page 134
Rom 13:8–10	*Princess Caraboo*	1	Page 21
1 Cor 6:15–20	*Unfaithful*	6	Page 165
1 Cor 7:1–5	*American Beauty*	9	Page 239
1 Cor 13:4–13	*Save the Last Dance*	6	Page 151
2 Cor 4:6–12	*Cider House Rules, The*	5	Page 140
2 Cor 9:6–14	*Glengarry Glen Ross*	10	Page 265
2 Cor 12:7–10	*Bruce Almighty*	2	Page 45
Eph 2:13–18	*Cold Mountain*	3	Page 87
Eph 2:13–22	*Pianist, The*	5	Page 127

Movie Ratings Chart*				
Movie Title	**MPAA (1)**	**BBFC (2)**	**OFLC (3)**	**USCC (4)**
Absolute Power	R	15	M	A-IV
American Beauty	R	18	MA	O
Boiler Room	R	15	N/A	A-III
Bruce Almighty	PG-13	12A	M	A-III
Business of Strangers, The	R	15	MA	O
Cider House Rules, The	PG-13	12	M	O
Client, The	PG-13	15	M	A-III
Cold Mountain	R	15	MA	L
English Patient, The	R	15	M	A-IV
Finding Nemo	G	U	G	A-I
First Wives Club, The	PG	PG	PG	A-III
Gift, The	R	15	MA	A-III
Glengarry Glen Ross	R	15	M	A-III
Glory	PG	15	M	A-III
Italian Job, The	PG-13	12A	M	A-III
Jackie Brown	R	15	MA	O
Jerry Maguire	R	15	M	A-III
Lantana	R	15	M	A-IV
Liar, Liar	PG-13	12	M	A-III

Movie Title	MPAA (1)	BBFC (2)	OFLC (3)	USCC (4)
On Golden Pond	PG	PG	PG	A-III
Ordinary People	R	15	N/A	A-III
Phone Booth	R	15	M	A-IV
Pianist, The	R	15	MA	A-III
Princess Caraboo	PG	N/A	N/A	A-II
Save the Last Dance	PG-13	12	M	A-III
Simone	PG-13	PG	PG	A-III
Ten Commandments, The	G	U	G	A-I
Time to Kill, A	R	15	M	A-IV
Tuesdays with Morrie	N/A	PG	N/A	N/A
Unfaithful	R	15	MA	A-IV
Veronica Guerin	R	18	MA	A-III
Witness	R	15	N/A	A-IV

* Information regarding the rating codes may be found on each organization's website.
  1. MPAA: Motion Picture Association of America, United States; www.mpaa.org.
  2. BBFC: British Board of Film Classification, United Kingdom; www.bbfc.co.uk.
  3. OFLC: The Office for Film and Literature Classification, Australia; www.oflc.gov.au.
  4. USCC: United States Catholic Conference; www.nccbuscc.org.

Suggested Scenes for Viewing/Discussion	
(alphabetical order)	
Absolute Power	The aftermath of the murder, the helplessness of the president, Gloria taking over and organizing the cover-up.
American Beauty	When Ricky shows Jane the video of the plastic bag in the wind.
Boiler Room	Jim Young's motivational speeches and the broker's and the recruits' responses.
Bruce Almighty	When God and Bruce meet and God tells Bruce that he cannot impose on anyone's free will; when Bruce throws his phone outside and it keeps going off until he answers it; when Bruce tries to handle prayers by computerizing all the requests.
Business of Strangers, The	Paula's story about Nick and the rape, leading Julia on to feelings of anger and their revenge on Nick and his humiliation.
Cider House Rules, The	Homer's dilemma about carrying out the abortion and his explanation for his own personal stance and the reasons for his final choice.
Client, The	When Reggie Love explains the compass to Mark and the end of the film when she gives it to him.
Cold Mountain	Inman and the woman with the caravan who takes him in; their talk about war; the final scene when Ada and her daughter prepare for the meal and the meal itself.
English Patient, The	Katharine alone in the cave facing her death and remembering what she had done.

Finding Nemo	Marlin and Nemo on the way to school; Nemo's being caught; Marlin's grief and his decision to find his son.
First Wives Club, The	When the women decide that helping other women is better than vengeance.
Gift, The	One of the scenes when Annie tells her client to get help.
Glengarry Glen Ross	Blake's speech at the beginning of the film.
Glory	The assault on Fort Wagner; Trip taking up the flag and the men, black and white, fighting and dying together.
Italian Job, The	Charlie trying to convince Stella to help them get the gold back; the final scene when Charlie outwits Steve and the crooks decide their future.
Jackie Brown	Jackie making her final decision to take the money, and Max deciding to remain honest.
Jerry Maguire	When the sleepless Jerry writes his mission statement and his remembering Dicky Fox's wisdom.
Lantana	Leon sitting in the car and listening to the tapes of his wife's sessions with the psychiatrist and learning about her feelings.
Liar, Liar	Max's wish; Fletcher telling the truth as he goes to work; Fletcher trying to get Max to "un-wish" the wish.
On Golden Pond	Norman and Billy in danger on the river when Norman faces the possibility of death.
Ordinary People	Any of Conrad's discussions with the psychiatrist (and the flashbacks during the sessions).
Phone Booth	Stu's public confession of the lies in his life.

Pianist, The	Wladyslaw Szpilman playing the keyboard silently in the abandoned house; the scenes with Wladyslaw and the German soldier in the house.
Princess Caraboo	At the end, when Mary tells her story to Mr. Gutch in the stable.
Save the Last Dance	The final dance audition after Derek arrives to the end.
Simone	Simone at the rock concert when people think she is really there, including Victor's wife and daughter who want to meet her.
Ten Commandments, The	Moses on Sinai and the giving of the Decalogue.
Time to Kill, A	Jake's closing statement to the jury
Tuesdays with Morrie	Any of the discussions between Morrie and Mitch about life.
Unfaithful	The finale as the couple waits at the traffic light deciding whether or not to go to the police.
Veronica Guerin	Veronica's visit to the home of the drug lord and his violence toward her and her continuing her work.
Witness	Daniel's grandfather explaining to him why the Amish do not use guns; Daniel ringing the bell at the end and the community coming to the family's rescue.

How to Use *Lights, Camera...Faith! The Ten Commandments* and Other Volumes in the Series

Liturgical Use

Preparation for the Leader

Remote preparation

- Obtain a copy of the book for the proper liturgical year cycle (*Lights, Camera... Faith! A Movie Lectionary* www.pauline.org).

- Read the chapter for the Sunday readings you wish to use with the lectionary.

- Locate the DVD/video.

- Research the film on the Web to consider several ways to "see" the film (start with www.imdb.org; see the handout for others).

- Arrange for refreshments.

- Prepare a parish bulletin notice or some kind of promotion.

- Secure viewing equipment and appropriate-sized space.

- Secure a license to show the film (www.mplc.com). (If you show videos, it's a good idea to get a yearly license for your institution.)

Proximate preparation

- Read and reflect on Scripture readings.

- Preview the film.

- Decide if the readings, especially the Gospel, can be read by multiple lectors to provide some dramatic background to the event.

- Preview the film.

- Read the chapter from the *Movie Lectionary* and reflect on the questions.

- Prepare the space and refreshments.
- Check equipment.

The Movie Lectionary Event

- Lower the lighting, play music from the soundtrack of the film softly in the background as people gather.
- Begin the event on time.
- Let the group know that it's important to let the film run through to the final credits at the end.
- Read the Scriptures; use various readers if possible.
- Only read the synopsis if it seems like the group "needs" it.
- Start the film and run the film through the last credits.
- Break for 10 minutes (wine and cheese for adults works very well).
- Gather again for the conversation; let people know they can bring their snacks with them.
- Read the commentary on the Gospel aloud.
- Ask the first question and be prepared to respond in order to get the dialogue going.
- Refer to the "Key Scenes and Themes" to help move the conversation along.
- Let the conversation continue as long as it seems appropriate (usually 30–40 minutes).
- End with the prayer.

How to Use Lights, Camera...Faith! The Ten Commandments

Remote preparation

- Preview the entire film in advance of a group screening (whether you show the film in its entirety or only a clip).

• Decide how you will integrate the film with your class presentation or theme of the group meeting.

Proximate preparation

• Make sure you have all the needed equipment and that everyone can see and hear.

• Make sure the room can be darkened, the air can circulate, and that outside noise will not interfere.

• Read the introduction to the section of the book in which the film is located (e.g., commandment, beatitude, etc.).

• Read the entire chapter about the film.

The Scripture-Movie Event

See "The Movie Lectionary Event."

Clips

Clips are appropriate to use

• within a homily or sermon

• for reflection at the end of Mass or service

• to introduce or reinforce the theme of a religious education class

• to use to prepare for the Sunday liturgy, as part of *lectio divina,* or other prayer service

Preparation

• Preview the entire film first and evaluate its use for your audience or congregation.

• Identify the location of the clip on the video or DVD.

• Try out all equipment ahead of time; make sure everyone will be able to see and hear.

• Decide on the best moment to use the clip.

Recommended Resources on Movies and Religious Themes

Books

Anker, Roy M. *Catching Light: Looking for God at the Movies.* Grand Rapids, MI: Wm. B. Eerdmans Publishing Co., 2005.

Barsotti, Catherine, Robert K. Johnston, *Finding God at the Movies: 33 Films of Reel Faith.* Grand Rapids, MI: Baker Books, 2004.

Baugh, Lloyd. *Imaging the Divine: Jesus and Christ-figures in Film.* Kansas City, MO: Sheed & Ward, 1997.

A thesis-based study of the Jesus movies and some selected Christ-figure movies; defines what Christ-figure means, extensive and thorough, if somewhat controversial in interpretation.

Belknap, Bryan. *Group's Blockbuster Movie Illustrator.* Loveland, CO: Group Publishing, 2001.

Over 160 film clips are presented according to theme. Includes Scripture references, cue times to start and end the clips, and questions. Suitable for teenagers.

———— *Group's Blockbuster Movie Illustrations: The Sequel.* Loveland, CO: Group Publishing, 2003.

More than 170 clips...

Blake, Richard A. *After Image: The Indelible Catholic Imagination of Six American Filmmakers.* Chicago: Loyola Press, 2000.

An exploration of imagination and its religious dimension in the movies of six Catholic-educated directors: Capra, Coppolla, De Palma, Ford, Hitchcock, and Scorsese.

Detweiler, Craig, and Barry Taylor. *A Matrix of Meanings: Finding God in Popular Culture.* Grand Rapids, MI: Baker Academic, 2003.

A closer look for God and meaning in advertising, celebrities, music, movies, etc.

Eilers, Franz-Joseph. *Church and Social Communication: Basic Documents.* Manila: Logos Publications Inc., 1993.

The texts of nine Vatican documents from 1936 to 1992 with the addresses for World Communications Day and quotations on communication from other official documents. Eilers provides introductions and some structural outlines of the documents.

Fields, Doug, and Eddie James. *Videos That Teach.* Grand Rapids, MI: Zondervan, 1999.

"Teachable movie moments from seventy-five modern film classics" suitable for use with teenagers. Offers clip selections, themes, reflections, and Scripture references.

———— *Videos That Teach 2.* Grand Rapids, MI: Zondervan, 2002.

"Teachable movie moments from seventy-five more modern film classics to spark discussion," suitable for use with teenagers. Offers clip selections, themes, reflections and Scripture references.

———— *Videos That Teach 3.* Grand Rapids, MI: Zondervan, 2004.

More of the same, suitable for use with teenagers, with added lists.

Focus on the Family Staff. *Movie Nights for Kids.* Carol Stream, IL: Tyndale, 2004.

Highlights twenty-five thought-provoking films to get parents and younger children talking and learning about life, faith, and family—while having fun. This useful guide shows parents how to use contemporary movies to teach eternal truths to their children in a fun, easy way.

Fraser, Peter. *Images of the Passion: The Sacramental Mode in Film.* Westport, CT: Praeger Publishers, 1998.

Selected movies are examined to illustrate how they implicitly dramatize aspects of the Gospel and the sufferings of Jesus.

Fraser, Peter, and Vernon Edward Neal. *ReViewing the Movies: A Christian Response to Contemporary Film.* Wheaton, IL: Crossway Books, 2000.

An application of the theory in Fraser's *Images of the Passion* to contemporary popular cinema in a wide-ranging survey.

Higgins, Gareth. *How Movies Helped Save My Soul.* City: Relevant Books, 2003.

Jewett, Robert. *Saint Paul at the Movies.* Louisville: Westminster/John Knox, 1993.

A New Testament scholar writes an enlightening book about the Greco-

Roman world of Paul. A movie enthusiast, Jewett has chosen ten popular movies to illustrate the virtues that Paul holds up to the Roman Empire.

———— *Saint Paul Returns to the Movies.* Grand Rapids, MI: Eerdmans, 1999. A sequel that is as good as or perhaps better than the original.

John Paul II. *Giovanni Paolo II e il Cinema: Tutti i discorsi.* Rome: Ente dello Spettacolo, 2000.

A collection of eight speeches by Pope John Paul II on cinema. Texts in Italian and in English with commentary articles on the Church and cinema.

Johnston, Robert K. *Reel Spirituality: Theology and Film in Dialogue.* Grand Rapids, MI: Baker Academic, 2000.

A theologian from Fuller Theological Seminary who loves cinema asks basic questions about the religious dimension of movies, opening up the spirituality implicit in many mainstream movies. It has a wide range of film references.

Johnston, Robert K. *Useless Beauty: Ecclesiastes through the Lens of Contemporary Film.* Grand Rapids, MI: Baker Academic, 2004.

Kinne, Matthew. *Reflections for Movie Lovers.* Chattanooga, TN: Living Ink Books (AMG Publishers), 2004.

Written for the Christian or the movie-loving fan who enjoys exploring the spiritual aspects of movies. This book of 365 devotionals compares and contrasts movie plots and themes with bible stories and biblical truth.

Larson, Craig Brian, and Andrew Zahn. *Movie-Based Illustrations for Preaching and Teaching: 101 Clips to Show or Tell.* Grand Rapids, MI: Zondervan, 2003.

Larson, Craig Brian, and Lori Quicke. *More Movie-Based Illustrations for Preaching and Teaching: 101 Clips to Show or Tell.* Grand Rapids, MI: Zondervan, 2004.

Lyden, John C. *Film as Religion: Myths, Morals and Rituals.* New York: New York University Press, 2003.

Maher, Ian. *Reel Issues: Engaging Film and Faith.* Swindon, U.K.: Open Book Bible Society, 1998.

Produced for the Open Book program of the British Bible Society, this booklet is designed for use with Christian groups.

——— *Reel Issue: Five More Films to Engage Film and Faith.* Swindon, U.K.: Open Book Bible Society, 2000.

Produced for the Open Book program of the British Bible Society, this booklet is designed for use in Christian groups and continues the approach of its predecessor by considering five new films.

Mahony, Roger M. *Film Makers, Film Viewers, Their Challenges and Opportunities.* Boston: Pauline Books & Media, 1992.

The text of Cardinal Mahony's pastoral letter to the diocese of Los Angeles, his synthesis of a contemporary Catholic approach to cinema.

Malone, Peter, MSC, with Rose Pacatte, FSP. *Lights, Camera...Faith! A Movie Lectionary, Cycle A.* Boston: Pauline Books & Media, 2001.

Scripture readings for each Sunday of the common lectionary in dialogue with popular Hollywood films. Cycle B, 2002; Cycle C, 2003.

Malone, Peter. *Movie Christs and Antichrists.* New York: Crossroads, 1990; Sydney: Parish Ministry, 1988.

A study of movies and meanings focusing on the Jesus movies (the Jesus figures) and the movies of characters who resemble Jesus (Christ-figures); also chapters on movies and antichrist symbols.

——— *On Screen.* Manila: Daughters of St. Paul, 2001.

An introduction to the study of movies and meanings.

——— *Myth and Meaning: Australian Film Directors in Their Own Words.* Sydney, Australia: Currency Press, 2001.

Fifteen interviews with Australian film directors like Bruce Beresford, George Miller, Fred Schepisi, Scott Hicks, and Gillian Armstrong on the values and spirituality underlying their films.

Marsh, Clive, and Gaye Ortiz, eds. *Explorations in Theology and Film.* Oxford: Blackwell, 1997.

A collection of theological essays exploring specific contemporary popular movies like *The Terminator, The Piano,* and *Edward Scissorhands.*

May, John R. *Nourishing Faith Through Fiction: Reflections on the Apostles' Creed in Literature and Film.* Franklin, WI: Sheed and Ward, 2001.

An American pioneer in the studies of cinema examines stories that evoke the presence and images of the Trinity, the Creator, the Savior, and the Holy Spirit, the Life-giver. Classic movies and novels are considered in reference to many contemporary movies.

———— *New Image of Religious Film*. Kansas City, MO: Sheed and Ward, 1997. A collection of theological essays that examine theoretical aspects of religion, society, and cinema.

McNulty, Edward. *Films and Faith: Forty Discussion Guides*. Topeka, KS: Viaticum Press, 1999.

As the title indicates, discussion material for forty films. They are designed for the non-expert in cinema and provide detailed information about each film as well as some theological background. There are extensive questions for reflection.

———— *Praying the Movies: Daily Meditations from Classic Films*. Louisville, KY: Geneva Press, 2001.

A collection of thirty-one devotions that connect movies and the spiritual life of moviegoers.

———— *More Praying the Movies*. Louisville, KY: John Knox Press, 2003.

A second collection of thirty-one (one for each day of a month) devotionals built around a film scene. Includes related passages from the Hebrew and Christian Scriptures, a film synopsis and scene description, questions for reflection, a hymn suggestion, and a closing prayer.

Pungente, John and Montey Williams, . *Finding God in the Dark: Taking the Spiritual Exercises of St. Ignatius to the Movies*. Boston, MA: Pauline Books & Media, 2005.

Romanowski, William D. *Pop Culture Wars: Religion and the Role of Entertainment in American Life*. Downers Grove, IL: InterVarsity Press, 1996.

A wide-ranging study of entertainment, including cinema, noting the hostile U.S. religious tradition as well as the movements to find the religious values in media and entertainment.

Rosenstand, Nina. *The Human Condition: An Introduction to the Philosophy of Human Nature*. Boston, MA: McGraw-Hill, 2002.

Uses examples from fiction and popular film to show applications of theories of human nature: What is it to be human?

———— *The Moral of the Story: An Introduction to Ethics.* Mountainview, CA: Mayfield Publishing, 2000.

This popular textbook uses film stories in particular to explore ethics and ethical theories.

Sanders, Theresa. *Celluloid Saints: Images of Sanctity in Film.* Macon, GA: Mercer University Press, 2002.

A search for "authentic accounts of saints and of the miracles, healings, ethical questions, and challenges to holiness," a masterful analysis of the finest cinematic presentations of holiness in the history of the movies.

Schreck, Nikolas. *The Satanic Screen: An Illustrated Guide to the Devil in Cinema.* London: Creation Books, 2001.

A book that documents the devil's twentieth-century celluloid history and locates three hundred or so films in the culture of the years in which they were made.

Scott, Bernard Brandon. *Hollywood Dreams and Biblical Stories.* Minneapolis: Fortress Press, 1994.

The author brings his scriptural background to modern, popular movies and highlights the links between the biblical stories and the new cinema stories to draw out their meanings and their myths.

Short, Robert. *The Gospel from Outer Space: The Religious Implications of E.T., Star Wars, Superman, Close Encounters of the Third Kind,* and *2001: A Space Odyssey.* San Francisco: Harper & Row, 1983.

The author of *The Gospel According to Peanuts* and *The Parables of Peanuts* offers the text of a multimedia presentation of Gospel parallels in popular science fiction and fantasy movies.

Solomon, Gary. *The Motion Picture Prescription: Watch This Movie and Call Me in the Morning: 200 Movies to Help You Heal Life's Problems.* New York: Lebhar-Friedman Books, 1998.

———— *Reel Therapy: How Movies Inspire You to Overcome Life's Problems.* New York: Lebhar-Friedman Books, 2001.

Dr. Gary Solomon has registered "Cinema Therapy" and "The Movie Doctor" as his trademarks and blends a popular approach to movies along with the academic. Though these two books are not specifically religious, he has selected a great number of films that can be used for "cinema therapy," that is, for healing and inspiration.

Smithouser, Bob. *Movie Nights: 25 Movies to Spark Spiritual Discussions with Your Teen*. Colorado Springs: Heritage Builders, 2002.

How to help teens critically evaluate films through twenty-five highly entertaining movies; Scripture connections.

Stern, Richard C., Clayton N. Jefford, and Guerric Debona. *Savior on the Silver Screen*. Mahwah, NJ: Paulist Press, 1999.

The authors have run courses on the principal Jesus movies from Cecil B. De Mille to *Jesus of Montreal*. This is the expanded course with a thorough rationale for studying these movies.

Stone, Bryan P. *Faith and Film: Theological Themes at the Cinema*. St Louis: Chalice Press, 2000.

The framework for examining a range of generally well-known movies is the Apostles' Creed, enabling the author to highlight religious themes in movies in a context of faith and the exploration of faith.

Vaux, Sara Anson. *Finding Meaning at the Movies*. Nashville: Abingdon Press, 1999.

The author wants to encourage study groups in schools, universities, and parishes by taking a range of popular movies and showing how they can be fruitfully discussed.

Voytilla, Stuart. *Myth and the Movies: Discovering the Mythic Structure of 50 Unforgettable Films*. Los Angeles: Michael Wiese Productions, 1999.

The author draws on the culture of referring to and using myths, especially the hero's journey, to look at a number of popular screen classics.

Film Websites

Film and Spirituality

www.signis.net

> The international Catholic association for communications includes current jury prizes for film festivals and reviews by Rev. Peter Malone, MSC, president of SIGNIS.

www.daughtersofstpaul.com/mediastudies/reviews/index.html

> Media literacy in faith-communities includes some in-depth movie reviews and links, sponsored by the Daughters of St. Paul.

www.nationalfilmretreat.org

> Information on the National Film Retreat, an annual interfaith gathering that screens and prays several films over a weekend (Friday evening to Sunday noon).

www.HollywoodJesus.com

> This ecumenical website is dedicated to finding Christian spirituality in movies, with a searchable archive.

www.catholic.org.au

> Four film reviews a month beginning in 2001 from the Australian Conference of Catholic Bishops.

www.chiafilm.com

> This site is named for *chiaroscuro,* the interplay of light and shade in an image, and seeks to move beyond the culture wars and encourage a conversation between the cinema and Christian spirituality. Contains new reviews, retrospectives, and essays.

www.beliefnet.com

> Comparative religion community includes movie reviews.

www.cityofangelsfilmfest.org

> Interfaith film-festival site with reviews, resources, and events.

www.spiritualityhealth.com

> Fred and Mary Brussat offer an e-course, "Going to the Movies as a Spiritual Practice," as well as current film and video reviews with a searchable database.

www.FilmClipsOnLine.com

 Hollywood filmmaker Michael Rhodes and industry colleagues and educators offer clips from popular films to use in educational settings.

www.christianitytoday.com/ctmag/features/columns/filmforum.html

 Christian film reviews that integrate and analyze commentaries from several sources, both from religious and from the mainstream press.

www.unomaha.edu/–wwwjrf/

 Articles and reviews by the *Journal of Religion and Film,* University of Nebraska at Omaha.

www.christiancritic.com

 The Christian critic's movie parables.

www.textweek.com

 Sermon helps with a movie concordance for the Catholic and Anglican lectionaries.

www.visualparables.com

 Visual Parables is a monthly review of films, videos, and the arts with lectionary links.

www.udayton.edu/mary/

 This site features the videos on Mary and Marian subjects archived by the University of Dayton's Marian Library/International Marian Research Institute.

Cineandmedia@yahoogroups.com

 E-group for those interested in cinema, spirituality, and theology.

Film/Media Education

www.chumlimited.com/mediaed

 Canada's BRAVO! Channel presents a media-education perspective based on the television program *Scanning the Movies,* hosted by Neil Anderson and Rev. John Pungente, SJ, with study guides.

www.filmeducation.org

 This U.K. film-education site is provided for secondary school teachers to encourage and promote the study, evaluation, and analysis of a wide range of media, including film, within the curriculum. Free online study guides and resources.

www.udayton.edu/~ipi

The Pastoral Communication and Ministry Institute (PCMI) of the University of Dayton is an annual summer program to prepare leaders to proclaim the Gospel using all the means of pastoral communications available today. The program includes courses on film, theology, and spirituality.

Film and Families

www.daughtersofstpaul.com/myfriend

Movie and video reviews by kids for kids.

www.americancatholic.org

St. Anthony Messenger's "Entertainment Watch—Movies" section and the *Every Day Catholic* newsletter's "Media Watch," feature movie reviews and articles.

www.moviemom.com

"Helping families share great times, great movies, and great conversations."

www.screenit.com

Entertainment reviews for parents with a searchable archive.

Film Review Sites

www.usccb.org

The United States Catholic Conference site includes current film reviews, searchable archives, and "information for guidance."

www.imdb.org

The Internet Movie Databases is the largest movie archive on the web and includes industry information and a multitude of links to sources and reviews.

www.suntimes.com/index/ebert.html

The index on this website contains famed movie critic Roger Ebert's film reviews since 1985, along with a searchable database of these reviews.

www.movie-reviews.colossus.net

Film reviews since 1996 by James Bernardelli.

Film Ratings

Please note: while all of these sites list film ratings, only a few list their criteria for judging films.

www.mpaa.org

The Motion Picture Association of America (U.S.A.) film ratings.

www.ccr.gov.on.ca/ofrb/

Ontario Film Review Board.

www.media-awareness.ca/eng

Film-rating links for all other provinces of Canada.

www.bffc.co.uk

The British Board of Film Classification.

www.oflc.gov.au

The Office for Film and Literature Classification, Australia.

Movie Licensing Information

For the United States and Canada

If you wish to show a video/film in a group setting that is not included in the regularly structured curriculum of an educational institution, then you need to acquire a license.The Motion Picture Licensing Corporation/Christian Video Licensing International can issue an umbrella license for many of the studios. Please visit them on the Web, www.mplc.com, or call 888-771-2854.

Swank Motion Pictures can issue licenses for films from Miramax, Warner Bros., and HBO: 800-876-5577.

Twentieth Century Fox can be contacted directly: 310-286-1056.

For all films/studios that are not covered by the licenses these companies can provide, please contact the studio directly and ask for the licensing or legal department.

Movies That Refer to the Commandments
in *Lights, Camera...Faith! A Movie Lectionary*, Cycles, A, B, C

FIRST COMMANDMENT

Theme: Worship of false idols

Amadeus	C
Beach, The	A
Bob Roberts	A
Bram Stoker's Dracula	B
Cool Hand Luke	C
Cry Freedom	A
Devil's Advocate, The	A
Edward Scissorhands	B
End of Days	A
Evita	C
Exorcist, The	B
Godfather, The	B
Harry Potter and the Sorcerer's Stone	B
Insider, The	A
Jesus of Montreal	B
Jesus' Son	A
Lord of the Rings, The: The Fellowship of the Ring	B
Mad City	C
Pleasantville	A
Quiz Show	C
Remains of the Day, The	B
Restoration	C
Road to Perdition	C
Truman Show, The	B

SECOND COMMANDMENT

Theme: Presumption by individuals or institutions

Agnes of God	B
AI: Artificial Intelligence	B
Apostle, The	A
At First Sight	B
At Play in the Fields of the Lord	A
Chocolat	B
Cookie's Fortune	A
Crucible, The	A
Deep Impact	C
Doctor, The	A
Few Good Men, A	C
Fisher King, The	A
Flatliners	B
Gods and Generals	C
Groundhog Day	C
Mass Appeal	B
Matrix, The	B
Shoes of the Fisherman, The	A
Snow Falling on Cedars	A
Third Miracle, The	B
Titanic	B

Touch	A
True Confessions	A

THIRD COMMANDMENT

Themes: The sacred and the nature of work and rest

2001: A Space Odyssey	B
Alive	B
Babette's Feast	C
Black Robe	B
Brother Sun, Sister Moon	B
Cast Away	B
Chariots of Fire	C
Close Encounters of the Third Kind	C
Contact	C
Eat Drink Man Woman	C
Grapes of Wrath	C
Horse Whisperer, The	A
It's a Wonderful Life	A
Kundun	B
Lilies of the Field	B
Meet Joe Black	C
Message in a Bottle	A
Mission to Mars	A
Mission, The	B
Molokai	B
Paradise Road	A
Places in the Heart	A
Simply Irresistible	B
Spitfire Grill, The	B

Stanley & Iris	B
Straight Story, The	C
Tender Mercies	A
Truly, Madly, Deeply	C
What Dreams May Come	C
Wit	C

FOURTH COMMANDMENT

Theme: Family relationships

About Schmidt	C
Angela's Ashes	B
Billy Elliot	B
Bronx Tale, A	B
Deep End of the Ocean, The	C
Disney's the Kid	B
Family Man, The	A
Frequency	C
Girl, Interrupted	A
Home for the Holidays	C
Joy Luck Club, The	B
Life as a House	C
Life Is Beautiful	B
Little Women	B
Little Man Tate	C
Lorenzo's Oil	A
Marvin's Room	A
Mighty, The	B
Mr. Holland's Opus	B
My Left Foot	B
One True Thing	C
Powder	C

Rain Man	B
River Runs Through It, A	C
Second Best	B
Secrets and Lies	A
Shine	C
Simon Birch	A
Sound of Music, The	C
Steel Magnolias	B
Test of Love, A	
(Annie's Coming Out)	B
What's Cooking?	B
What's Eating Gilbert Grape?	A
When a Man Loves a Woman	C

FIFTH COMMANDMENT

Themes: Violence, killing, war, and peace

Beyond Rangoon	C
Bless the Child	C
Born on the Fourth of July	A
Braveheart	C
Bringing out the Dead	C
Changing Lanes	C
Crossing Guard, The	A
Dead Man Walking	A
Falling Down	C
Far East	C
Gallipoli	C
Green Dragon	C
Green Mile, The	C
Killing Fields, The	A

Last Valley, The	B
Magnificent Seven, The	B
Men with Guns	A
Outlaw Josey Wales, The	C
Pale Rider	C
Prince of Tides	A
Saving Private Ryan	A
Savior	B
Schindler's List	C
Shawshank Redemption, The	C
Star Wars: Episode IV	C
Terminator 2: Judgment Day	A
Thelma and Louise	C
Thirteen Days	B
Unforgiven	A
Year of Living Dangerously, The	C

SIXTH COMMANDMENT

Theme: Sexual betrayal, violation, and marriage

Accused, The	C
Bed of Roses	B
Bridges of Madison County, The	A
End of the Affair, The	B
Moonstruck	B
Where the Heart Is	A

SEVENTH COMMANDMENT

Theme: Honesty, social justice

Civil Action, A	A
Erin Brockovich	A

Firm, The	B
Simple Plan, A	B
Wall Street	C

EIGHTH COMMANDMENT

Themes: Truth and lies

Absence of Malice	B
Beautiful Mind, A	B
Burning Season, The	B
Catch Me If You Can	C
Elephant Man, The	C
Entertaining Angels	A
Leap of Faith	C
Legend of Bagger Vance, The	B
Les Miserables	A
Long Walk Home, The	B
Matewan	A
Mumford	B
On the Waterfront	C
Phenomenon	A
Philadelphia	C
Romero	B
Shipping News, The	C
Sixth Sense, The	C
Sommersby	B
To Kill a Mockingbird	B
Winslow Boy, The	C

NINTH COMMANDMENT

Themes: Desire, sexual temptation

Keeping the Faith	B
Oscar and Lucinda	A

TENTH COMMANDMENT

Themes: Envy, jealousy, charity, and empathy

As Good as It Gets	C
Baghdad Cafe	A
Big Night, The	A
Chorus Line, A	A
City of Joy	A
Dances with Wolves	B
Daylight	B
Finding Forrester	B
Forrest Gump	A
Good Will Hunting	C
House of Mirth, The	B
Hurricane, The	A
Pay It Forward	A
Regarding Henry	C
Remember the Titans	C
Saint of Fort Washington, The	C

Index